THE POWER OF A
WHISPER

Books by Bill Hybels

Axiom

Holy Discontent

Just Walk Across the Room

The Volunteer Revolution

Courageous Leadership

Rediscovering Church (with Lynne Hybels)

Honest to God?

Fit to be Tied (with Lynne Hybels)

Descending into Greatness (with Rob Wilkins)

Becoming a Contagious Christian (with Mark Mittelberg and Lee Strobel)

The New Community Series
(with Kevin and Sherry Harney)

Colossians

James

1 Peter

Philippians

Romans

The Sermon on the Mount 1

The Sermon on the Mount 2

The InterActions Small Group Series
(with Kevin and Sherry Harney)

Authenticity

Character

Commitment

Community

Essential Christianity

Fruit of the Spirit

Getting a Grip

Jesus

Lessons on Love

Living in God's Power

Love in Action

Marriage

Meeting God

New Identity

Parenting

Prayer

Reaching Out

The Real Deal

Significance

Transformation

THE POWER OF A

WHISPER

HEARING GOD. HAVING THE GUTS TO RESPOND.

BILL HYBELS

ZONDERVAN.com/
AUTHORTRACKER
follow your favorite authors

ZONDERVAN

The Power of a Whisper
Copyright © 2010 by Bill Hybels

This title is also available as a Zondervan ebook.
Visit www.zondervan.com/ebooks.

This title is also available in a Zondervan audio edition.
Visit www.zondervan.fm.

Requests for information should be addressed to:

Zondervan, *Grand Rapids, Michigan 49530*

ISBN 978-0-310-52019-1

International Trade Paper Edition

Cover design: Hanon McKendry
Cover photography: Getty Images / Guy Edwardes
Interior design: Beth Shagene
Edited by Sandra Vander Zicht, Bob Hudson, and Elaine Schnabel

Printed in the United States of America

10 11 12 13 14 15 16 /DCI/ 24 23 22 21 20 19 18 17 16 15 14 13 12 11 10 9 8 7 6 5

To Dick and Betsy DeVos
and
Ron and Sharon VanderPol

Only on the other side will the four of you know
how much your friendship and support
have meant to the Hybels family
and to the global Willow family.

CONTENTS

ACKNOWLEDGMENTS

THIS WHOLE "WHISPERS" JOURNEY BEGAN FOR ME WITH MY second-grade Christian schoolteacher, Miss Van Soelen, who took the time to counsel a young boy and challenge him to reflect on a simple four-line poem.

The opportunity to put this material in a book was graciously extended to me by Moe Girkins, president of Zondervan.

Ashley Wiersma helped me conceptualize the content for this book and reworked manuscripts until the day of the deadline.

My wife, Lynne, and her friend September Vaudrey teamed up with me to do the final edit.

My daughter, Shauna, now an author in her own right, inspired me to make this book my best work yet.

My son, Todd, has been a living example of a young man who takes whispers seriously.

And what can I say about the congregation of Willow Creek Community Church? They have heard me talk about whispers and promptings for more than thirty-five years. More importantly, they have had the guts to obey the leadings of the Holy Spirit, even when the price got high.

To you, my colleagues, family and faith community, I offer my deepest gratitude.

FOREWORD BY
WAYNE CORDEIRO

I N THE 1970S, BEFORE DIGITAL GUITAR TUNERS WERE ON THE
market, I was a budding musician (who, after a few decades,
is still waiting to bloom), preparing for a song-set at a youth
convention. Tuning your guitar in those days required match-
ing tones on one string with another. It's not a difficult task, but
another band slated to perform on the same program was really
rocking their sound check. My meager Martin was no match for
the muscular Marshall amps of these adrenaline-fueled scream-
ers. I had to bend my ear increasingly closer to the sound hole
with the loudest plucks I could manage, and yet the blare of the
competing system still overpowered my best attempts. Until,
that is, I resorted to laying my ear flat on the spruce top of my
instrument. Then, no matter how blatantly the rockers attacked,
the tender strains of my acoustic guitar could be heard—readily,
effectively, sweetly.

It's a lot like that with God. When it comes to being heard by
his children, our Father does not compete, nor does he contend
for our undivided attention. Often he delivers nothing more
than a nudge—easy to dismiss if you don't recognize the Source.

He *whispers*, soft undertones that invite us to bend an ear—or an entire life—until it is pressed flat against his lips.

THE EARLIEST RECOLLECTION I HAVE OF HEARING FROM GOD occurred when I was in the seventh grade, a young Catholic boy living with my family in Japan. Back then I knew my catechism, but I didn't know the person of Christ. I knew that God was "out there," but I had not yet learned the sound of his voice.

It was around that time that I went with a missionary couple who were family friends to visit an adjacent city for a few days. As I watched them work with a group of helpless and hopeless orphans, I sensed a divine message from above: "This is what you will be doing, Wayne. You will be helping people the rest of your life."

Still today, I can remember sitting in that little orphanage, listening to the conversations, observing the mutual love, enjoying the thrill that comes from meeting another person's deepest need, knowing that from that moment on, my life would drastically change. And over time, as I surrendered myself to Christ, I would learn that it was God's voice I had heard that day.

There is a frequency that your life was designed to be tuned to, and that frequency is the unique voice of God. Once you learn to hear it—and you actually *can* get better at picking it out—you will find that your craving for it intensifies as your soul strains to hear more from him. I experienced it first as a twelve-year-old and have known it consistently since: the ability to absorb heaven-sent input fills the sails of your life like nothing or no one else can.

RECENTLY, MY JOURNEY TOOK ME HEADLONG INTO A DEEP pit of burnout. I could no longer hear God's voice and believed earnestly that my heart for ministry had collapsed. My future was foggy, faded and dim. But during that season of near silence I learned firsthand the power of a whisper. I learned to perceive the sound of stillness, and in the midst of that stillness I finally heard God speak. "Train leaders," he seemed to prompt.

Train leaders? Was God serious?

I was experiencing the most intense emotional pain I'd ever known, and God's solution to my overtaxed state was to give me yet another task to accomplish?

What God knew that I couldn't have known at the time was that his beautiful words of wisdom weren't intended to give me comfort. They were meant to infuse me with *confidence*, something I sorely needed right then. God wasn't airlifting me out of my situation; rather than a way out of my pit, he was offering me a way *through*. He knew that in my heart of hearts I didn't want to abandon my calling, my family, my life. What I really wanted was to be assured that I still had a kingdom contribution to make. A life of leisure might have appealed to my flesh, but what I was truly and desperately in need of was something that would fuel my soul.

Isaiah 30:21 says, "Whether you turn to the right or to the left, your ears will hear a voice behind you, saying, 'This is the way; walk in it.'" I found that during those difficult days, I would hear God one step at a time. I would start each day soaking up a passage from his Word in order to position myself to hear from him again. And once I'd receive a bit of instruction, I would charge off into my day. But at the first slippery slope or craggy precipice I encountered, I'd realize I needed another infusion of help. "I'm at the far edge of the light," I'd admit to God. And each time, he'd expand the area of illumination so that I could take another small step.

Today, out of sheer obedience to that divine whisper I heard in the pit, I divide my time between my home church in Hawaii and a Bible college in Oregon, where I help shape young men and women into the shepherds of tomorrow. But despite the evident successes that have come by heeding God's request of me to train leaders, I think the real thing he was after was my life pressed flat against his lips.

It's probably true for you too. You may have picked up this book because you long for circumstantial input from God: What are his intentions for your future? Will the job you want *ever* pan out? What's he going to do about your exasperating spouse? Won't life just once cut you a break? But I believe the real reason you hold these pages in hand is to learn how to lean more on God.

The Power of a Whisper is the tractor-beam of the soul that prophets of old heard daily. And in the modern-day cacophony of cell phones, email and instant messaging, what will distinguish God's people from others will be hearing and heeding whispers from above. I hope you'll work through this slowly and thoughtfully. Afford yourself a renewed ability to distinguish the tender timbre of your loving Father's voice. Tune yourself to the only frequency that truly can satisfy your soul. And start today boldly responding as you hear the gentle whispers of God.

A FIFTY-YEAR
WHISPER-FUELED ODYSSEY

I MAGINE MY SURPRISE WHEN AFTER A WEEKEND SERVICE AT our church I looked into a pair of eyes I had not seen in nearly fifty years. "Do you remember me?" the lanky businessman— about my age—asked, tears pooling in the bottom of his lids. Truthfully, I did not.

He offered a few clues, and it all came flooding back. I remembered not only his name but the names of six other boys who had shared a cabin with us at the summer camp of our youth.

We caught up for a few moments, trying to cram five decades of updates into a terribly brief span of time. Then, as he took in the spacious auditorium surrounding him, he looked me square in the face and asked, "How did all of this happen?"

I began to describe how we had started Willow Creek Community Church in the mid-1970s in a rented movie theater, and how, many years later, we'd purchased property and broken ground on permanent facilities.

"No," my former cabin mate interrupted, "I didn't mean how did this *building* happen. I meant how did your *life* turn out the way it did?"

He went on to say that I probably wouldn't enjoy hearing how some of the lives of the rest of those guys from camp wound up—and that he surely wasn't going to bore me with the details of his own life's saga. "But frankly," he said, "I never would have guessed that your story would have unfolded like this." He eyed the line of people still waiting to greet me and then suggested we catch up over dinner sometime. We exchanged a warm handshake, and he was gone.

Later that night in bed, I pondered how I would help my childhood camp mate understand the truth about the unlikely course my life has taken. How could I tell this savvy, cynical business guy that my fifty-year odyssey unfolded as it has because of a series of whispers from God? *Inaudible* whispers, at that. I imagined the mere use of such language would shorten our upcoming dinner considerably, but no other explanation exists. My entire journey comes down to a series of unplanned promptings from heaven that have charted a course for my life even I never could have foreseen.

I have chosen to wait thirty-five years before writing a book about how God's whispers have affected my life—hesitant in part because of the controversy this subject tends to arouse. Even today, when I make public reference to the whispers of God, I barely make it off the stage before half a dozen people approach to remind me that ax murderers often defend their homicides by claiming, "God told me to do it." Conservative Christians question my orthodoxy when I describe my experiences with the promptings of the Holy Spirit, and secularists either are humored or quietly tell their spouses that Hybels has lost his marbles. Or both.

Still, I've come to believe that hearing the quiet whisper of the transcendent God is one of the most extraordinary privileges in all of life—and potentially the most transforming dynamic in the Christian faith. When people hear from heaven, they are rarely the same again. When the sovereign God chooses to communicate with someone—whether eight, eighteen or eighty years old—that person's world is rocked. Without a hint of exaggeration, I can boldly declare that God's low-volume whispers have saved me from a life of sure boredom and self-destruction. They have redirected my path, rescued me from temptation and reenergized me during some of my deepest moments of despair. They inspire me to live my life at what boaters call "wide-open throttle"—full on!

So, why go to the trouble of penning the words in the chapters that follow? Because I firmly believe that God whispers to you too. If you lower the ambient noise of your life and listen expectantly for those whispers of God, your ears will hear them. And when you follow their lead, your world will be rocked. Let's get started.

BILL HYBELS
South Haven, Michigan
August 2009

CHAPTER 1

SAMUEL'S EAR

I GREW UP IN A CHRISTIAN FAMILY AND AS A KID WENT TO A Christian school, which admittedly had its advantages and its disadvantages. As an adult who now appreciates having received a sturdy spiritual foundation, I have greater appreciation for one of the clear plusses: Each day before recess, my classmates and I would have to sit and listen to our teacher read a short story from the Bible. The better we listened, the faster she read—and the faster she read the sooner we'd be out on the baseball fields. With that as my motivation, I was all ears every day.

One such day, when I was in the second grade of that school in Kalamazoo, Michigan, my teacher read a story from the Old Testament about a man named Eli—an older worker in the temple —and a young boy named Samuel, whom he mentored. As the story goes, one night after Samuel had gone to bed, he thought he heard Eli calling for him. He got out of bed, ran to where Eli was lying down and said, "I heard you call. Here I am."[1]

Eli looked at young Samuel, confusion creasing the old man's forehead. "I didn't call you," Eli said. "Go back to bed."[2]

Samuel, of course, complied. But moments later, he heard his name again. "Samuel!" the voice called. Samuel rose from his bed, hurried to Eli's side and said, "Here I am; you called me."

Again Eli told the boy he was wrong. Again Samuel returned to his bed.

When it happened a third time, the old man finally realized what was going on. "Samuel, maybe God is trying to get a message to you," Eli explained. "Go back and lie down. If the voice calls again, say, 'Speak, God. I am your servant, ready to listen.' "[3]

And so, the text says, "Samuel returned to his bed,"[4] where soon thereafter he heard his name yet again. "Samuel! Samuel!" the Lord called, to which Samuel replied on cue, "Speak, for your servant is listening."[5]

The message that the Lord then spoke to young Samuel was a prophetic promise that would radically impact an entire nation. But the content of that message is not what struck me as I sat in my wooden grade-school desk. What struck me was the fact that the content got conveyed through the ears and lips of a little boy!

The recess bell rang. Miss Van Soelen stood, and my classmates made a rush for the room's single door. Typically I was the first kid on the field, picking teams and filling positions and generally organizing the sport of the day. But not today. Today I found myself glued to my seat. The story she'd read had leveled me for reasons I didn't fully understand.

When the room had emptied save for Miss Van Soelen and me, I eased out of my desk, stuffed my hands deep in my pockets and walked up to my teacher.

"What is it, Billy?" she asked—probably fearing the worst, given that it was recess and I was still indoors.

"Miss Van Soelen," I said as my throat began to choke up, "does God *still* speak to little boys?"

She smiled and let out a relieved sigh. Placing her two hands on my small shoulders, she looked me square in the eye.

"Oh, *yes*, Billy," she said. "He most certainly does. And if you learn to quiet yourself and listen, he even will speak to you. I am *sure* of it."

I felt a swell of release as I considered for the first time in my seven years of life that perhaps Christianity was more than ancient rules, creeds and other stiff-necked ways. Maybe God really *did* speak. And maybe he'd speak to me.

Satisfied by her answer, I turned to head out to the baseball fields. "Billy," Miss Van Soelen called after me, "I have something for you." She reached into the top drawer of her desk. "For some reason I've kept this poem here, but I think you should have it now. It might help you, given what we talked about today." She slipped a folded piece of paper into my palm, and with her knowing nod I was dismissed.

As I pulled on my pajamas that night, my mind kept drifting back to the idea that maybe God would someday speak to me. I rummaged through the pockets of my school pants and pulled out the paper Miss Van Soelen had given me. Opening its folds and flattening out its creases, I discovered a poem—words about having Samuel's ears to hear God, every single day. I read the poem and then read it again. I read it a third time, and then figured I might as well memorize the thing. And so I did.

The next day just before recess, Miss Van Soelen read a Bible story that meant absolutely nothing to me. I faked attentiveness, knowing this would help my baseball game come sooner, and when the beloved bell finally sounded its alarm, I flew out of my desk and lunged for the classroom door.

"Not so fast, Billy," Miss Van Soelen's singsong voice rang out. I felt my shirt collar caught in her grip. As my friends pushed past either side of me and headed out to recess, Miss Van Soelen asked, "What did you think of the poem I gave you?"

"I really liked it," I said.

"You mean you actually read it?" she asked.

"I memorized it," I said with a straight face and a shrug.

"No *way*," she said, flabbergasted.

"*Yes*, way, I did," I countered.

She called my bluff. "Can you say it for me?"

I took up the dare.

"Oh, give me Samuel's ear," I said, "an open ear, O Lord, alive and quick to hear each whisper of Thy Word; like him to answer to Thy call, and to obey Thee first of all."

As I finished my recitation, I thought Miss Van Soelen might faint dead away, right then and there. As a pride-infused smile beamed across her face, again I felt those two hands on my small frame: "You keep listening for God to speak, Billy," she said, "and I believe he will use your life in a very special way."

※

After that experience, I tried to listen for the whispers of God. I didn't do it well enough or often enough, but as I walked down the road of my young life and faced the right-or-wrong choices that all adolescent boys face, sometimes I'd recall that rhyming refrain.

> *Oh! give me Samuel's ear,*
> *An open ear, O Lord,*
> *Alive and quick to hear*
> *Each whisper of Thy Word;*
> *Like him to answer to Thy call*
> *And to obey Thee first of all.*[6]

Each time the plea for Samuel's ear floated through my mind, it was as if I could hear God cheering me on—at least as much as I understood "God" at the time. I'd be standing at the crossroads of the paths marked yes and no and would sense him say, "I'm rooting for you, Billy! Take the high road here; you'll never regret your yes." It shouldn't have surprised me that God's way would prove best. But each time I'd head off on the high road and feel the good feelings that his way always brings, I'd look heavenward and with a shake of my head think, "God, you were right again!"

As I grew into the teenaged version of myself, an insatiable craving for adventure grew inside me too. My dad had discerned a thrill-seeking temperament in me from an early age, and he knew that if he didn't do something to channel all that energy in a positive direction, I'd likely wind up wrecking my life. Before I was even ten, he sent me off all alone on a cross-country train bound for Aspen, Colorado. Evidently he wanted me to learn how to ski, which would have been fine had he actually been present on that trip to teach me. The real goal, I would later surmise, was learning how to navigate the big, blue world around me. And navigate it I would.

When I was sixteen, my admittedly eccentric father came home from work one day and announced, "Billy, I think you ought to see even *more* of the world." It was the middle of the school year, a reality I felt sure my incredulous expression conveyed. Reading my expression, he added with a grin, "Obviously, you must never allow school to interfere with your education."

Clearly we wouldn't want that.

The following week, I boarded a plane headed for Europe. For eight weeks straight—again, all by myself—I traipsed from Scandinavia to the Middle East, and then headed for Nairobi, Kenya.

Having no idea what else to do when I arrived in Nairobi, I decided to take a walk. It was a decision that—five minutes in—I deeply and desperately regretted. I began down a bustling dirt road, and as I rounded the first corner, I came face-to-face with a level of human suffering I hadn't known could exist. I peered down the street and took in scores upon scores of people leaning against broken-down, battered buildings. The effects of rampant disease and malnutrition were obvious; I breathed in the open-guttered stench; I felt the staleness, the thickness of the air, and I knew I'd never again be the same.

As I made my way around a row of gaunt, downcast faces, my stomach started to lurch. "I'm a Dutch kid from Kalamazoo, Michigan," I thought. "What am I doing *here*?"

Turning the next corner, I saw a boy about my age. The leprosy that racked this part of the city had found its way to this young kid. The bottom half of his arm was missing, and on the nub of his upper arm he'd rested a tiny tin cup. I took in his situation, trying not to be too obvious about it. Our eyes met, and he uttered a single word.

"Penny?"

I thrust my hands in my pockets but discovered I had nothing for a situation like this. My fingers found the stiff, rounded corners of my dad's American Express card—useless to this kid—and then a wadded up stack of traveler's checks that were tucked around a folded airline ticket for wherever I was headed next.

"Sorry," I mumbled, showing him my empty hands. Embarrassed, I hurriedly stepped away.

When I was safely out of the young man's sight, I ran as fast as my legs could carry me back to my hotel. Rushing inside my room, I emptied my pockets, fell to my knees and buried my head in the rug. I began to pray, although I had little relationship with the One I was praying to—and no idea what to say. All I knew was that I had never before seen suffering like I'd seen on the streets that day, and the only person I figured would know what to do about it was the God I'd heard hates suffering too.

As I sat crouched there, tears streaming down my hot cheeks, I heard an inaudible whisper from God: "If you will allow me to guide your life, one day I will use you to relieve some of the pain you see."

I quickly sealed the pact. "That would be great," I said to the silence all around. "That would be *absolutely* fine with me."

The following summer, I surrendered my life to Christ. I had been going to a Christian camp in Wisconsin since I was in single digits, but it wasn't until I stood on its familiar hillside at age seventeen that I finally connected with God for real. In the perfect stillness of a late-night hour, the words of Titus 3:5—a verse that I'd been told to memorize as a boy in Sunday school—crept back into my consciousness. "Not by works of righteousness which we have done, but according to his mercy he saved us, by the washing of regeneration, and renewing of the Holy Ghost."[7] In a flash of divine insight, I heard God's still, small voice: "You will never earn your way to my approval, Bill, but it is yours without condition right now." His whisper reflected a depth and purity of love that was so rich and real, I wondered if I was making the whole experience up.

I rushed back to my cabin, awakened my friends and dragged them all out of bed. "I don't have language to describe what just happened in my heart," I panted, "but I took a step of faith and invited God into my life—for real. For good. He came in, and I feel different on the inside!"

My groggy cabin mates glared at me with eyes that said this was a no-good reason to interrupt their sleep, but I knew the truth in my heart. I hadn't made up that hilltop experience. The decision I'd made that night was undeniable, irreversible and *good*. I've never looked back.

SHORTLY AFTER MY LATE-NIGHT GRACE-ATTACK, I BEGAN TO wrestle with how seriously I was going to take my newfound faith. I grasped that Jesus had died for me on a cross, forgiven my sins and promised me a place in heaven. I even gathered that it would be a good thing to invest a few minutes a day reading my Bible, saying some prayers and perhaps getting involved with a church. But in the midst of all my low-balling, I kept hearing about people my age who were going all-out for God. Fully committed and truly devoted, they were allowing their faith to affect things like their morals, their relationships, their money management and in some cases even their *career path*, which seemed a little over-the-top to me.

God had whispered into my boyhood years, helping me learn to act on what is right. He had whispered again to me in a slum in Kenya, encouraging me to pay attention to suffering wherever I see it. He had whispered to me in Wisconsin, asking me to give him the whole of my life. On and on these whispers continued, and thankfully as God was speaking more regularly, I grew increasingly aware of my need for input from above.

I *wanted* to live wide open to God, but I couldn't reconcile my sin. The truth about me is that for as long as I can remember, I have possessed an awe-inspiring, southbound gravitational pull that makes me rationalize doing something that is wrong as though somehow it were right. I am prone to justify my behavior when I cross lines that clearly I should not cross. I want to stay put when God asks me to move, to go right when God suggests a left-hand turn, and to speak my mind when I sense silence would serve me better.

He prodded me toward being a young man of my word, toward releasing judgment and revenge-seeking. "Love your enemies," he'd whisper, just when things were heating up. "Never return evil for evil, but return evil with good."

"Seriously, God?" I wondered.

I worried that devoting myself more fully to God would only make battles such as these more intense. I had wanted to hear directly from heaven since the second grade, but now that such input was frequent—and often contrary to my reflexive reaction to things—I was second-guessing my childhood request.

About that time, an older Christian man approached me and offered to buy me dinner. As a teenage boy and a frugal Dutchman, I regarded his offer of a free meal as a no-brainer.

Five bites into my burger the man said, "So, Bill, all the signs seem to be pointing to you heading into your family's business. And while that's a fine choice to make, I have a question for you. What are you going to do with your life that will last *forever*?

"I have no doubts about your making money and racking up a ton of achievements," the man continued. "You're a bright kid who will probably set records in whatever you choose to do. I'm just curious what you'll do that will *outlive* you and all of those earthly accomplishments."

I made eye contact with the guy with each bite of burger, careful to chew thoroughly so that I wouldn't have to speak. How was I supposed to respond to an assessment like *that*? I was just a teenager, and teenage boys by definition are only concerned with three things: food, thrills and girls. And in my case, God too, but *how much* of God was still up for debate.

Undaunted, the man continued. "What are you going to do to serve people—because people are the only commodity that makes it to the next life, you know...."

Sensing the questions wouldn't stop until I offered some semblance of a response, I put together a few words to get this guy off my back. But the effects of that supposedly free dinner held me captive the rest of the night.

As I crawled into bed a few hours later, I had a strong sense of God's presence. It was as if he walked right into my room, sat on the edge of my mattress and in the sightless shadows of the night repeated the older man's words. "What are you going to do with your one and only life?" I sensed him whisper. "What difference will you make for eternity? Faster cars, more cash and toys—none of those will make it beyond your grave."

As I stared at the ceiling, I felt my thrill-seeking days slip through my fingers like sand. I was being asked to make a choice: Would I choose a future I could generate and control myself—or would I sign on for the vagaries of a God-guided life? I was not even sure what a "God-guided life" would look like, but I was fairly sure the fun factor would be dialed back further than my liking.

I then recalled my dinner companion's closing words: "Bill, I'm going to issue you a challenge," he had said just before we left. "Why not put your *whole life* in God's hands? Why not trust him fully? I challenge you to give him full clearance to lead your life—*every* area of your life—until the point that he proves himself to be untrustworthy. At that moment, you can bail. But until then, give God total control. I challenge you to push the throttle as far as you can push it, and live your life wide open to God. See where his way takes you. I have a feeling you'll never regret it."

In the quiet of my room, the man's words kept replaying in my mind, gaining energy every time. There *was* something a little intriguing about seeing what God might do with my life. Where would he direct me to go? Who would he direct me to become? I could bail as soon as he muffed his part of the deal, right?

As I lay there, I redirected the man's challenge to me back to something of a challenge to God: "You want to lead my life fully, God? Alright, then. Let's see what you can do."

A fter those sometimes-tumultuous high school days— during the time when I was still working for my family's fresh-produce business—my dad presented me with another stack of airline tickets.

"Billy," he announced, "it's time to enlarge your world a little further." This time he was sending me to Latin America. Was I really so stubborn that God has to take me to the farthest reaches of the earth to get my attention? Regardless, with the American Express card in my pocket and a slightly more open mind this time around, I boarded a plane for Brazil.

When I arrived in Rio de Janeiro, I learned that I'd be staying overnight at a hotel overlooking Copacabana Beach, which in those days was the jet-set capital of the world. After walking the beach and taking in the local scene, I went to the restaurant at the top of my hotel, sat down at a table overlooking the water and ordered dinner.

A retired couple from the United States was seated at a table a few feet from me, speaking to one another in a volume I couldn't ignore. At one point in their conversation, the husband looked at his wife with a self-satisfied gaze and said, "Honey, being here tonight, at *this* hotel on *this* beach, makes all of life's efforts worthwhile. I mean, *look* at this! *Copacabana* Beach! The long hours at work, the overtime, the business travel.... It was all worth it to be able to be right here, right now."

His words hit me like a sledgehammer. I was *nineteen years old* and was already "here." The thought of spending the next fifty years enduring a passion-killing job only to come back to this same hotel overlooking this same beach and have dinner at this very same table seemed insane to me. My disillusionment rose as I silently fumed. "This is not enough of a payoff for five decades of life lived," I thought. "This can't be enough for people!"

Hearing my thoughts, God responded with a whisper. "Bill, almost everyone you know is living for additional income, and yet you have not even spent the last two bonus checks that are still tucked inside your wallet. How many checks will you need to pile up before you get it? If money fired you up, you would have used your last two bullets by now. Paychecks are *never* going to energize you, Bill. That is not who I wired you to be."

I was so rattled by this experience that I left my uneaten steak on the table and headed for my hotel room a few floors down. My mind replayed one question over and over again: "If paychecks will never scratch the itch, God, then what's going to do it for me?"

Inside my room, I sat with my palms upturned on my lap. With the most sincere words I knew how to say, I prayed, "God, guide my life toward a purpose that really will count. I am wide open to how you would choose to lead my life!"

I heard no audible response. Nothing. Instead, an odd feeling swept over me—the kind of feeling that race car drivers must feel when they're barreling into a turn at high speed and they start to lose control of their cars—a feeling of pure adrenaline mixed with terror.

Within months of that monumental evening, I would walk away from my family's business, leave the comfortable life I had known in Kalamazoo and move to Chicago where I would help a friend lead the youth ministry that eventually gave birth to Willow Creek Community Church. I was finally beginning to grasp that whispers matter. They matter a *lot*.

And decades later, I still shake my head in wonder at the power of a single whisper I received after not eating a meal while overlooking Brazil's most famous beach.

THREE YEARS INTO THAT YOUTH-GROUP LEADERSHIP, ATTEN-dance had exploded from an original collection of twenty-five to more than a thousand kids. As is always the case in ministry, there were challenges, but what I recall from this era is *life* and *peace*. I was watching the promise of Romans 8:6 play out powerfully in my young, twenty-something world. "The mind controlled by the sinful nature is death," the verse says, "but the mind controlled by the Spirit is life and peace." The youth group was growing, people were coming to Christ, I had a beautiful wife, we were expecting our first child—life was firing on all pistons.

Whenever I had fought God's guidance in my life, I'd experienced feelings of anxiety and "death." But here? Now? In the midst of teaching kids I loved? I was right where I was supposed to be for the rest of my life. Or so I thought. But uneasy feelings began. I was sensing God's guidance in a new direction.

Imagine the conversation I had with my young, pregnant wife when I suggested that we put our recently acquired house up for sale because I was hearing whispers from God about starting a church from scratch in a distant suburb. Suffice it to say, it was a long night!

Enter Willow Creek Theater.

~

Holding church in a movie theater might sound like a fun gig to you, but when that movie theater regularly shows scary movies on Saturday night and assumes that—since you're coming in on Sunday morning anyway—you might as well be the ones to clean up the fright-induced pools of vomit that wind up coating the floor, it loses a bit of its luster.

What's more, those of us who had been called to start Willow were flat-broke teenagers and early twenty-somethings who knew nothing of starting a church. In this case "life" and "peace" would come by way of selling tomatoes door-to-door to fund a meager sound system, and cashing in on every penny of credit we could get, just to keep the lights on.

But to no one's surprise, God proved faithful each and every step of the way, despite rookie leadership errors on my part that several times threatened to utterly do us in.

Eventually, after countless decisions for Christ, recommitments, baptisms, heartfelt prayers, growth opportunities seized and acts of service given, God would bless Willow Creek with a permanent property to call home. And over time, that little band of tomato sellers—who had been so committed to hearing and heeding God's promptings—would be handed an opportunity to influence people on a scale no one ever could have imagined.

Somewhere in the late 1980s, I noticed a trend in the kind of phone calls coming my way at church. Pastors from Dallas to Orlando, LA to Seattle began hearing about what God was doing at Willow Creek, and they called to ask for help. "Would you train us?" was the most common refrain. "Would you show us how you 'do' church like you do?"

These phone calls came with increasing consistency, but I was busy leading Willow at the time and didn't feel I had much to say that could help these other pastors. Willow's leaders and I were so focused on trying to accomplish the mission we had been given by God that I never stopped to assess *how* we were doing what we were doing. We were quite content to keep forging ahead in South Barrington and let others sort out their own stuff.

But along the way, one pastor made an offer I couldn't refuse. I was sitting in my office when his call came through, and after a few seconds of pleasantries, this pastor made his pitch.

"I am so determined to glean from the leadership lessons your team has learned," he implored, "that I'll fly to Chicago at my own expense on any day of your choosing if it means that such a meeting could occur."

I rattled off reasons why his plan wouldn't work: I was too busy. I didn't have anything substantive to share. My focus was set on South Barrington.

It was a lame litany of excuses.

"Surely I am not the first pastor who has called....," he said.

"Well, no," I admitted.

"Then why don't you compile a list of the next dozen or so pastors who call you," he suggested, "and invest just one day in training us all at the same time? I'd be happy to coordinate the event. We could rent a conference room at a local hotel so that you wouldn't have to use up one of Willow's rooms to get this done. All you would have to do is show up and answer questions all day long. I'll handle the rest!"

This guy was determined. There was no way I could say no.

"If you're willing to do all that legwork," I conceded, "I will be happy to show up. Send me a few date options, and let's go."

Several weeks later, I stepped into the hotel conference room and found twenty-five serious-minded pastors who were committed to getting better in their leadership roles. The engagement level was high, the questions were intelligent and the interaction around the table was catalytic to each of us. By the time I looked down at my watch, it was four o'clock in the afternoon. The day had flown by.

I had a commitment at the church that night, and as I pulled away from the hotel and made my way back up Algonquin Road, I sensed a two-word prompting from God that was as clear as any I have ever received: "Serve pastors," he said. That was it. "Serve pastors."

As I absorbed that whisper, I said to God, "If what you mean by that is doing what I just did today, I'm in! I now see the value of investing in other leaders this way, and if this is how you would have me spend a portion of my time and energy, I'll do it." I realized that living out this whisper might very well complicate my life and ministry, but I couldn't deny the clarity of God's input, nor could I refute the power of what had unfolded before me in the conference room that day. God's bidding was clear, and I was determined to see where it would lead.

In the coming years, the Willow Creek Association would be birthed from this desire to usher in help for as many local church pastors as possible, so that *every* congregation could prevail. And as the number of those banded-together churches crested one thousand, five thousand, ten thousand and more, I would catch myself thinking, "I love that God willingly speaks to us, that he cares enough for us as his kids to whisper the path that he'd have us walk."

"Spiritually alive" and "filled to the brim with peace"—these are the two descriptors that mark this season of life for me. But as is often the case when walking closely with Christ, the tides of our world can shift quickly, and in some pretty significant ways.

WITHIN SEVERAL YEARS, I NOTICED A NEW TREND IN THE PHONE calls we were receiving. The calls that once came in from Dallas, Orlando, LA and Seattle now originated in London, Frankfurt, Sydney and Singapore. Our international foray had begun.

I began making trips to various global locations where committed pastors were hungry to grow in their leadership skills. One year, during an especially rigorous trip through Western Europe, I arrived in Lucerne, Switzerland, where I was to speak to four hundred pastors at a regional leadership conference. Fighting exhaustion, I seriously questioned if I should be saying yes to so many of these international requests.

After nearly six hours of teaching, my session was followed by a worship leader who took the stage. From my seat in the front row of the centuries-old Swiss sanctuary, all I could think about was getting back to my hotel and crashing on the bed. But tonight, that just wasn't meant to be. The worship guy had more than a final song in mind.

"I think we should linger here a few more minutes," he said, strumming his guitar quietly, reverently, with a spirit of worship I clearly did not share.

I eyed him suspiciously, as though his impromptu extension was in direct challenge to my silent cry for sleep. My throat was sore, my back ached, my head was foggy and all I wanted was a mattress. His words again interrupted my thoughts: "I'll keep playing as long as I need to, in order for God to have the chance to speak to those of us who need to hear from him now."

"Nooo!" my mind revolted. "Don't play *that* card." I let my head fall into my hands. I was beside myself with exhaustion. "Just do us all a favor," I thought, "and end this session now."

No luck. This guy was convinced that God was trying to speak to someone. In total exasperation I mumbled quietly, "God, if I'm the guy keeping us from ending this conference, then speak to me and let's get this over with."

And with my hand on a Bible, I would tell you that God unmistakably spoke to me. "For reasons you do not have to understand," he said, "I am calling you to serve church leaders beyond the borders of the United States. I am making no promises that it will be easy. In fact, it will require more sacrifice than anything else I have asked you to do, but I am asking you now … serve church leaders wherever I give you opportunity around the world."

There it was, in about fifteen seconds flat—one innocent whisper that would upturn a major part of my life.

As daunting as it all sounded to me that day in the front row of that historic sanctuary, I had walked with God long enough by then to know that even his tough assignments are precious entrustments. And when he calls us into sacrificial roles, it is never without his caring presence or affection. That lone whisper complicated the next twenty years of my life in ways that I never could have imagined: the time away from my family has been tougher than I ever imagined; the toll on Willow is a story in itself; and the emotional and physical price of crossing time zones thousands of times is higher than I ever calculated. Truly, living out the "whisper in Lucerne" has taken me to levels of loneliness and despair that I didn't know existed. More often than I care to admit, I have asked God to amend or rescind that whisper. Interestingly—and sometimes annoyingly—I get no response to that prayer.

As I write this, I still am recuperating from jet lag from a recent trip to Asia. Did I feel God's presence and favor? Absolutely! Did I feel obedient to his bidding? Yes. Were there moments of exhilaration? Yes. But would I gladly receive an updated whisper releasing me from all international responsibilities starting today? You better believe I would.

Whispers can be dangerous things. They can come with huge price tags. God's whisper to his Son, Jesus—to make a redemptive visit to planet Earth—was a costly one, and as we will see in the next chapter, high-cost whispers are a huge part of what has kept the kingdom dream alive throughout the centuries. Therefore it should come as no surprise that a certain number of whispers that come our way will drive us to our knees and stretch our faith like nothing else can. So be it. We only live once, and I much prefer the idea of standing before God one day, having done his bidding to the best of my understanding than to face him knowing full well that I ignored his voice and sidestepped the tougher promptings I received. What started for me with the reciting of a poem to Miss Van Soelen is what I cling to still, to this day:

> *Oh! give me Samuel's ear,*
> *An open ear, O Lord,*
> *Alive and quick to hear*
> *Each whisper of Thy Word;*
> *Like him to answer to Thy call*
> *And to obey Thee first of all.*

CHAPTER 2

OUR
COMMUNICATING GOD

Recently I flew to Minneapolis, Minnesota, to help a Willow Creek Association church raise money for a building that would soon be under construction on their newly acquired plot of land. This wonderful church has grown from a small nucleus of people seven years ago to nearly three thousand today. As I understood my role for this event, I was to come speak to a thousand or so of their core members—who were going to be squeezed together in the ballroom of a local Radisson Hotel—about sacrificing time, talent and resources so that this first "real" building could be built.

Now, I do this sort of thing a lot. I love to help churches make their facilities more useful or advance new ministry initiatives. Typically in these settings, all I bring with me is a single sheet of paper with a few reminders of pertinent points.

This particular night in Minneapolis—about fifteen minutes before the program was to begin—I was talking with the senior pastor about the background of the church. While he was giving me a little history lesson, I sensed a definite whisper from God.

It wasn't an audible voice I discerned, but I knew unmistakably that heaven was trying to break through.

"The talk you brought is not the one I want you to give," God seemed to say.

The senior pastor kept going, but by then his voice was being drowned out by an inaudible conversation in my head. "The talk I *brought*," I countered to God, "is the only talk I *have*."

Still more details from the senior pastor. And still the Spirit kept speaking. "I'll give you another talk," he said, as if that was supposed to give me comfort when I was twelve minutes from taking the stage.

Knowing nothing else to do, I interrupted the senior pastor mid-syllable. "Excuse me, but is there a private room where I can be alone for a few minutes?" I asked.

Concern swept across his face as he undoubtedly wondered whether his keynoter was going to follow through or flake. "Are you okay?" he asked. "Are you feeling alright?"

Knowing my response would do nothing to reassure him, I shot straight anyway: "I'm not sure. Can we just find that room?"

Once huddled in a side room to the right of the stage, I took out a pad of paper and a pen. "God," I said aloud, "I'm very willing for you to give me a different talk than the one I came prepared to deliver. *Very* willing. But here's the deal: You've got nine minutes and nothing more. How about making this quick?"

I began writing furiously as the heaven-sent ideas came to me, formulating a rough outline as I went. Partway through my frenetic process, there was a rapid knock on the door. "Pastor Hybels," someone called, "they've already begun the music. You've got to get out there."

With the ink still wet on the page, I took the stage and began to deliver my new talk. Thirty seconds in, it was obvious to me that this message was exactly what God had wanted me to say.

These ideas—the ones he had shot through my mild state of panic—were precisely the ideas he wanted delivered to the group that had gathered on this night.

Throughout my entire thirty-five-minute talk, I couldn't help but think, "If these people only knew...."

After the event dismissed, and just as I was heading for the side door to catch my plane back home, the pastor stopped me and shook my hand. "I can't thank you enough for coming, Bill," he said. "And what an incredible message! It was so ... *fresh*."

I laughed out loud. "You don't know the half of it!"

Moments later in the car, I thought, "For fifty-some years, I've tried to train my ear toward heaven, and yet it still amazes me when God actually chooses to speak."

Throughout history God has spoken. For millennia, he has forged his children's faith by promising parted waters, empowering unlikely leaders, declaring world-changing prophecies—and imparting last-minute sermons to pastors who questioned whether he really would deliver. In short, our God is a communicating God. Always has been, and always will be. And if there is one story in Scripture that goes to great lengths to prove this point, it's the story of Elijah, the prophet described in 1 Kings as a man who was "zealous for God."

There comes a point in Elijah's remarkable ministry when his zealotry has fizzled to zero. He is ready to call it quits. "I've been working my heart out," he says to God, and for what? "The people of Israel have abandoned your covenant, destroyed the places of worship and murdered your prophets. I'm the only one left, and now they're trying to kill me."[1]

Elijah felt undone, and perhaps the only thing that could improve his mood was a firsthand encounter with God.

As the story goes, Elijah trekked into the desert and eventually collapsed from exhaustion under the shade of a tree. It was here that an angel who happened to be in the area gave him specific instructions for where he could go to experience the presence of God. The instructions took Elijah forty days and forty nights to follow, but eventually he ended up at Horeb, the mountain that the angel had told him to find. He crawled his way into a cave and got some much-needed sleep.

The next day, the Lord said to Elijah, "Go, stand on the mountain at attention before God. God will pass by."[2] Enter whisper number one. Elijah's weariness gave way to wonder. I imagine his heart beating a little faster as he considered what it would be like to meet *firsthand* the One he had served all these years.

Elijah obeyed the whisper and hiked up the mountain. The Bible describes a hurricane-force wind howling past Elijah as he stood on that mountain's face. Strength, might, power, brute force—"That's probably God," Elijah must have thought. Yet the text says, "But God wasn't to be found in the wind."[3]

Next up came a full-fledged, mountain-trembling earthquake. But again, God was not there.

A fire then blazed by, consuming everything on the side of the mountain but Elijah himself—yet to his sure surprise, his God was not to be found in the flames.

Finally, the text says, following the fire came a "gentle and quiet whisper."[4] And amazingly, *that's* where Elijah found God.

The wind, the earthquake, the fire—none of these conduits of God's company would have shocked Elijah as much as the still, small voice that emerged. In response, he "muffled his face with his great cloak, went to the mouth of the cave, and stood there."[5]

"So Elijah, now tell me, what are you doing here?" God whispered. Elijah then told God all of his frustrations, unburdening himself from the emotional poundage he'd been carrying. I envision Elijah—enveloped by God's audible whisper, his shoulders relaxing with each syllable he spoke—thinking, "Am I glad you're here!" Nothing else can ease the soul like the presence of our Holy God.

On Mount Horeb that day, Creator convened with creation, and one man's life was forever changed. Regardless of what else Elijah might have later told his friends about this encounter—and about God himself—undoubtedly he had been a witness to two attributes at the very core of who God is: he's relational and he is near.

He is all-powerful, yes. He is righteous and holy too. He is sovereign, he is majestic, he is magnificent, he is just. But what stunned Elijah on the side of that mountain—and what will stun you someday if it hasn't already—is that the same God who is all-powerful, all-knowing, all-*everything*, yearns to be in relationship with us. The God of the Scriptures is irrepressibly communal, hopelessly familial, and his whispers are still ours to hear.

FROM TODAY'S VANTAGE POINT, I CAN LOOK BACK ON MY SPIRItual life thus far and see two distinct eras. The first era was defined by my thinking of God in non-relational ways: Like Elijah, I looked for God in the passing weather patterns of my life, oblivious to the fact that he was right by my side all along. I thought of him as a distant businessman, holed up in a corner office somewhere or off on an important trip. The CEO of the Universe—that's who I took God to be.

During that era, Christianity was nothing more to me than a compilation of theoretical ideas about God: There were beliefs to be memorized, doctrines to be mastered and a moral code that at all costs must be maintained. But aside from that? My faith system could be whittled down to a simple rule that I hoped would keep my nose clean: *Do not disturb the CEO.*

If you were to study the major religions of the world, you would discover that most of them rely on an impersonal dynamic with their deity. Like the version of my Christianity of old, there are beliefs to be mastered and codes and rituals to be followed—and perhaps some rewards in this life or the next. But the stuff of genuine relationship between God and humankind? It is nowhere to be found.

Biblical Christianity is a far cry from those systems, as I would eventually learn. From Genesis to Revelation, the constant refrain of Scripture declares that our faith is relational—God listens when we speak through prayer, and we are to listen when he speaks through his whispers. In that earlier era, I longed for a sense of whispers like those, and thankfully, over time, I would learn to hear them.

The second of my spiritual eras has been marked by a far different understanding of Christianity than the first. As I would scour the Scriptures—the *logos*, the authoritative, infallible, inerrant, eternal Word of God—to find out what God was really like, I discovered a deity who couldn't have been more different from the CEO-type I had dreamed up. I began to understand that God was near to me, and that a relationship with me was on his mind.

You don't get very far in the pages of Scripture before you begin to see evidence of God's whispering ways. Bear with me as we take a look throughout history at God's stellar track record of communication. I think you will be struck, as I have been, at how prevalent his whispers have been:

The beginning of the Bible tells us that God communicated within the holy Trinity—the Father, the Son and the Holy Spirit—and that when he decided to establish the physical world, it was a whisper that got the job done. "Let there be light," God says in Genesis 1:3, and as is always the case when the recipient of divine direction is open to input from above, creation found a way to comply.

Soon thereafter, the people he'd created became the recipients of God's whispers. Adam and Eve "heard the voice of the LORD God walking in the garden in the cool of the day."[6] God spoke to Noah about the coming flood and his need to build the ark for the safety of his family.[7] Abraham, still going by the name Abram, heard the words of God's promise and trusted them.[8] Jacob, Isaac's mischievous son, heard from God during a vision as a young man. Later, he would receive another "visionary" whisper after moving from his homeland to Egypt to escape a devastating famine.[9]

The great leader Moses heard the voice of God from a bush that wouldn't stop burning.[10] An entire nation heard the voice of God when he delivered the Ten Commandments through Moses.[11] God told Moses what to say to Pharaoh, the Israelites' captor. He gave Moses detailed instructions on how to build and decorate the tent where the people would worship him.[12] It is obvious from Scripture that there was *intimacy* between God and this man Moses: "The LORD would speak to Moses face to face," Exodus 33:11 (NIV) states, "as a man speaks with his friend."

Later, the prophet Balaam said, "I must speak only what God puts in my mouth."[13] And who can forget when Balaam's talkative donkey received some divine direction of her own?

When Moses led the Israelites through the wilderness, Scripture tells us that still more people could hear the voice of God: "Surely the LORD our God has shown us his glory and his greatness," they said, "and we have heard his voice from the midst of the fire."[14]

God clearly communicated with Joshua, after his mentor Moses had died. He talked to Gideon, giving the warrior specific instructions about how many (or rather, how few) men to take into battle in order to secure a swift victory.[15] Then there was the wife of Manoah, who came to her husband one day and informed him that God had spoken to her through an angel. She learned she would conceive and give birth to a son—a boy she would name Samson, who would be dedicated to the Lord's work and rescue Israel from the Philistines.[16]

Young Samuel—another yearned-for child born to a woman in tune with God's whispers—certainly heard a word from the Lord, as I mentioned in chapter 1. In this same biblical era, God whispered specific direction to shepherd-turned-king David. According to 2 Samuel 2:1, "In the course of time, David inquired of the LORD. 'Shall I go up to one of the towns of Judah?' he asked. The LORD said, 'Go up.' David asked, 'Where shall I go?' 'To Hebron,' the LORD answered." Specific questions, specific answers.

A lesser known prophet, Micaiah, said, "As sure as God lives, what God says, I'll say."[17]

God even spoke to Satan and then to Job during the well-known story of Job losing it all, only to gain far more from God.

The prophet Isaiah testified to the presence of God's still, small voice. "Whether you turn to the right or to the left," he told the people of Jerusalem, "your ears will hear a voice behind you saying, 'This is the way; walk in it.'"[18]

Earlier in the book of Isaiah, the prophet responded to God's whisper with now-famous words. "Also I heard the voice of the Lord, saying, 'Whom shall I send, and who will go for us?' Then said I, 'Here am I; send me.'"[19] That one whisper alone has compelled many Christ-followers across the globe to leave the lives they know and avail themselves of an adventure that could only be orchestrated by God. I've known executives, accountants, mechanics, teachers, doctors, full-time students, at-home moms and people who fill almost every other profession imaginable who one day decide to radically shift gears in favor of following a whisper from God. Leaving the lives they knew behind, they embark on a journey that only God himself could have dreamed up. "Here I am, Lord. Send me!"—it's a powerful prayer to pray.

This same prophet Isaiah said of God's whispers: "The Sovereign LORD has given me an instructed tongue, to know the word that sustains the weary. He wakens me morning by morning, wakens my ear to listen like one being taught. The Sovereign LORD has opened my ear; I have not been rebellious, I have not turned away."[20]

It seems God prepared another prophet, Jeremiah, early in life to pay attention to heaven-sent wisdom he would receive along the way: "But the LORD said to me, 'Do not say, I am too young.' You must go to everyone I send you to and say whatever I command you."[21]

God has spoken clearly to *many* of his followers: "Surely the Sovereign LORD does nothing without revealing his plan to his servants the prophets."[22]

SWEEPING INTO THE NEW TESTAMENT, GOD SPOKE TO THE elderly priest Zechariah through the angel Gabriel, who delivered good news: Zechariah would soon father a son, John the Baptist, who would be called the greatest human ever to live.[23]

The same angel then spoke to Mary, the mother of Jesus. "The angel went to her and said, 'Greetings, you who are highly favored! The Lord is with you.'"[24]

An angel spoke to a jittery Joseph in a dream, telling him not to be afraid to take a very pregnant Mary as his wife.[25] And

God communicated in multi-part harmony—through angels, shepherds and prophets—to announce the birth of his Son, Jesus Christ. He spoke to shepherds through an angel: "Do not be afraid. I bring you good news of great joy that will be for all the people. Today in the town of David a Savior has been born to you; he is the Messiah, the Lord."[26]

God spoke to his own Son as well. "As soon as Jesus was baptized," says Matthew 3:16–17, "he went up out of the water. At that moment heaven was opened, and he saw the Spirit of God descending like a dove and alighting on him. And a voice from heaven said, 'This is my Son, whom I love; with him I am well pleased.'"

John 1:1 refers to Jesus as "the Word," and through the Messiah incarnate, God would whisper countless times—to city officials, religious leaders, tax collectors, fishing-industry workers, hard-working moms and more. Even the natural world received its fair share of input, such as when Jesus said to the storm, "Be still!"[27]

As you'd expect, the storm obeyed.

Jesus spoke to his disciples the unknowable truth about the death of Mary and Martha's brother. "So Jesus then said to them plainly, 'Lazarus is dead, and I am glad for your sakes that I was not there, so that you may believe; but let us go to him.'"[28]

God spoke clear, practical instruction to Philip. "Now an angel of the Lord said to Philip, 'Go south to the road—the desert road—that goes down from Jerusalem to Gaza.'"[29]

Later in the book of Acts, God spoke to Peter while the apostle was on the roof waiting for lunch. God said, "Do not call anything impure that God has made clean."[30]

The leaders of the early church understood God's propensity to whisper. After making a decision concerning the Gentiles' entry into the church, Scripture records their words, "It seemed good to the Holy Spirit and to us...."[31]

God sometimes spoke through the evidence of divine providence. In Acts 16:7, the author writes, "When they [Paul and his traveling companions] came to the border of Mysia, they tried to enter Bithynia, but the Spirit of Jesus would not allow them to."

During an awful storm that caused his ship to go down, the apostle Paul heard from the Lord, and addressed the passengers and crew: "Last night an angel of the God whose I am and whom I serve stood beside me and said, 'Do not be afraid, Paul. You must stand trial before Caesar; and God has graciously given you the lives of all who sail with you.' So keep up your courage, men, for I have faith in God that it will happen just as he told me."[32] And it did.

Both Paul and Peter understood their roles to include the responsibility of speaking for God. Paul wrote, "But we speak the wisdom of God in a mystery, even the hidden wisdom, which God ordained before the world unto our glory."[33] "For we are not as many, which corrupt the word of God: but as of sincerity, but as of God, in the sight of God speak we in Christ."[34]

God spoke to the apostle Paul during an especially long and dark night of the soul. "Three times I pleaded with the Lord to take [the thorn in my flesh] away from me. But he said to me, 'My grace is sufficient for you, for my power is made perfect in weakness.'"[35]

The writer to the Hebrews reminds us that God speaks to us through his Son. "In the past God spoke to our ancestors through the prophets at many times and in various ways, but in these last days he has spoken to us by his Son, whom he appointed heir of all things, and through whom also he made the universe."[36]

In 1 Peter 4:11 (NIV), we read this counsel from one man who lived wide open to God: "If anyone speaks, he should do it as one speaking the very words of God ... so that in all things God may be praised through Jesus Christ."

And finally, God spoke to his church through the advocacy of the Holy Spirit. The Message transliteration of Revelation 2:7 says this:

> Are your ears awake?
> Listen.
> Listen to the Wind Words, the Spirit blowing through
>   the churches.
> I'm about to call each conqueror to dinner.
> I'm spreading a banquet of Tree-of-Life fruit, a supper
> plucked from God's orchard.

Listen to the "Wind Words," that verse suggests—the whispered promptings of God. Still today he is speaking, as evidenced by John 14:26: "The Advocate, the Holy Spirit, whom the Father will send in my name, will teach you all things and will remind you of everything I have said to you."

It is by these whispers, John 15:5 says, that we are led toward a productive and fruitful life. By the still, small voice of God, our lives are flooded with personal assurance, correction, insight, guidance from above.[37] By our heavenly Father's wisdom, we are directed, aided, changed and eventually grown up.[38] And aren't you and I both grateful for that!

If there is a pattern in Scripture regarding whispers, it is that we serve a communicating God—a God of words. He created with a word, he healed with a word, he encouraged with a word, he rebuked with a word, he guided with a word, he prophesied with a word, he assured with a word, he loved with a word, he served with a word and he comforted with a word. Throughout all of history, God has communicated, and he still is at it today. The issue isn't whether or not God is speaking; it's whether we will have ears to hear what he says.

As I hope you have seen in this little trek through biblical history, Scripture is packed with powerful texts that demonstrate the whispering ways of God. But perhaps my favorite is the story of a murderer-turned-minister, a man known to us as the apostle Paul.

For the majority of his early days, Paul went by the name of Saul, a righteous Pharisee consumed with bitterness and rage toward people of "the Way," as Christ-followers were known in those days. Saul hated Christians and everything they stood for, and he plotted to find legal ways to have them arrested or even killed. One morning, his revulsion having reached fever pitch, he decided to pay a visit to Damascus, home of many converts to Christianity. Before departing, Saul asked the high priest in Jerusalem for permission to capture and perhaps kill any Christians he happened to encounter along the way. "Permission granted," Saul must have thought. "Nothing can stop me now!"

Little did he know, a minor diversion awaited him as the Damascan skyline came into view.

Acts 9 tells the tale of Saul and his entourage riding along the road, when suddenly a bright, terrifying light from heaven consumes Saul, knocks him off his horse and throws him to the ground. Once he catches his breath, he tries to get his feet back under him. But the task gets a little more complicated when Saul discovers he can no longer see.

Some texts refer to the light that blinded Saul that day as possessing the brightness of the sun—think of the piercing intensity of a welder's torch, and then multiply that by a thousand. Understandably, the concentration of that shaft of light sent Saul staggering to the sand, which is precisely where he received whisper number one from God. "Saul, Saul," a voice said, "why do you persecute me?"[39]

Face down on the ground and blind, Saul had no idea where

the voice came from. "Lord, who are you?"[40] he asked. It was a reasonable question, really. "I am *Jesus Christ*," came the declaration in response, "the one you have been persecuting!"[41] Jesus might as well have added, "I am alive and well, thank you very much. I am resurrected, and here I am, with you on this road. And today, my friend, I have a few things I'd like to say."

NOW, ANOTHER PART OF THIS STORY ADDS CRITICAL DIMENSION to its plot. In the same city of Damascus, where Jesus told Saul to go and await further instructions, there lived a man named Ananias, who likely was on Paul's short list of people to capture and kill; Ananias was not only a Christ-follower, but a devoted one at that.

Acts 9:10–12 says that God spoke to Ananias in a vision, telling him to go to Saul and deliver a message. God even provides the address where Saul is staying—the house of Judas on Straight Street. "He's there praying," God explained. "He has just had a dream in which he saw a man named Ananias enter the house and lay hands on him so he could see again" (MSG).

God may have been calm, cool and collected about the whole deal, but Ananias thought differently of things. "Hey, God," he essentially said, "I don't know if you've neglected to keep up with the daily news or what, but Saul's name is all over the headlines. He's a *terrorist*, and the whole reason he's in town is to destroy the church that I attend. If you think I'm going to actually *seek him out*, well, then one of us is crazy!"

Ananias delineated all of the reasons why his answer to God's instruction was no, but God stood by his one-word reply: "Go." And Ananias went.

God instructed Ananias to tell Saul that Saul was a "chosen instrument," that he would be used to proclaim the name of

Christ to many people, and that in doing so, he would suffer greatly for Jesus' sake—that's it, just three little messages that needed to be delivered—by a Christian, to the greatest Christian-hater of the day.

HAD SAUL NOT OBEYED *HIS* WHISPER FROM GOD, ANANIAS could not have obeyed the one he himself received. Back on the road to Damascus as Saul lay there blinded by the light, God had issued him a triad of instructions, as well: "Get up, Saul. Go into the city. And wait."

Saul now had a decision to make. What would he do with the direction he'd been given? He's a tough guy—should he just stand up, shake his fist at heaven and say, "Is that your best shot?"

In perhaps the wisest move of Saul's life to that point, he chose the other path. The text says that he rose, he was led into the city by his band of brothers (who were probably shocked to be leading their once-fearless, now-helpless leader), and he waited for whatever would happen next.

I am convinced that one of the major reasons a one-time terrorist wound up becoming one of the most impactful Christian leaders in history is because he chose the path of obedience. On day one, when Jesus asked him to do three little things, *he did them*. And that step of initial obedience began a pattern of submission to the will and ways of God. Despite the eventual respect among believers that Saul—now Paul—would come to enjoy, the apostle Paul never got too seasoned, sophisticated or smart to do anything less than that which Jesus whispered for him to do. How I wish the same always could be said of me!

There are seasons when I am "meticulously obedient" to the will and whispers of God, and then there are times when I'm sure I know a better way. Still, I try to keep coming back to my heavenly Father with open hands, an open heart and a keener interest in whatever insights he is willing to share. "God, if there is something you would like me to do," I prayed recently, "then please say so. It doesn't matter what it is; I'll do it."

Wouldn't you know it? He actually took me up on that prayer.

Lynne and I had just come from a funeral home across town after saying our final farewells to my aunt. As we approached our car, I spotted a frail, elderly woman pulling into the nearby apartment complex. She parked her car and began to slowly and laboriously pull grocery bags out of her trunk. "How about helping that woman with her groceries?" the Holy Spirit seemed to prompt.

I initially brushed past the whisper because Lynne was with me and we were ready to go. But I had just made that offer to God, "If there is something you would like me to do...." I knew I had to comply.

"Lynne," I said, "I've got this little pact going with God, and I need to go help that woman with her groceries for a minute...."

My wife tried to conceal her dumbfounded expression, but I saw it peeking through. You probably know the look, the one that says, "*You?* Living at your pace? Helping someone you don't even *know*? Wow. It *must* be God."

I approached the elderly woman. "Can I give you a hand with your groceries?" I asked.

"Oh, yes! Thank you!" she said, relieved.

The driveway leading back to her apartment recently had been seal-coated and was roped off, meaning residents had to walk a few hundred yards just to get from their cars to their homes. I knew that this small act of kindness would honor God and help meet a real need; what I didn't know was that those grocery sacks boasted thirty pounds of fresh peaches each.

Pretending the added weight didn't affect me a bit, I said, "All set here. You lead the way."

She began winding through backyards that had become swamps due to recent rains, but drenched dress shoes would be the least of my worries that afternoon. The woman was extremely arthritic and slow-moving. On top of that, she had some sort of emphysema that forced us to take a breather every forty-five seconds or so. It took us a full thirty minutes to make our way to her apartment, and by the time we arrived, we were *tight*. I had learned more about this dear woman's life than I could ever have hoped to know.

We entered her modest home, and I made my way to the kitchen, where I set the sacks on the counter before turning to shake her hand and then let myself out through the front door. The woman left her bony, wrinkled hand in mine long after the handshake was done. "I will believe to my dying day that God sent you to help me just now," she said.

The whole deal felt so inglorious—the wet feet, the longer-than-expected trek, the lack of any earth-shattering results—and yet as I walked away from the apartment complex, something in my spirit felt right. God had whispered a simple instruction my way, and this time I had actually slowed down enough to listen. There is no greater feeling in the world than to hear—and heed—God's voice.

I often talk with people around Willow or in the community who are exploring the Christian faith. During those conversations, it is not uncommon for me to hear tales about how they are going about their normal daily routines when "weird stuff" starts happening to them. They report feeling restless in life or less satisfied with the direction they're headed. The "fun" they used to have doesn't feel quite as fun anymore. They grow weary of the way things are and wonder if there might be more to life. And typically it's in a moment like this when they finally agree to come to church.

On some occasions, I'll ask folks like these, "Do you think anyone is orchestrating those ideas that float through your mind? I mean, do you think your thoughts are just random, or is it possible that God is trying to communicate to you in some way?"

Usually, they think it's all random. Which *usually* is when I beg to differ.

"When the circumstances of your life start to shift," I suggest, "at least consider that it might be due to God. When you find yourself in a state of confusion or curiosity about the way things are going, go ahead and ask him if there's something he'd like to say to you. Open your hands, open your heart, heighten your attentiveness to any small way he might want to communicate to you, and then agree in advance that you will comply with whatever he says. Why not give it a shot? What's the downside?"

I have come to believe over time that it is the little acts of obedience that invite God's power to fully flow in our lives. When you and I prove ourselves faithful with the small whispers, he entrusts us with bigger ones. And when we follow through on those big ones, *big* kingdom results can be gained. This is what Ananias experienced firsthand, on that day when Saul became Paul. Back to our text.

ACTS 9:17–19 SAYS, "THEN ANANIAS WENT TO THE HOUSE and entered it. Placing his hands on Saul, he said, 'Brother Saul, the Lord—Jesus, who appeared to you on the road as you were coming here—has sent me so that you may see again and be filled with the Holy Spirit.' Immediately, something like scales fell from Saul's eyes, and he could see again. He got up and was baptized, and after taking some food, he regained his strength."

God had whispered specific instruction to Saul, and Saul had followed through. God also had told Ananias what he wanted him to do, and despite his initial hesitancy, that man too would cooperate.

I have read this passage of Scripture many times, and with each reading I find myself trembling just a bit. Think about it: a highly intelligent (though completely misdirected) man—who will someday become a powerful force in the hand of Almighty God—is lying blind on a bed with no clue what he is to do next—other than to wait. If someone could only deliver a small dose of knowledge—a divine insight to him—the blind man not only will regain his sight but will eventually change the whole world for good. Ananias delivers that small dose of knowledge, and Saul goes on to write two-thirds of the New Testament; he plants churches that will have lasting impact; he leaves a legacy, not of bitterness and rage, but of boldness and righteousness and faith. Lost people are saved, believers are encouraged, churches are strengthened and entire communities experience times of great peace, all because two men hear God's whispers and have the guts to respond.

I imagine God cheering from heaven's balcony as he watched Ananias enter the home where Saul lay anxiously awaiting the arrival of a man he'd never met. "You were so ecstatic about your license to kill," I picture God saying to Saul, "but I can do you one better than that! You're about to be granted a license to help millions of people throughout history *live*. You now have full access to grace. Full access to love. Full access to power. Full access to fulfillment. Stay close to me, Saul, and you will want for nothing. I will care for you. I will protect you. I will provide for you. And while we're at it, I'll even give you a new name. *Paul*—that's who you are now ... Paul, my brand-new creation."

Some time ago, on the heels of re-reading Paul's story, I held coaching meetings in Chicago with several pastors from across the nation. Typically we just talk pastor stuff—how to lead effectively, how to survive a down economy, how to balance the needs of discipleship amid very busy schedules—but that day I decided to start the session by taking a different tack. "How did you come to faith in Christ?" I asked the group. We went around the room and each person told their story, an hour comprising fascinating tales of faith. Eventually, the last pastor took his turn. "I came from a family that had no use whatsoever for God," he said, "but there was a devoted Christian family that happened to live next door."

This Christian couple had received a prompting from God to invite his family to come to church with them. Not surprisingly, his parents said no. "Actually," the pastor explained, "they said, 'We want nothing to do with your God, we want nothing to do with your church and we want nothing to do with *you*. Now leave us alone.'"

While his parents spewed their response at the next-door neighbors, this pastor, who was a young boy at the time, happened to be standing in the entryway of his house, hearing every discourteous word. He walked up to his dad, yanked on his dad's untucked shirt and said, "Hey, Dad. I'll go."

In a flash of insight, it occurred to the parents that if they allowed their son to go to church, they'd get free babysitting for much of the day. Suddenly, they weren't so opposed to the idea of these "crazy Christians" coming to their home. "You will?" his dad asked. The son nodded sincerely. "Oh. Well, then ... okay," the father said, eyeing the Christian couple. "I guess you can take our boy with you, if that's what you want to do."

Every week—week after week—all through that boy's junior high years, the next-door neighbors stopped by on Sunday morning and gave the son a ride to church. Once the young man was in high school, he surrendered his life to Jesus Christ. From there he went to college, earned his degree and decided to start a church—a church that now includes thousands of worshipers on the east coast of the United States.

Again, it all traces back to one whisper that one couple chose to obey. They made it a priority to live life with one ear open to heaven, and since then, through their impact on one young man, many have come to faith.

And the same God who whispered a word to them wants to help direct your every step too. Just like the kings and prophets and apostles who have gone before us, you and I can hear straight from God. He will dwell among us, Exodus 29:43–46 promises. He will remain the Lord our God. And it is this God of whom author Dallas Willard writes, "People are meant to live in an ongoing relationship with, speaking and being spoken to."[42]

SEVERAL YEARS AGO AT A RESTAURANT, I WAS HELPING A NEW believer pray aloud for the very first time. "Just close your eyes, think of God and tell him what is on your mind," I assured this man. "He will listen to you. Just say whatever you're led to say."

He stared at me incredulously for a few seconds with a look that seemed to convey, "But *you're* the pastor! Don't I have to hook something up to you? Aren't you going to sprinkle some magic dust or light some sort of incense to help me get this thing done?"

Essentially the guy was wondering if he *actually* had access to God. He knew what kind of life he had led, and it was a colorful one to be sure. What's more, he now understood just how holy and righteous God is, and he couldn't reconcile the two. "Who am I, to be given speaking rights with the King of the universe?"

he wondered. "Why would God listen to me and talk to me? Why would he give me the time of day?"

Our lunch had come and my food was getting cold. I closed my eyes and bowed my head to communicate my silent response: "Sink or swim, buddy. You're on your own."

He sat there uncomfortably for a few seconds before his shaky voice finally piped up. It was a simple prayer but it was sincere. And when at last he said, "Amen," he opened his eyes, looked at me overjoyed, and said, "I did it! I talked to God!"

I bet he remembers that prayer still today.

It's a concept I believe was at the heart of Jesus' message to his disciples when he preached the Sermon on the Mount. "Ask and it will be given to you," he says in Matthew 7:7–8. "Seek and you will find; knock and the door will be opened to you. For everyone who asks receives; those who seek find; and to those who knock, the door will be opened."

When I read that passage, I imagine Jesus looking into the eyes of people who said they loved the Father and thinking, "I only wish you knew him better."

Jesus had taught his followers how to live for God, how to stack up treasure in the right places, how to avoid sexual immorality, how to serve selflessly and so forth. But if only they *really* knew the heart of his Father more, their own hearts would absolutely melt. "If you knew of my Father's strong inclination toward you," I imagine him thinking, "it would alter your entire spiritual orientation. You would give him all of your life. You would worship him in spirit and in truth. You would trust him with your days and weeks. You would *strain* to hear his voice. My Father is available, he is approachable and he is waiting to talk to you now."

Keep in mind that for the group to whom Jesus was speaking when he delivered his hillside talk, this news came as a real surprise. The idea that ordinary people could talk directly to God was staggering. It went against hundreds of years of religious tradition in which they needed an intermediary to talk to God for them. "No priest is required?" they must have asked, just to be sure they had the new deal straight.

"No priest required," Jesus' message confirmed. "There are no hoops to jump through, no rituals to entertain, no sacrifices to tend to and no ceremonial purification rights to respect. You can come boldly before my Father's throne and receive an audience with Almighty God."

I can only imagine the inner turmoil this caused for the crowd that day. Perhaps it is causing you a little trauma as well. Depending on what faith system you grew up in, it is possible that what you are reading on these pages seems downright illegal, or at least blasphemous and brash. But I promise you it's the truth of Scripture: because of Jesus Christ's work on the cross, there is *no* red tape between you and God.

He is available.

He is approachable.

And he stands ready to talk to you now.

The writer of Hebrews put it this way: "Therefore, brothers and sisters, since we have confidence to enter the Most Holy Place by the blood of Jesus ... let us draw near to God with a sincere heart in full assurance of faith."[43] In the next chapter, you'll meet a handful of men and women who are striving to live this way. They are working to improve their batting average of hearing—and heeding—the whispers of God. Whatever aspect of life seems to be weighing you down today, you can bring that burden before God. What Jesus was so sure of, we can know for sure too. God is *available*. He is *approachable*. And he is ready to talk to you now. Your move!

CHAPTER 3

EVIDENCE
FROM EVERYWHERE

O N THE MORNING OF SEPTEMBER 11, 2001, ROB CATALDO was copiloting a Boeing 767 for a major U.S. carrier, en route from Chicago to San Francisco. The day began as they all do when Rob is flying, with a preflight briefing with the captain, a thorough check of the aircraft and completion of the paperwork that authorizes them for departure. But soon enough, assumptions of "all things usual" quickly would fade away.

Somewhere over eastern Nebraska, Rob received a message from his airline via the jet's onboard computer that a Cessna and a Boeing 737 had collided over lower Manhattan. The information seemed questionable at best. A quick check of the weather in the New York City area—bright sunshine and cloudless blue skies—made Rob wonder if the single-engine plane had wandered into New York's airspace without having permission from air-traffic control.

While his mind turned over the data, further messages would clear things up. Within minutes the dispatcher reported that there was "trouble with a plane from our fleet." Rob immediately searched for the flight records for the troubled plane, only to discover that those records had been secured by his company and were inaccessible.

"That's when I knew that something was terribly wrong," Rob says. "And the worst was yet to come."

As Rob deepened his breathing and put his senses on high alert, another message suddenly came through. "Every aircraft that is on this frequency will land at the nearest suitable airport as soon as possible," came the instruction from air-traffic control. Simultaneously his airline sent their own instructions: due to suspected terrorist hijacking activity, every pilot was to secure their cockpit immediately. Under no circumstance were they to permit entry to anyone. Throughout the company's fleet, pilots closed and locked their cockpit doors and began planning their descent.

Rob and the captain had a perfect diversion airport in Denver, but it would take another hour to get there. That remaining hour is one they won't easily forget. "My stomach is in knots," the captain told Rob. But Rob felt strangely calm; moments before the fearful admission from his flying mate, Rob had received a one-sentence whisper from God. "Rob, I have never let you down before," the whisper said, "and you can trust me that I never will."

"God undeniably whispered to me that day," Rob says. "I should have been a basket case, but my Father gave me a deep sense of peace." Rob flew to his destination confident in the truth that whatever happened, God was with him.

Note that for Rob and his teammate, the circumstances had not suddenly improved. The hijacking threat still existed, and the pilots still had to get the plane on the ground quickly and safely—which they did. But the team in the cockpit were flying with two totally different perspectives: one fear, one faith. Hearing God's whisper matters.

Rob is part of Willow's congregation, and for years he has heard my challenges to live in every circumstance of life with one ear toward heaven. For him, doing so made a huge difference during one of the most frightening experiences of his life. Amazing!

Several months ago, I sent an email to the entire congregation at Willow, asking them to describe a time when they had heard a whisper from heaven and then to explain how they had responded to that whisper.

I sent the email on a Friday afternoon; by Monday my inbox was bulging with more than five hundred heartfelt replies.

Some of the respondents described the recent promptings they had received, and others ventured back in time, explaining that some of the most important, meaningful input they've been given in life happened years or even decades ago. The topics ran the gamut—vocational, relational, spiritual, physical, medical, financial and more. The tone of the whispers varied as well— sometimes God offered words of gentle affirmation, and other times he issued stiff challenges.

Far more women than men sent in their responses, which I found interesting and actually a little troubling. It may be that women are simply more willing email correspondents, but I fear that the "I can handle anything" worldview claimed by many men gives them a bias *against* outside help—even when that help comes in the form of a whisper from God. So if you're of the male persuasion, I'm offering you a special challenge to take this chapter seriously.

As I soaked up the extraordinary evidence of God's interactions with us, I thanked him for speaking not just during creation and throughout the course of biblical days, but also "today," in our fast-paced, high-tech twenty-first-century world. A sampling of those modern-day whisper stories appears in the pages that follow, and my hope is that these nudges from God will help you make more sense of the nudges you receive. As well, I hope that reading these firsthand tales will inspire you to start living "wide open" to God in *all* areas of your life. I've lumped them into broad categories—whispers of assurance, whispers of admonition, whispers of action—for continuity's sake, but I trust as you plow through them, you'll see how uniquely God speaks to the men and women who have devoted their lives to him.

Whispers of Assurance

"God did whisper to me once," Jane wrote in her email reply. "I'm absolutely sure of it." Shortly after her husband passed away, she was in bed crying herself to sleep—again—and sensed God offering specific words to soothe her soul. "You are not alone," he said, which was all Jane needed to know. Hearing from the One who never will leave your side stems loneliness every time.

Another woman, Lisa, said she knows God spoke to her too. She had been prompted to start a Mothers of Preschoolers group at Willow but was unsure of her skills and available time. Still she pressed on, believing it was what God had asked her to do. Everything seemed to be going smoothly until she was due to give a talk at the first meeting of the year.

"I seriously thought I was going to be sick," Lisa wrote. "I had prayed and prayed for weeks beforehand, and had prepared carefully, but now that the occasion was upon me, my throat was closing up."

Moments before Lisa was to take the stage, she sensed God say, "Lisa, you've done the faithful work of preparation. Now all you have to do is go out there and open your mouth. Once you do that, I'll take it from there."

With renewed confidence, Lisa walked out on the stage and gave a talk that ministered to many young mothers.

Jill used to work at a Fortune 500 company. At one point, she was given a special project that had her reporting directly to the CEO. Suffice it to say, with visibility like that, the pressure to "get it right" was intense. The project timeline was aggressive, and the people involved disagreed at every turn. Partway through her leadership of the project, Jill began to unravel.

"One day I went into the ladies' room," Jill said. "Given that I worked mostly with males, this was the safest place to fall apart. But in the midst of that river of tears, I sensed God's whisper to me: 'Be still and know that I am God,' he said. And then he whispered it a second time."

From that moment until the end of her project, whenever Jill faced seemingly overwhelming stress, rather than falling apart she would focus on the reality of God's presence in her life. This provided her a "still" center from which she could continue her work.

And then there was Jeanne, who said she clearly heard God's voice in the midst of her company's layoffs. "I was so concerned about my work status that I was having trouble sleeping," she said. "I would play out hypothetical scenarios over and over again: What if I lost my job? What if I couldn't afford rent? What if I wasn't able to find employment again? What if? What if? What if?"

Suddenly God cut through the noise in her head and simply said, "Worry not." It was such a straightforward and obvious solution, but it made *all* the difference that night. Two simple words: *Worry not!*

Many of the stories I received showcased God's tenderness toward his followers. A woman named Susan received this type of whisper from God at a Cubs game, of all places.

"The bases were loaded," Susan said, "and all of a sudden I was aware of how many people were sitting inside that stadium. There were a lot. I then thought about how many people were in the city, the state, the nation and the world. Again, a lot! Too many people to count, even.

"In that moment, and for the first time in a long time, I considered the fact that despite all of those people to care for, God was aware of *me*. He whispered, 'I know all about you, every detail of your life. And I love you.'"

Just as God was imparting this message to Susan, the Cubs hit a grand slam, which explains to me why the memory was so vivid—the Cubs *never* hit grand slams.

A Willow dad named Paul wrote in and said, "My family and I were on vacation on the island of Kauai when I decided to take a hike by myself. I got to the top of a mountain and sensed God's presence in such a strong way that I stopped moving altogether and listened for what he was trying to say."

Paul and his wife had just adopted a baby boy named Evan, and what God conveyed to him that day was this: "As much as you love your brand-new son, I love you infinitely more."

The realization almost melted Paul, a man who had never considered God's love in that way. All Christ-followers could use reminders like that.

Reading through all of the email replies was like riding an emotional roller coaster—one minute I was soaring on people's highest highs and the next minute the bottom would fall out. A woman at our church named Candace wrote about an excruciatingly painful situation she had endured, resulting from some bad choices she had made. "I kept waiting for some horrible consequence to my sin," she said, "thinking that the shame I was experiencing was going to be with me the rest of my life."

Then she came across Romans 8:34, which says, "Who can say God's people are guilty? No one, because Christ Jesus died, but he was also raised from the dead, and now he is on God's right side, appealing to God for us" (NCV).

Candace said, "As I read those words, I sensed God saying, 'My conviction is not meant to crush you. I will not let you be destroyed by the feelings you are carrying over your sinful situation. You have my word.'"

I devote an entire chapter of this book—chapter 6, "Light for Dark Nights of the Soul"—to this idea that God meets us at our deepest point of need. Candace's experience proves that, as do the next two that you'll read.

A woman wrote to tell me that earlier this year, her husband of thirty-five years committed suicide. She heard a gunshot, she ran into the room where he had been and she found her beloved husband dead on the floor. He had no history of depression, no known illness and no obvious cause for wanting to die. And yet now he was gone.

Two hours after she discovered her husband's lifeless figure, and in the midst of a flurry of emergency-personnel activity, she was walking through the foyer of her home toward the kitchen when something almost tangibly stopped her short. "It was like a force actually prevented me from moving," she said. "Once I was perfectly still, I felt a warm, almost liquid feeling move from my head all the way to my toes."

She went on to explain that there in the foyer, God whispered, "I will walk with you." There was no assurance of a quick walk, an easy walk or a pain-free walk. But even if the walk proved long and agonizing, she knew that her God would be by her side, every single step of the way. Today, this faithful woman is involved in Willow's grief-support workshops. She says that although there are sad moments and difficult days, she lives with a heart that is open to God and to whatever he might say.

I don't know what a story like this does to you, but it does wonders for my faith. Hearing how God is upholding a broken-hearted sister in Christ reminds me how ready he is to steady me too.

One more, and then we'll move on.

A man named Troy in our congregation responded to my plea for God-whispers with a story that truly was incredible to read.

Several summers ago, Troy arrived home on a typical Friday afternoon. He had endured a rigorous week at work as a day trader and decided to jump on his motorcycle and head to his health club so he could relieve a little stress. As he describes it, minutes after that seemingly innocuous decision, Troy found himself lying in the intersection of two neighborhood roads, his skull fractured and his brain exposed. He had been hit by a sixteen-year-old girl who pulled out from an adjacent gas station and into oncoming traffic before looking both ways. Witnesses relayed that the girl had been fighting with friends in her car over a cell phone. Her blood tests later came back positive for various illegal drugs.

After someone called 911, a fatality crew was deployed to the scene. Troy doesn't remember seeing anyone from that crew; he only remembers a woman kneeling over him, grabbing a shirt from his gym bag and holding his head together in a makeshift tourniquet until "official" help arrived. "The only thing she said to me was, 'Can you lift up your head?' I told her that I thought I could, but then I blacked out."

The woman would be unaccounted for in the police record, but Troy knows she was present that day—God's whisper of tender care sent in the form of a mystery woman with a crumpled shirt holding up his wounded head. "By God's grace I recovered from that incredible ordeal, and by his Word my heart was healed too. When I think back on that situation, I recite Psalm 3:3: 'But you, LORD, are a shield around me, my glory, the one who lifts my head high.'"

For guys like Troy—and people like you and me as well—I imagine there is nothing like being passed out on death's doorstep to reveal what we really believe about God. In those harrowing moments and in mundane ones too, I hope we'll remember the truth. He is the lifter of our heads *and* our hearts.

Whispers of Admonition

If there's ever a time when you and I employ "selective listening," it's when we're on the receiving end of a dressing-down, courtesy of God himself. Have you noticed this dynamic along the way? God suggests that you *stop* doing something or *start* doing something or, for once in your life, act your age, and instantly, God gets tuned out. "Surely that piece of insight wasn't from *God*," you think. "I was probably just making it up."

You go on your pre-planned way, thinking everything is copasetic once more, until minutes or days or a few weeks later, when you careen face-first into the brick wall known as God's wisdom, and realize it was *his* voice you actually ignored.

As I scrolled through hundreds of emails from our congregation, I was impressed by how many of these God-whisper stories dealt with tough, admonishing promptings. It takes real maturity to make significant changes in our lives, but for those who are gutsy enough to do so, rich blessings await.

If you're up for a challenge, I dare you to read the brief stories that follow and then give God your wide-open ear. It just might be that he has a few love-fueled rebukes lined up for you as well.

"I GREW UP IN A FAMILY WHERE YELLING WAS PROTOCOL, AN accepted behavior," Linda writes. "If something happened that was aggravating, or if an honest mistake was made, we didn't talk about it. Instead, someone just yelled.

"As a young mother of two toddlers, I never hesitated to raise my voice at spilled milk, upended dishes or unexplained crying from my little girls. One evening as I was preparing dinner, the girls were playing in the food pantry—stacking cans, in an attempt, evidently, to climb to heaven and see our dog that recently died. Somehow, in the midst of their childlike construction project, a large container of vegetable oil opened and oozed out everywhere—on clothes, hair, little fingers and feet, and through the cracks of the beautiful wood floor.

"I turned from the stove where I was cooking and literally was about to verbally pounce at my daughters with a raised and angry voice. But in the split second it took for me to turn, I distinctly heard God's voice say these words: 'Linda, no more yelling. Deal with the situation. Correct the children, but do so without ranting.' In that moment I found myself incapable of raising my voice and unable to find disparaging words. To this day, it's almost physically impossible for me to erupt in anger. Thank you, thank you, God."

As I read Linda's story, I thought, "The fact that she heeded just one simple whisper during a critical moment likely will change her family's legacy forever." Amazing what can happen when one believer listens to God.

Other examples of succinct whispers radically altered their recipient's errant attitudes. Fara wrote in to tell me about the first time she sensed God "speak."

"I was in my car, crying over a painful breakup I'd just gone through, and felt devastated at a deep level. I wasn't even a Christian yet, but for some reason, I cried out, 'God, why does it hurt so much when I'm just trying to love someone?'

"I wasn't really talking to God, but to my surprise he is the one who answered me. 'Fara,' he said, 'that's exactly how I feel when I keep trying to love you.' *Thud.* That one hit dead center."

Fara soon surrendered her life to Jesus Christ and as a result, began to hear from God *far* more frequently.

A woman in Australia named Liz recounted the experience of hearing God's admonishing whisper after visiting the brand-new home of her sister-in-law. "After I left," Liz wrote, "I sat in my car outside and felt deep pangs of jealousy and self-pity welling up. I wanted the beautiful home and perfect furnishings that my sister-in-law now enjoyed, but as soon as I let myself entertain those thoughts, God broke in with a simple request: 'Liz, make me your treasure,' he said. 'I am everything you need.'"

A covetous heart had been rebuked and redirected with a single whisper.

Donna also received words of admonishment, in the midst of tough economic times. She wrote: "It was becoming more apparent that my husband's construction/remodeling business was not going to make it through the downturn, and my own job at a commercial-construction firm would be ending soon as well. I desperately tried to find a new job that would prevent us from losing our home, but after many failed attempts things only became worse.

"Bills I couldn't pay stacked up as my fears multiplied and my anxiety level reached an all-time high. It was in the middle of that reality that I heard a whisper, straight from God. 'Stop striving,' he said. It wasn't a suggestion; it was a command. 'Stop striving. Stop striving to work so hard. Stop striving to fix this situation. Stop striving to fix your *husband*. Stop striving and just trust me.'"

Donna did just that and for the first time in a long time, she felt sweet relief from stress. Note again that her circumstances had not changed. She was still facing serious financial challenges. She still had to look for a new job. But the destructive inner anxiety that drove her obsessive striving had lessened. Such whispers have rescued me from destructive levels of stress more times than I can count.

AFTER DONNA'S EMAIL, AN INTERESTING TRIO OF EMAILS caught my eye. They all had to do with receiving admonishment from God, but it was the *conduits* for those corrections that were fascinating to me. One of them came via Oprah Winfrey, one through an iPod, and one by way of a Hawaiian pastor I happen to know and love.

Here's what Dick wrote: "Fifteen years ago I was a practicing alcoholic. One day I was working out and saw Oprah on TV. Her guests were an alcoholic and a physician, and she was trying to facilitate healing for the addict that day. It was the start of four or five random occurrences like that, where I'd be flipping television channels and happen upon someone who also was struggling to find sobriety. After that troublesome sequence, I sensed God say, 'I've shown you the source of your problem. What will you do with what I've revealed? The ball is now in your court.'"

The next night Dick showed up at a Christian twelve-step-ministry meeting at Willow and has been sober ever since. What's more, as a result of that initial divine encounter, Dick surrendered his life to Jesus Christ and was baptized in June of that year. Only God.

A young woman named Keri Lynn wrote to tell me that God spoke to her through her iPod. I raised my eyebrows in skepticism, until I got to the details of what happened that night.

"My parents were away for the weekend," she wrote, "and I was driving home from a friend's house late at night. I was on the back roads, which can get a little twisty, and eventually made my way to Elbow Road, a street where lots of people sadly have died from taking the curves too fast.

"I admit I was a little preoccupied, and as I rounded the elbow that gave the street its name, I took the bend a bit too sharply. I hadn't noticed my speed until my iPod shuffled to the song, 'Real Gone,' from the Disney movie, *Cars*. The lyrics talk about slowing down before you crash, and as I sang along to the catchy tune, I realized it was advice I should immediately take.

"I looked down at my speedometer and took things down a notch (or ten). When I looked back up, I saw a truck barreling toward me from the other side of the road. The load it carried was oversize and barely could fit on one side. I inched to the right to give him more room, but the shoulder was uneven and rough." The truck passed, but Keri Lynn was not out of the woods yet.

"As soon as I heard my right tires hit the gravel, I knew things would not end well," she continued. "The wheel jerked out of control, and before I could grab it to steady it again, my car swung wildly to the left, onto the other side of the street. In a matter of seconds I careened headfirst into the far-left ditch, flew back out of that ditch and somehow came to a dramatic stop. I stepped out of my car unharmed, which is when I saw a massive telephone pole up ahead. Who knows the damage I could have done if I had not slowed down? And who knew God spoke through iPods?" Keri Lynn surely feels he did.

The third story was from Cathie, a woman who had a difficult relationship with her mom. "In her heart I know she loves me," she explained, "but growing up it didn't feel that way because of the choices that she made."

Cathie had not spoken to her mom for six full years and said that the Mother's Day card she would send each year was the only communication they had. "I kept praying that God would change her," she said. "I can't tell you how often I prayed that prayer, but still, God chose not to act."

At the end of that six-year run, Cathie was at church one weekend and heard a friend of mine named Wayne Cordeiro speak. "He challenged us all to read our Bibles daily," Cathie remembers, "and my husband and I decided to give it a try. We read every morning and every night, and over time I noticed that something was shifting in me regarding my mother. Was God answering my prayers through his Word?

"Shortly after that experience my mom became a widow. In the clearest prompting I have ever received, the Holy Spirit instructed me to write her a letter that would hopefully encourage her sad heart. Slowly, she and I began to write each other back and forth until the day dawned when I realized that God hadn't answered my prayers by changing my mother; he had answered them by changing me."

Cathie admits that her relationship with her mom is still fragile. But she is quick to add that she knows as long as she stays tethered to the power of God's Word, his Spirit will have room to work. You and I both could probably learn a thing or two from Cathie's example.

THERE ALSO WERE STORIES THAT CENTERED ON GOD'S DESIRE to be first in his children's hearts. Tara recounted, "I gave my life to Christ at a young age but drifted away from him during my college years. After graduation, I moved away from family and friends, stopped attending church altogether and began making poor choices with my life. I longed for intimacy with God but couldn't seem to get out of my own way. It went on like this for two years before I stepped foot inside a church again—this time with my family at Christmas. During the singing portion of the service, I sensed God almost audibly say, 'Enough!' He said it over and over again, to the point that I literally was shaking where I stood. God had a purpose that I wasn't fulfilling in life, and I knew my only option was to surrender to him for real.

"After that worship service, my 'next steps' became perfectly clear. I knew I needed to move back to the Midwest, I knew I needed to find a new job and I knew I needed to get connected with a local church. And that's exactly what I did."

In another case, a guy at Willow named Jim said that on the heels of his wife's untimely death from ocular melanoma he decided to take his RV from Ohio to Colorado. He felt stuck in the overwhelming pain of fresh grief and thought it might help to get away for a while. On the first Sunday morning of his trek, he found his way to a local church. Though he felt disconnected from God, he yielded to his habit of church attendance. While singing half-heartedly during a congregational worship song, Jim felt as if God were saying, "If you cannot worship me with all that you have, do not worship me at all. I do not want your halfway heart."

As Jim then engaged with full voice, he felt his heart settling back into the full devotion to God that he had known in the past. As he sang, his tears flowed freely and his grieving soul was steadied once more.

I received other stories of admonishment—how God corrected a course, reversed a deadly habit, asked for fuller commitment from one of his kids—and each time I'd get to the end of the story, I would think of the power of going God's way in life instead of insisting on following our own path. Before you get to the final story, please carefully read this next phrase: *There is no more critical goal in life than to keep a pliable heart before God.*

God cannot be seen by spiritual eyes that are shut.

God cannot be heard by spiritual ears that are plugged.

And God cannot be followed by a heart that stubbornly stays hard.

A WOMAN NAMED JAN SENT IN A STORY THAT WAS SOBERING to read. When Jan was only eighteen years old she decided to get married. "I knew the guy was someone I should not have married," she wrote, "but I was young and thought that 'love' would make everything right."

The night before the wedding, during the dress rehearsal of the big event, Jan felt a "very strong prompting" from the Holy Spirit that she should call the whole thing off.

"I did not listen," she said. "And for many, many years after that decision, I found myself stuck with a husband who was emotionally abusive, a practicing alcoholic and extremely fond of being with women besides his wife."

I got to the last line of Jan's email and just sat there staring at the screen. She wrote, "I thought you might like to hear from someone who refused to listen to God."

I don't know the rest of Jan's story. I do know that God is in the business of redeeming the messes we make in life, but that doesn't mean there is not a price to pay—often a very steep price—for ignoring God's whispers of counsel. I don't know how Jan has experienced God's redemptive intervention in her life, but I am confident she has learned a vital lesson: that many of God's whispers are offered to save us from difficulties and pain that we don't have the wisdom or maturity to foresee. I pray that we will all keep that lesson in mind.

Whispers of Action

Divine promptings that spur you to action are some of the most important words you'll ever hear. I can remember times when God prompted me to write a letter, place a call, avoid a particular route home, give a job candidate a shot, engage a grumpy neighbor in friendly conversation and more. Sometimes the whispers are fairly involved and sometimes they're short and sweet. On more occasions than I can possibly count, his most profound words of needed wisdom have been one-word commands like "Go!" or "Stop!"

A terrifying example of this happened one time when I was in my car in our driveway. Running late for a meeting at church, I threw my car into reverse and was backing down toward the street, when I received a very strong prompting from God. "Stop. Right now!" he urged.

I slammed my foot on the brake and then sat there, thinking, "Did I forget something in the house? Was Lynne supposed to come with me?"

Figuring I must have just gotten my wires crossed, I glanced in my rearview mirror and was lifting my foot off the brake as I caught sight of our neighbor's three-year-old son, who was riding his tricycle right behind my car. He was so close that all I could see was the top of his little blond head, and had I not stayed planted on those brakes, he surely would have been seriously injured or killed.

I put my car in park, rested my head on the steering wheel and said, "Oh, God, that you would be this merciful to that child and to both of our families is beyond me. Thank you."

Minutes later my neighbors expressed equal gratitude as I stood on their porch with their son and explained the narrow escape.

How important are whispers of action? I'll let you be the judge.

By far the most common stories I received from folks at Willow dealt not with words of assurance or admonition but with whispers that prompt action in accomplishing kingdom good. Ephesians 2:10 says, "For we are God's handiwork, created in Christ Jesus to do good works, which God prepared in advance for us to do," and it seems that one of the primary ways God helps us to get these good works done is by divinely guiding our steps.

So what do "good works" look like? Based on the hundreds of emails I scoured, they include healing a relationship, impacting a neighborhood, encouraging a friend, expanding a horizon, giving tangible resources, seizing opportunities to serve, sacrificing comfort and more. I wish I had room to share every story I read, because by the end of our time together I think you'd be revved up to go out and do some good!

What follows are a few excerpts, arranged in general categories. As you take in each story, ask God if there is a "good work" in this area that he'd like for *you* to complete. Everyone below testifies that there is no better feeling in all of life than being used for good by God.

Relational Actions

One woman, Debbi, wrote in to say that it was during her mother's final days on earth that she was prompted by God to act. She and her sister had interviewed several hospice options, and although her sister was comfortable with a couple of them, Debbie wasn't so sure. She committed the matter to prayer and several days later sensed God saying, "It is *you* who should be the caregiver for your mom."

Debbi made the necessary arrangements and cared for her mother until her dying day two months later. "It was a wonderful journey I would not trade for anything," she wrote. "I shared meals and chats and moments with my mom that otherwise I never would have known."

Another powerful story came from Linda, who wrote, "A friend of mine from our college days had become pregnant outside of marriage and was tormented daily with the stress of weighing whether or not she wanted the child."

To Linda's dismay, her friend decided that she would have an abortion. "I begged her to come visit me for a week, so that we could shop and play and talk. We had an amazing time together, followed by something more amazing still. After I had hugged her goodbye at the airport and was walking back to my car, I got the distinct impression from God that I was supposed to deliver a message to her.

"I ran all the way back to the terminal, yelling her name through the crowd like a crazy person. Finally I found her. I embraced her in a hug and then pulled away, clasped her elbows and said, 'I'm supposed to tell you this: Even if you get all the way to the doctor's office, you're already lying down on the table and your feet are in the stirrups, you still can change your mind. You can get up, walk out and choose to give this little one life.'"

A week later, Linda received a phone call from her friend, who had done just that. Today the child that woman chose to keep is healthy, beautiful and thirteen *lively* years old.

I heard from a woman named Alison who had been eagerly anticipating a job interview for several weeks. A few hours before the interview, her mom called and invited her to lunch. She was about to explain why it wasn't a good day to meet, when God prompted her to take another tack. "I cancelled my interview and went to lunch with my parents," Alison said. "To my utter disbelief, the next morning my mom suffered a fatal heart attack. How grateful I am for that last lunch date, when I could lavish her with praise and love."

An email from a man named Todd read, "During my prayer time not long ago, I asked God how I could serve him that day. It was like he was sitting right next to me. He whispered, 'Love my people.' That firsthand interaction caused me to look at people differently that day, and also every day since."

A man named Kevin wrote about a series of unexpected actions he was prompted to take. One summer he had taken a large group of students to a conference and partway through the week decided he needed a break. (Teenagers will do that to a guy.) Kevin begged off of an afternoon excursion with the kids, and instead headed to his room to take a nap. En route, he passed a park where a young boy was kicking around a soccer ball all by himself. "Why don't you play with him for a while?" came the whisper.

While playing soccer for half an hour, Kevin would learn that the boy's name also was Kevin, that he had just turned eleven, and that the two of them shared the same birthday—the eleventh of June. Kevin the elder sensed that God was up to something big. The birthday discussion led the older Kevin to mention the fact that he has a physical birthday *and* a spiritual birthday, which he celebrates in honor of surrendering his life to Christ. The little boy was interested in knowing more, and in that moment a would-be nap was transformed into an evangelistic appointment set by the God of the universe himself.

Financial Actions

I read dozens of powerful stories having to do with people releasing their grip on money. See if the three that follow inspire you to do the same!

James wrote, "I've never felt very in tune with the leadings of the Holy Spirit, but one particular prompting was unusually strong. A few years ago I was asked to support a ministry initiative in Guayaquil, Ecuador, and I quickly said no. In fact, my standard answer to requests for money has *always* been a very quick no. The subject then would be dropped.

"But over the next three months," James continued, "the Holy Spirit went to work on me. Increasingly, I felt a strong sense that I was supposed to provide the support I had been asked to donate. I called the man back and for the first time in my life said yes to a financial request.

"Several months later I had the opportunity to visit the people of Guayaquil, and as I watched them engage in heartfelt worship and saw them learn about the God I love, I was overwhelmed with gratitude that he had let me play a part."

A woman named Mikki wrote that several years ago, after receiving an inheritance from her dad, she sensed God telling her not to tithe on the monies quite yet. "I waited and waited," she explained, "but soon I began to doubt if I had heard God's voice at all. I wondered whether I was being prudent or greedy—I didn't know what to do."

Within days of all that wondering, Mikki received an email asking for her to consider offering a large one-time gift to an international church. Immediately her heart skipped a beat. "As I read about the program, I sensed God saying, 'Now, Mikki. Now is the time.' I was so excited by the prospect of giving to this particular initiative that I picked up the phone, called the number of the man who had sent the email and said, 'Count me in!'

"If I had written my tithe check without asking for God's input, I would have missed the bigger blessing he had in store. In the end I gave away far more money than I had planned to give, and I received *vastly* more in return."

Spiritual Actions

Whispers that prompt us to take spiritually oriented action—surrendering a life, praying a prayer, speaking an encouraging word—can be heard all throughout the Christ-following life. (And even beforehand, as we just read in the life of the apostle Paul, when "Saul" was still his name.) When I first read the stories that follow, I couldn't help but wonder what would happen if all believers upped their batting averages on receiving and obeying whispers like those. Perhaps more than through any other means, *here* is where hearts truly get changed.

A man named Webb wrote to say that the Easter following his wife's death from breast cancer, he and his three young sons were attending Willow's Easter musical *The Choice*. There was a point in the production when the entire congregation was standing as a worship leader led a series of songs. It was then that Webb heard from the Lord.

"All of a sudden everything became quiet around me," he said.

"People were everywhere, but although their lips were moving, there was no sound. Instead, I heard what I guess is the voice of God. In a kind, fatherly tone, he said, 'It's time,' to which I quietly replied, 'I know.'" You see, though Webb had been a churchgoer for many years, he had never given his life to Christ.

As the volume of the room's noise resumed its previous pitch in Webb's ears, tears streamed down his face. His boys looked at him with worried eyes, wondering what was wrong with their dad. "I told them, 'Nothing is the matter, boys. In fact, everything is very, very right.'" The God of the universe had just invited him to become one of his children and he had joyfully said yes.

Verna wrote that her "spiritual action" was to be directed toward her difficult and degrading boss, a man named John. "My whisper was telling me to go into his office and invite him to church," she said. "But I continued what I was working on and told the whisper, 'No way.'"

Verna and the whisper would go back and forth for a while, her "no" following each new request. Finally "the whisper" won: "I got out of my chair, walked directly into my boss's office, asked him if he and his wife would like to join my husband and me at church on Saturday night, walked right back to my desk and collapsed back into my chair. 'There,' I said, to nobody in particular. 'I did what you asked me to do.'"

A few days later, Verna's boss said yes to the invitation. Not only that, but he and his wife then actually came! Verna looks back on that entire experience now and grins, because her simple step of obedience led to an astounding turn of events. John and his wife began attending church regularly and eventually surrendered their lives to Christ. They were baptized a few weeks after that and serve in a volunteer capacity today.

Another responder, Sheri, wrote, "I had taken a break from

being a small-group leader during a time in my life when several crises were happening at once. Without knowing I had entered a season of spiritual stagnation, the ministry's leaders asked me to step back into leadership. Before I could even pray about it, God whispered, 'Get back to it. You experienced the most dramatic spiritual growth of your life when you were a small-group leader. Don't cheat yourself out of that.'"

As soon as Sheri obeyed the prompting, she began to grow in intimacy with Christ once more.

And then there was Susan's story, which is sobering to any parent who has a teenage child. "I stepped into the garage to put away an extension cord and saw my son's motorcycle standing there. I heard God say, 'Lay your hands on that bike and pray for your son's safety.' I'd received promptings like that before but had just ignored them. What normal mom lays hands on a bike?

"This time, though, the leading would not desist. I walked over, placed both hands on the motorcycle, and asked God in the name of Jesus to surround my son with angels each time he went out for a ride.

"Later that evening, my son told my husband and me that he was going out on his bike. I told my husband about the prompting I had received, and together we prayed yet again. It wouldn't be until the next day that we would learn of our son's near accident. The buddies he had been riding with were over at our house and said, 'We didn't believe there was a God until we saw what we saw last night.'" They described last-second, spectacular maneuvers to avoid a collision—maneuvers that seemed beyond human skill.

The last line of Susan's email to me read, "I'll never ignore a whisper again."

Acts of Service

Many of the action-oriented whisper stories I received fall into what I call the "acts of service" category. Those service-acts can be simple and immediate, like Cecelia's. She wrote, "A couple of months ago I came home from the grocery store and heard God say, 'Give it all away.' I jumped back into my car and drove directly to the church's food pantry." And she gave it all away.

Or whispers can be longer-term in nature. Barbara's story provides a perfect example:

Several years ago during the Christmas season, Barbara visited Willow with friends who already attended the church. She says, "I was feeling sad and missing my two-year-old grandson, who lives in Arizona. But at some point during that service I received a prompting I could not ignore. God focused my attention on a ministry at Willow called Promiseland, where volunteers play with and minister to children during each church service. I sat up in my seat and determined that I would become part of the church immediately—and that my Sundays would be spent loving on kids who needed my care. This grandma may miss her own sweet one, but she's filled with joy nevertheless!"

A woman named Bev wrote of a time when her daughter decided to rent a nearby condo that she and her husband owned. One night some kids were throwing mud balls, one of which happened to hit the condo's front window and shatter it. "Our daughter got the name and phone number of the young man who threw the mud," Bev said, "but when she finally reached the kid's mother, it was apparent the woman didn't have available funds to pay for a replacement pane. The mother promised she would send the money when she could, but with both her husband and her being out of work, the likelihood of that happening was slim." Bev and her husband paid to have the window repaired.

Several months passed, and Bev's daughter still had not heard a word from the kid's mom. Bev decided to call the woman herself. "It was a couple of days before Thanksgiving," she explained, "and I was preparing to do our final grocery shopping. But something prompted me to place the call before I left the house."

Bev wound up reaching the woman that day, but instead of pressuring her into making good on the funds for the replacement pane, Bev heard herself ask, "I was just heading out to the grocery store. May I bring you a Thanksgiving meal?"

Shocked by her own spurt of compassion, Bev went to the store, purchased two of everything her family would be enjoying on Thanksgiving, and with a genuine sense of joy dropped off overflowing bags at the woman's house en route back home. Can you imagine how deeply this unemployed mother must have been marked by a spontaneous gift of generosity from a woman she'd never met—and to whom she owed money?

Mark is a man who worked on staff with the Willow Creek Association and says that ever since he married his wife, Sandy, God frequently has whispered to him. Sandy has Type 1 diabetes, and as Mark soon would learn, the disease caused an hour-by-hour struggle for Sandy, who must ensure a "normal" blood-sugar level to avoid the perils that come when it is too high or too low.

Mark says that in the early days of their marriage, God would sometimes prompt him during the middle of the night to wake up and test Sandy's blood-sugar level. On those occasions, he would discover Sandy in the throes of an insulin reaction. She would be sweating profusely, shaking uncontrollably, confused and unable to function. The solution was as simple as a glass of juice, but Mark recounts time after time when Sandy needed help holding her head up and pressing the cup to her quivering lips.

"Over time," Mark wrote, "it became very clear that one of God's purposes for me in my wife's life is to stay open to his promptings so that I can protect her when she is vulnerable. Nine times out of ten, when God whispers, 'Wake up!' there's a real problem at hand. I know that it is his grace at work that provides input like that for me."

Again, I ask you, how important are whispers that prompt people to actions God wants them to take? They are absolutely *critical*, my friend, and are the crux of the Christ-following life.

O ne of the most meaningful exhortations in the New Testament comes from 1 John 3:18. It says, "My dear children, let's not just talk about love; let's practice real love. This is the only way we'll know we're living truly, living in God's reality. It's also the way to shut down debilitating self-criticism, even when there is something to it. For God is greater than our worried hearts and knows more about us than we do ourselves" (MSG).

The goal of the Christ-following life is to grow to the point that we live in God's reality—that we love like he loves, serve like he serves, give like he gives, show compassion like he shows it. And that's a way of life we'll only maintain consistently by hearing from heaven on a regular basis. Take to heart the stories you've just read. Tell God you too want to live wide open to his whispers of assurance, his words of admonition and his promptings to take kingdom-building action in your world. I promise he will deliver on his commitment to guide your steps.

I should mention that the dominant emotion I experienced as I read through these hundreds of emails was pure joy—joy regarding how often God is speaking, and joy over how gutsy so many believers are becoming, in taking action when he speaks. But there was one message that made my heart sink. A physician named Charles who has been part of our congregation for quite some time wrote, "I am now in my eighth decade of life, and despite my lengthy time as a believer, I'm still waiting for God to speak. I've tried to remain open to such things, but so far, no luck. I truly envy those who assert that they've had conversations with God. Honestly, I'm starting to feel left out. I continue to muddle along, trying to do the right things … suffice it to say I'll be interested in learning what others report on this matter."

If you're reading along, Charles, don't bail on me now. The next two chapters were written with people just like you in mind.

CHAPTER 4

HOW TO KNOW WHEN
YOU'RE HEARING FROM GOD

S O, BY NOW YOU MAY HAVE A NAGGING QUESTION: CAN divine direction be misunderstood or lost in translation as it makes its way from heaven down to earth? Put more forthrightly, can human beings make it up or mess it up once it arrives?

The honest answer is yes. Hearing from God is not like receiving a text message or reading an email. We humans can get in the way. Believe me, I am more than capable of hearing what I *wish* God were saying rather than what he is actually telling me—and perhaps you are too. Discerning God's direction is somewhat subjective, but it's not arbitrary. Even though God's whispers are rarely tangible, there are concrete steps we can take to help us discern if we're hearing from God or hearing from the bad sushi we ate last night. What we are about to explore in this chapter can *significantly* lower the likelihood of us hearing a message that is not God's.

Acts 13 offers a window into how a first-century prompting arrived on the scene and how the leaders of the church processed it. There is something we both can learn from evaluating this episode.

Acts 13:1–3 says, "Now in the church at Antioch there were prophets and teachers: Barnabas, Simeon called Niger, Lucius of Cyrene, Manaen (who had been brought up with Herod the tetrarch) and Saul [who would become the apostle Paul]. While they were worshiping the Lord and fasting, the Holy Spirit said, 'Set apart for me Barnabas and Saul for the work to which I have called them.' So after they had fasted and prayed, they placed their hands on them and sent them off."

Before we jump into the rest of the passage, let me provide a little context. Antioch was an incredibly diverse city where the Christian message had recently arrived. People crossing many racial and ethnic lines were receiving Christ and flowing naturally into the church. Saul was a Jew. Barnabas was from Cyprus. Simeon was a black-skinned man from northern Africa. Lucius most likely was also black-skinned, from Cyrene, which is present-day Libya. And Manaen grew up in royalty, living with the family of Herod. It would have been a challenge to find five men more different from one another, but here they are—in the same church—together in heart and mind, leading a dynamic community of faith at Antioch. Then one day, while they were in a spirit of worship, a whisper from heaven came their way.

We read in Acts 13:2 that the Spirit tells the five leaders of this local church that Saul and Barnabas should be "set apart." In other words, these two guys should stop doing what they have been doing in the Antioch church, and they should prepare to be sent out on a new kingdom assignment. Nothing more specific is offered by way of helpful information, but the leaders test the whisper, find it to be authentic, and before you know it Saul and Barnabas are packing their bags.

IN ORDER TO RECEIVE MY DEGREE IN BIBLICAL STUDIES AT Trinity College in Deerfield, IL, I was required to write a senior dissertation on a Scripture passage of my choosing, As you might guess if you're familiar with the core theme of my teaching over the years, I selected Acts 2:42–47, the classic text about the rapid and radical development of the early church.

At the time, I was leading the youth group I mentioned earlier, believing with all my heart that I was going to give the rest of my life to those kids who had become like family to me. Lynne was pregnant with our first child, Shauna, and we had just purchased a tiny house in Park Ridge, a few blocks away from the church. Our plan was to settle down, dig in and serve the students for a long time. The last thing I was expecting was a life-altering whisper.

My father owned a lakefront condominium in downtown Chicago, which he offered to me as something of a writer's retreat so I could complete my dissertation in peace and quiet. I gathered up my study materials and headed downtown where I planned to hunker down and write for four days straight.

On day three of my writing, the Holy Spirit impressed the following message on me: "What you are passionately writing about—the beauty and power and potential of the local church—is going to become the thrust of your life. I am going to release you from the responsibility of leading this youth group so you can start a church—an Acts 2 church. I will bless that church so that eventually it will become a community of faith that offers the hope of Christ to many people, young and old."

Although I hadn't heard an audible voice, the refrain of that impression washed over me again and again that day. It seemed clear to me that something big was up.

After I completed my required writing assignment, I packed up my things and drove home to Park Ridge. That night, I invited Lynne out to dinner where I nervously recounted the promptings I felt I had received. I think my closing remark—delivered in my classically compassionate style—was something like, "Hope you haven't unpacked all the moving boxes yet, honey."

My wife is truly a saint.

What's more, the whisper I'd received rang true to her spirit too, and she became as excited about the dream of starting a church as I was.

Within a few months, we said goodbye to those thousand students and began looking for a place to launch a church. We walked into our future having no secure job, no support from any organization and no idea if our new plan would strike a responsive chord with anyone. What we did have was the confidence that stems from receiving a clear whisper from God. We had placed our trembling hands in his strong ones and were confident that it was *his* lead we were following. It was not lost on me that the entire series of events could be traced back to a few days of solitude, when I was quiet enough to hear God's voice.

BACK IN ACTS 13:2, WE READ THAT IT WAS WITHIN THE CONtext of worship and fasting that the Antioch leaders heard their whisper from God. In this position of surrender before their Lord, they were able to hear him speak.

In the course of ministry life, I meet many people who claim to have never heard the promptings or whispers of God. Not even once. Sometimes when I probe a little deeper, I discover that their lives are so full of noise that they can't possibly hear the Holy Spirit when he speaks. Cell phone calls during their commute, boisterous restaurant gatherings with friends, a houseful of excitable toddlers or countless hours of reality TV provide a constant roar of distraction that drowns out any whisper that might be sent their way.

Time and again, the Scriptures tell us to be still. *"Be still*, and know that I am God....,"[1] Psalm 46:10 encourages. Reduce your speed. Stop multitasking. Lower the ambient noise of your life— and *then* listen for God to speak.

Jesus himself adopted this practice during his ministry here on earth. The biblical record shows that Jesus wove into the fabric of his everyday life the disciplines of prayer, solitude, reflection, fasting and worship. He had favorite places to be alone with his Father and favorite places to pray in private. When he faced major decisions, his pattern was to withdraw from the crowds around him and to devote time to solitude and prayer. Not surprisingly, the net effect of a lifestyle like that was the increasing likelihood of hearing from his Father.

Before selecting his twelve disciples, Jesus went off alone and spent an entire night in prayer. He needed to hear from his Father regarding the individuals he planned to select and knew he must quiet himself so God's wisdom could come through. Later, when Jesus was preparing to endure the agony of the cross, he withdrew to the garden of Gethsemane, where he and the twelve disciples had often prayed. There he and his three closest friends prayed; then he prayed alone. His devotion to hearing from God motivated him to take purposeful, intentional action in order to create a space where God's whispers could be heard.

That's the same level of devotion—and action—I recommend for you and me.

There is a God who loves you and who would gladly whisper to you words of encouragement or direction, wisdom or well-timed warning, if only you would carve out the space to hear from heaven throughout the course of your day.

I've said those exact words to many people over the years and sometimes I have sensed in their response, "Thanks, but no thanks. I'd rather make my own judgment calls." In my view,

THE POWER OF A WHISPER

these people are running the risk of missing out on some of life's greatest God-guided adventures.

God tends to speak to people who want to hear from him. He tends to offer divine direction to those who are willing to order their daily lives around receiving input from him. So, what does that look like?

I would recommend reading and reflecting on a biblical passage and then saying to God, "If you have anything to tell me, I am very eager to hear it." Then, just listen. People whom I most respect spiritually are those who integrate this kind of practice into their lives. In everyday conversation, they talk about their spiritual disciplines with ease because their habits actually back up the claims they make.

For many years I have been fascinated by the specifics surrounding where people tend to quiet themselves in the course of their day. Some have a favorite chair in the living room. Some head to the office an hour early and simply close the door. Some journal and pray on a commuter train as they make their way to work. Some venture into a neighborhood coffee shop and hole away at a corner table. The time and place tends to vary, but for all these people the practice is absolute. And what happens as a result of their consistency is that they consistently hear from God.

For what it's worth, my own daily practice involves reading a portion of Scripture, mentally chewing on it for a few minutes, then writing down my observations and reflections on what I've read. After that I close my time in prayer.

To that last point, it works better for me to write out my prayers. Especially on work days, I've noticed that when I get down on my knees and try to pray silently to God, my mind focuses more on upcoming meetings than on the divine communication at hand. The solution for me is to write things down.

Once I jot down a page or so of petitions and points of thanksgiving, I then read my entry to God. Afterward I always say, "God, I am going to be listening for you all day long, but knowing me, I'll be moving pretty fast today, so I might miss a prompting or two. While I'm in my current unrushed state, if there's anything you'd like to say to me, I'm all ears." Truth be told, some days I sense a message coming from him—an impression, a word of encouragement, a nudge to say or do something specific that day—and some days I don't. Either way, I close out my quiet time with God and then do my best to listen for his voice throughout the rest of the day.

On some occasions the promptings I think I have received from God make perfect sense, but on other occasions they leave me totally confused. This is where discernment with whispers comes into play. Christ-followers must carefully test every impression they receive to be sure it is from God and aligned with his purposes. But how does one do that?

Let's revisit our text. Remember, the church leaders were worshiping and fasting when the Holy Spirit told them to set apart for him Barnabas and Saul for the work to which he had called them. Most scholars agree that Acts 13:3 suggests that after the leaders received that initial message, they did a second round of fasting and prayer, then "they placed their hands on them and sent them off."

I think there is a lesson here for us to learn.

Before these leaders rushed to action, they slowed down to be sure they correctly understood what the Spirit was asking them to do. They turned again to the disciplines of fasting and prayer. They double-checked the prompting they were about to act on. And *then* they obeyed without delay.

OVER THE YEARS I HAVE COMPILED A SHORT LIST OF FIVE filters that help me "test every whisper" I receive. If a whisper fails to make it through one of these five, I question whether the whisper is really from God. At the very least, I move slowly to confirm the whisper's validity. At other times, a whisper makes it through these filters with no problem. In this case, no matter how confusing, challenging or unsettling a prompting may be, I attempt to obey it.

FILTER #1: Is the Prompting Truly from God?

The first filter is to simply ask God, *"Is this message truly from you?"*

Years ago, when my kids were junior-high age, a man whom I did not know approached me and told me that within thirty days my children were going to be "struck down" because of my style of ministry, which welcomed nonbelievers into the "house of God." He looked sophisticated and was very articulate, and I remember his opening statement being, "Pastor Hybels, I have a prophetic word from God to deliver to you." He had my attention from the get-go, but as soon as I understood what he was saying, I knew we were going to have a very difficult conversation.

As he spoke, the first thing I had to assess was whether his warning aligned with what I knew of the character of God as revealed in Scripture. Thankfully, it did not. His underlying premise for stating that my kids were going to suffer was that I was violating Scripture by attempting to use our public church services to point non-believing people to faith in Jesus Christ. From Genesis to Revelation, God extends himself to human-kind at every turn; I felt confident that my evangelistic efforts through Willow were not in violation of Scripture. Because this man's opening assertion was patently false, I didn't think I could trust his further comments.

What's more, even if his underlying assumption *had* been correct—even if I had somehow been violating the mandates of Scripture—I would have discounted his warning that my kids would be asked to pay for my mistakes with their lives. Although there are a few times in Scripture when God disciplines children for the sins of their fathers, usually God disciplines the wrong-doer himself.

I believed this man's "prompting from God" was probably of his own making, a belief that was affirmed when my children—thankfully—were still alive and well at the end of that thirty-day period.

Whenever you receive a prompting—whether from God directly, or through the lips of another—be sure to test it. Take whatever time is necessary to ask, "God, is this message from you? Does this square with who I know you to be? Is it consistent with your character? Is it aligned with your attributes? Is this *you* trying to convey something to me, or are there other voices getting into my head?" Before taking a single step to obey the whisper you've received, be sure you get the all-clear that the voice you have heard could be from God.

FILTER #2: Is It Scriptural?

Next, run the prompting through the *Scripture filter*.

Several times a year someone will tell me that the reason their life is in shambles is because God "told" them to do something absurd.

"God told me to cheat on my wife."

"God told me to drop out of school with one semester left."

"God told me to quit my job, even though I have four kids to support and no other source of income."

I can't tell you how many jobs have been lost, educations have been foregone, marriages have been destroyed, bank accounts have been blown, all because someone felt sanctioned by God to take a particular action.

Scripture is replete with examples of how God would behave in any given life situation, and the Example's name is Jesus Christ. Whenever I sense a prompting from God, I ask myself if I could imagine Jesus taking whatever action I am considering taking. If I can't envision Jesus following suit, I fear my wires somehow must have gotten crossed.

If you need a straightforward starting point in this regard, check out Galatians 5:16–26, which says:

> So I say, walk by the Spirit, and you will not gratify the desires of the sinful nature. For the sinful nature desires what is contrary to the Spirit, and the Spirit what is contrary to the sinful nature. They are in conflict with each other, so that you are not to do whatever you want. But if you are led by the Spirit, you are not under the law.
>
> The acts of the sinful nature are obvious: sexual immorality, impurity and debauchery; idolatry and witchcraft; hatred, discord, jealousy, fits of rage, selfish ambition, dissensions, factions and envy; drunkenness, orgies, and the like. I warn you, as I did before, that those who live like this will not inherit the kingdom of God.
>
> But the fruit of the Spirit is love, joy, peace, patience, kindness, goodness, faithfulness, gentleness and self-control. Against such things there

is no law. Those who belong to Christ Jesus have crucified the sinful nature with its passions and desires. Since we live by the Spirit, let us keep in step with the Spirit. Let us not become conceited, provoking and envying each other.

Now, in case you glazed over these verses because of their familiarity, let me give a portion of the passage to you again, this time in *The Message* transliteration.

> Live freely, animated and motivated by God's Spirit. Then you won't feed the compulsions of selfishness. For there is a root of sinful self-interest in us that is at odds with a free spirit, just as the free spirit is incompatible with selfishness. These two ways of life are antithetical, so that you cannot live at times one way and at times another way according to how you feel on any given day.
>
> But what happens when we live God's way? He brings gifts into our lives, much the same way that fruit appears in an orchard—things like affection for others, exuberance about life, serenity. We develop a willingness to stick with things, a sense of compassion in the heart, and a conviction that a basic holiness permeates things and people. We find ourselves involved in loyal commitments, not needing to force our way in life, able to marshal and direct our energies wisely.

You and I both could do worse than to commit these ideas to memory. When we are motivated by God, we walk in freedom. When we are motivated by selfish interests, we will be inclined to interpret as "messages" from God messages that we have, in fact, created to satisfy something or someone other than God.

Check every prompting you receive against the thematic teachings of Scripture. Messages that contradict Scripture are not from God.

FILTER #3: Is It Wise?

A third filter I use in determining the veracity of various whispers is the *general-wisdom test*.

Jesus was fond of telling his followers to be *wise* at all times. "Behold, I send you forth as sheep in the midst of wolves," he says in Matthew 10:16. "Be ye therefore wise as serpents, and harmless as doves."[2] The entire book of Proverbs is devoted to dissecting wisdom and all her attributes. For example, the wise one loves knowledge, while the fool hates it; the wise one practices gentle speech, while the fool uses harsh, incendiary words; the wise one lives blamelessly, while the fool is utterly corrupt; the wise one follows a straight path, while the fool rejoices in the perverseness of evil; the wise one inherits honor, while the fool is held up to shame. Scripture is relentless in exhorting us to be wise in all our dealings, to be wise in all our ways.

A young couple thinks of buying their first house. They love the one that is priced fifty-thousand dollars higher than their budget will allow. The real-estate agent lowers his voice and says, "If we don't make an offer right now, it's going to be gone forever."

"Well," the couple thinks, "maybe this is God telling us to act quickly...."

Or maybe not.

What would the path of wisdom tell them to do? Slow down. Walk out. Cool off. Stick to the budget that you wisely set.

Another couple tells their pastor in excited tones, "We're getting married!"

"Great!" the pastor replies. "How long have you known each other?"

"Three weeks," they say.

"Wow ...," comes the pastor's less-than-enthusiastic response.

Again, slow down. Cool off. Give this thing a chance to bloom.

A businessman says, "I'm going to cash in my life savings and buy lottery tickets because God said I needed to make a huge contribution to the church."

Any guesses as to wisdom's response?

Be sure you're not sidestepping what is wise in favor of acting quickly on whispers. If God is indeed in the plan, it will likely not involve blatantly unwise action. God's direction rarely violates the wisdom test.

FILTER #4: Is It in Tune with Your Own Character?

Okay, on to filter number four. One of my favorite filters for verifying divine direction is what I call the *wiring test*.

Three years ago, my son Todd, then 28, decided to sail a forty-two-foot sailboat around the world. One night, he came over to the house and formally laid out for Lynne and me what he intended to do, providing us with a two-year plan he had clearly thought through in great detail. Mere seconds into his presentation, I received a word from God. "Todd's entire life has been leading up to this adventure," the prompting went. "This trip is perfectly consistent with the man I created him to be."

As Todd kept talking, I thought, "This plan isn't outrageous at all." I considered all the parents I knew who would have been coming unglued if their kid was laying out such a scheme—they wouldn't be able to see past their (quite understandable) fears regarding storms, tsunamis, rogue waves, gear failure, shipping traffic, piracy threats and more—but all I could focus on was the fact that Todd had been oriented toward the water since he was a very young boy. He took small boats out alone when he was five years old. He sailed a thirty-five-foot sailboat across Lake Michigan when he was only fifteen, and he captained yet another boat from Michigan to the Bahamas a few years after that. Circumnavigating the globe in a sailboat was likely his next big challenge. This was probably something Todd—to be true to the person God created him to be—just had to do. The prompting he believed he had heard from God passed the wiring test in spades, which was an important step in helping his parents embrace what would be a *very* long two years.

I've seen the other side of the coin turn up as well. One weekend following a service at Willow I spoke with a man who said he had been so moved by a particular music number during the service that he was contemplating quitting his job as a successful stockbroker and going full-bore into the Christian-music industry. "I really feel like that's what God wants me to do," he said. "I just can't shake the sense that this is my new calling in life...."

I waited until he finished his determined explanations of this new career and then threw a few softball questions his way. "Do you have any musical training?" I asked.

After some hemming and hawing, the answer, it turns out, was no.

"What about any experience in singing or songwriting? I mean, was there ever a time in your youth when you were drawn toward the arts?"

Again, no.

"Hmmm. Sing in the shower at all?"

A third time, no.

I looked at the stockbroker and said, "Not trying to burst any

God-ordained bubbles here, but is it possible that you were simply moved by a powerful song, and that maybe God just wants you to reflect on that wonderful experience without upending your entire world in order to pursue a new vocation?"

I caution people against running headlong into a field that is totally foreign to their wiring patterns, their education, their expertise and their experience in life thus far. It's not that God can't endorse a dramatic 180-degree turn. It's just that typically when he does so, it gets affirmed in a variety of different ways.

FILTER #5: What Do the People You Most Trust Think about It?

There is a fifth filter I use, which is based on Proverbs 11:14. "Where there is no counsel, the people fall; But in the multitude of counselors there is safety."[3] I call this the *godly counsel test*. The idea here is that whenever you sense that God is speaking to you, find two or three veteran Christ-followers—preferably people who know you well and who are further down the spiritual path than you are—and take some time to describe the situation to them in detail. Humbly ask them, "Do you think God really did speak to me? Is this the voice of God I'm hearing, or in your estimation did I get my wires crossed?"

Listen openly and intently to the answers you receive, because they might just save your hide. I speak from experience here.

In the early 1990s, I was in the process of recuperating from a time of burnout and over-commitment. At my lowest point during that season of extreme exhaustion—when I was emotionally fried—a business friend of mine from out of state made an offer for me to join his company. It was an exciting and lucrative offer, and I truly thought that God might be calling me to leave church work and re-enter the marketplace.

I was quite confident that I had heard God's voice, which meant that the opportunity successfully passed filter number one. It also passed filter number two, since nothing in Scripture would prohibit me from going back to my original career in the marketplace. Regarding the wisdom test, financially, the move would have been extremely wise for my family and me. And obviously it aligned with at least part of my wiring, since I had studied business and loved the thrill of closing the big deal.

But there was still the nagging "godly counsel test," which I'd conveniently ignored.

Somewhat begrudgingly, I called together a few spiritual mentors and other people whose opinions and perspectives I genuinely trust, and who understood my current state of exhaustion. I described the offer I was considering, then sat back and listened to their response. To a person, they said, "Bill, you are in no condition right now to make such a sweeping decision about your future. Even if you believe that God is steering you in this direction, we implore you to wait three months and then reevaluate at that time."

They begged me to rest up, heal up and get my wits about me before taking even one more step. I will forever be grateful that I heeded their wise advice.

Within a couple of months I did get healthier, and I began to see things more clearly. As I fell in love with my ministry role once more, I realized how much I would have missed if I had gotten that one decision wrong.

Subject every prompting to the godly counsel test. It will save you from boatloads of heartache and just might affirm God's best will for your life.

H aving those five filters at the ready helps tremendously when you're trying to make sense of a whisper from God. (See the appendix on page 267 for a consolidated list of them all.) But what about when you feel like heaven has fallen strangely silent and months go by without a single word from above? What do you do when it seems God has stopped speaking, despite your deep desire to hear from him?

One day a few summers ago, I decided to spend an afternoon alone with God. I hopped on a boat, headed out on the lake and prepared to hear meaningful words from heaven. I sat there for an hour and heard nothing. I sat there for a second hour and heard precisely nothing. Partway through hour number three, I thought, "I love being on the water, but what's with the silence, God?"

I was going through a tough time at Willow and desperately needed a little encouragement from above. But hour after hour I sat there, hearing nothing but the wind and the waves.

Just as I was ready to haul up the anchor and motor back toward the harbor, I saw a Bud Light beer can float by. I stood there staring at the can, wondering, *Is this a message from God? If so, what could it mean? Am I supposed to drink Bud Light? Am I supposed to tell my congregation not to drink Bud Light? Is there a message inside the can?*

After a few wasted minutes of silent inquisition, I figured God was probably just telling me to respect his creation, fish the can out of the water and toss it in the garbage.

I got back to the house, and my family, all of whom knew I was investing an entire afternoon in some "meaningful dialogue" with God, said, "So, what did God say to you?"

"Pick up the beer can—that's what he said."

We laughed, but there was little more to report. I had watched and waited and listened, but apparently God had nothing to say to me that day—or at least I couldn't hear it, despite my best efforts.

Can I offer you a few words of encouragement, based on countless firsthand experiences like that one? If you aren't sensing many promptings from God throughout the course of your day, your week, your month, check one of the following areas of concern. For me, one of these four culprits is usually to blame.

First, fervently and frequently ask God to improve your hearing. Pray every day for God to give you ears like the prophet Samuel's. Ask him for increased capacity to discern his voice and for heightened attentiveness to his promptings.

Second, reduce the ambient noise in your life. For me, a sure way to get quiet before God is to head off solo on a boat. For you, it might be listening for him while you are driving, exercising or enjoying the quiet of your bedroom at night. Wherever it is, be sure to carve out moments in your day when you can practice listening for the voice of God.

Third, you simply *must* fill your head with Scripture. As we will cover in the next chapter, most of the promptings we receive at critical decision points in life come as the Holy Spirit reminds us of Scriptures we already know. We hear whispers that reinforce biblical truths and we understand immediately what the Spirit is trying to say to us. So, saturate yourself with God's Word and see if his whispers don't increase over time.

Finally, the Bible makes it clear that any ongoing pattern of wrongdoing compromises our communication with God—in both directions. Our prayers don't get through to God and God's promptings don't get through to us. If you are stuck in a rut of sinfulness and deceit, confess your sin and turn away from it today. Let the laser light of truth permeate every corner of your life. Don't truncate your communications with the Father because you're unwilling to let go of a sin pattern in your life.

ONE OF THE MOST GUT-WRENCHING BOOKS I HAVE READ IN the past few years was the published series of personal letters to and from Mother Teresa that make up the book, *Come Be My Light*. So many things about this book touched me deeply, but one section in particular wrecked me. Her letters describe a season that lasted for some years, during which this extraordinary, godly woman could not hear the voice of God. Throughout this painful season, Mother Teresa begged God to cast light on her very dark night. But for reasons she did not understand, God seemed to be strangely silent.

Her chosen course of action during this disappointing season was incredibly instructive to me. Instead of growing resentful or hard-hearted, Mother Teresa chose to continue obeying the last whisper she had received from God. Eventually God began whispering to her again, but throughout that long season of silence, Mother Teresa continued obeying his most recent marching orders. It's worthy advice. If you're not hearing much from God these days, go back to the last whisper you received and follow it to the letter. Perhaps by faithfully executing his last command, a new nudging will have space to emerge.

A llow me one final point. While it's true that God sometimes seems silent and his whispers seem few and far between, there are plenty of times when he does choose to speak—as evidenced by the themes of this book. Whenever you find yourself on the receiving end of God's promptings, be sure to obey—no matter the cost. Don't let fear or doubt rob you of one bit of what God has in store for you. Whenever you hear from God, do precisely what he asks for you to do.

I've staked my entire adult life on following the still, small voice of God, and though my faithfulness has been flawed more times than I care to count, I have not for one second regretted this approach. I walked away from a three-generation family business and moved away from my hometown, my family, and my childhood friends because of a whisper. Willow Creek and the Willow Creek Association exist because of a whisper. I'm still in ministry today because at low points in my life God graciously whispered to me. Because I take whispers incredibly seriously, life is rarely dull. I live most days with a sense of anticipation, knowing that I could be one spiritual nudge away from once again having my world radically altered and redirected. Who would want to miss out on a ride like that?

Back to Acts 13 one last time. After Paul and Barnabas were "sent off" by the leaders at Antioch, the two men launched out on a trip around that region of the world to spread the message of Christ. In some villages townspeople warmly embraced the Good News and their lives were miraculously transformed. But in others areas, people weren't as thrilled to see Paul and Barnabas and terrible riots burst out.

In fact, after Paul delivered his message of grace in one city, the crowd was so incensed they hurled stones his way, leaving him close to death's door. By God's grace, he didn't die. He eventually recuperated, remembered his calling and resumed his God-whispered assignment, preaching from town to town.

My point is this: Don't ever buy into the idea that everything God prompts his followers to do will be uncomplicated or low-cost. Sometimes God asks his children to carry heavy loads, as he did with the apostle Paul. But even—and often especially—under those backbreaking burdens, God's purposes are fulfilled. When our whispered task is tough, the reward of knowing we've helped further his kingdom and bettered our broken world is all the sweeter.

If you ever find yourself with a difficult assignment, why

not try giving God thanks for trusting you with something that needs your particular strength. He assigns tasks to the right person every time. He did it throughout history, and he still does it today. As you walk whatever potholed path he has asked you to walk, never forget the tough journey that Jesus himself once made. As we'll explore in a later chapter, Christ was asked to bear the most difficult assignment of all—to lay down his life as a redemptive sacrifice for humankind. He chose to obey. And because of his obedience, you and I enjoy our redemption today.

Remember Christ's courage. Remember his obedience. Remember how his uncompromising cooperation with the Father altered the course of history, affording us freedom and peace with God. Remember guys like Paul (formerly Saul) and Barnabas, whom God frequently nudged into enemy territory— but who stayed the course anyway.

It could be that right here, right now, as you are reading the words on this page, God has something to say to you. He might be telling you that it wasn't only Paul and Barnabas he chose to set apart for something new—he also is choosing *you* to accomplish something new for him. Is it a new opportunity? A new assignment? A new adventure? A new start in life? Is he asking you to ditch a bad habit; adopt a good one; serve the poor, your spouse, your best friend? If you sense God is trying to tell you something, let him know your ears are open, your heart is pliable and your hands are ready for action. Tell him you're ready to get gutsier about doing what he says. And commit to him that whatever the whisper, you stand ready—right now—to obey.

CHAPTER 5

GOD'S WRITTEN WHISPERS

D URING A RECENT TEN-DAY PERIOD, I NOTICED A SPIRITUAL pattern in my life that I hadn't reflected on in quite some time. It has been ingrained in me for so long that I sometimes forget it is even there. I'll explain its importance in a moment, but first, to the pattern itself.

It was the final week of an annual three-week initiative at Willow called "Celebration of Hope," when we as a church put our faith into action by directing practical and financial resources toward people in dire need around the world. I had told the congregation that on the final weekend of Celebration of Hope, we would be collecting a special offering to ease the plight of people struggling against extreme poverty in various countries where Willow has ministry partnerships. With that final weekend just days away, I received an email from a man in our church who wasn't too thrilled with the idea of this special offering.

"I'm still gainfully employed," his message read, "but I haven't received a cost-of-living adjustment or wage increase in more than eighteen months...." He expressed how ridiculous he thought it was to take money from our church and give it to the poor, when there were so many "real needs" right here at home.

Now, my reflexive reaction to a message like that is to defend the decision of our church leaders (which is laudable) and then—in a move that on most occasions has proven something *less* than laudable—to inform the sender of such a note that there is a *big* difference between not getting a raise and watching your children slowly starve to death because of water-borne illnesses they can't prevent, detect or treat.

I wanted to give this guy a piece of my mind. As I framed my thoughts, pulled my desk chair up to my computer and was about to hit Reply, the Holy Spirit sent me a message instead: "Be kind to one another, tenderhearted, forgiving one other, even as God in Christ forgave you."[1]

Still focused on the cursor that was blinking invitingly on my screen, I pretended I didn't hear what God so obviously had said. I poised my fingertips above the keyboard and tried to focus on the retributive task at hand. But the whisper crept in again.

"Be kind and tenderhearted, Bill. Kind and tenderhearted...."

I knew the words well, because they form a verse of Scripture I had memorized forty years ago, Ephesians 4:32. I didn't grow up in a very nurturing home, and whatever thimbleful of gentleness I have collected over the years is due to having written that single line from the New Testament on my heart and then playing it over and over again in my mind like a CD on Repeat.

Back in front of my computer, my spirit protested, "But how am I supposed to zing this guy if I have to be *kind* and *tenderhearted*?"

No response. Not surprising, given my spirit.

I sighed, pushed my chair back and turned to stare out my window and think. When I re-approached my laptop a few moments later, I tapped out a response that was far different from the one I'd planned. That afternoon, I received a respectful reply from this man. I thanked God for his whisper, which once again had kept me from doing harm.

ONE EVENING THAT SAME WEEK, LYNNE STOPPED ME IN THE kitchen. "I've been thinking about the gift you and I will give toward Celebration of Hope this year," she said. "Maybe we ought to think and pray about it together, rather than just write out some sort of obligatory check merely because we've been challenging everybody else in the congregation to participate."

Now I know my wife did not mean to insult me by implying I would just write an "obligatory check." She was merely suggesting we mutually engage God in our decision-making process. But I had just returned from a multi-city trip and was exhausted. Or at least that's the excuse I'm giving myself to explain the stinging litany of responses that popped into my head. Thankfully, this time, my lips stayed shut. In the split second that those ugly comments festered their way through my brain, God impressed this verse on my heart: "Trust in the Lord with all your heart, and lean not on your own understanding; in all your ways acknowledge Him, and He shall direct your paths."[2]

God was reminding me through the words of a three-thousand-year-old psalm that he could and would direct our paths regarding how we should participate in the Celebration of Hope offering. Instead of responding with wisecracks, I said, "Yeah. Let's do that. If you pray fervently and I do too, then maybe God will direct us toward the specific amount he wants us to give."

Sure enough, several days later—again in the kitchen—I asked Lynne what she was sensing about the direction in which God was leading us. She stated an amount, and my jaw dropped. It was within two percentage points of the exact number God had been stirring in my mind. We gave the agreed-upon amount joyfully, confident that God had directed our path. And I thanked God for speaking to me through his Word—and for once again saving my marital hide.

DURING THAT SAME TEN-DAY SPAN OF TIME, MY SON, TODD, stopped by the house. He was in the process of rebuilding his own house, which had recently been destroyed by fire. (Thankfully, no one had been hurt). Most of our conversations of late had been centered on riveting topics like foundations, floor plans and finishing materials. On this particular day, the subject at hand was sump pumps; he was having some drainage issues and recalled that I'd faced similar problems with our home, some years back. As I bemoaned those decades-old challenges, Todd asked a reasonable question: "Why didn't you just route a drainage pipe from the sump pump to an external drainage ditch somewhere? Then you'd never have to run your pump at all."

His solution would have made perfect sense except for two minor details: first, if all the homeowners in our area had followed that solution, our neighborhood would have been declared a bona fide floodplain; and second, according to city ordinance, it was an illegal thing to do.

"One of my subcontractors actually suggested we do just that," I said. "We both knew that in function, it would be the perfect long-term fix. But, unfortunately, it was against code...."

"You were *that* fond of the building code?" Todd asked.

We laughed, but as I dug a little deeper inside myself for the real reason I had followed the rules, a realization came to mind. "You know, Todd, I was twenty-eight when we built this house," I said. "It was a big house for a kid in ministry who had walked away from a family business that would've left him set for life.

This house felt like a generous gift to your mom and me directly from the hand of heaven, and the last thing I wanted to do was screw that up. True, it was just a little building code, and no one would have been the wiser if I'd not followed it. But there's a passage in the Bible that says obeying the authorities is a big deal to God,[3] so sticking to that code, for me, was a tangible way that I could honor him."

Some thirty years ago, God had whispered his wisdom to me about obeying authorities, and it had stuck.

Once God's wisdom gets written on your mind and heart, your actions feel compelled to comply—which brings me to the pattern I mentioned at the start of this chapter. What I reflected on during that ten-day span of time was that throughout the course of my life, on an ever-increasing basis, my actions and reactions (or lack thereof) have been powerfully dictated by promptings that come directly from God's Word.

───

The most predictable way to hear from heaven is to read and apply God's Word. When you increase your biblical engagement, you increase the odds that you'll hear from God—that's as complicated as it gets. After all, if God already has written down his advice on the most common dilemmas we will face in this world—things like relationships, communication and money management—wouldn't we do well to take advantage of that? Psalm 119:105 says that God's Word is "a lamp to my feet and a light for my path." For more than four decades, whenever I've needed illumination in life, the Word of God has never disappointed.

ONE OF THE GREATEST GIFTS MY PARENTS GAVE ME AS A child was placing me in environments where I'd be motivated to memorize Scripture. Some of those opportunities panned out better than others—as a kid, those pizza bribes for reciting twenty verses correctly got a little old—but when all was said and done, I was given dozens of biblical sound bites that I still carry with me today.

Recently during a weekend service at Willow, I walked our congregation through many of those verses, which I'd arranged by topic. I'm including those same categories in this chapter, and feel free to add a few of your own. (A stripped-down listing appears in Appendix 1 on page 261 to make it easier to log these verses in your mind.) And I challenge you with the same promise I promised our congregation: The more devoted you become to learning and living God's Word, the more you'll sense his divine voice in your life.

The Truth about Salvation

In my view, every Christ-follower needs to know at least one key "salvation" verse. Think about it this way: if someone was to ask you about what made you devote your life to Christ, one of the clearest, most compelling ways you could answer them is by citing a passage of Scripture related to your spiritual transformation. I've explained how I came to faith in Christ hundreds of times over the years, and the single verse upon which it hinges is Titus 3:5: "Not by works of righteousness which we have done, but according to His mercy He saved us, through the washing of regeneration and renewing of the Holy Spirit."[4]

By quoting this verse, I remind whoever is listening that people can't save themselves by good works, that salvation is a gift of God's grace alone.

What's more, when I miss the mark of perfection in my own life (an astoundingly frequent occurrence), I can come right back to Titus 3:5 and remind myself that my sins have been washed completely clean. I was saved by God's grace, not by my good works—or lack thereof!

If my choice for a salvation verse doesn't stick in your memory easily, then find one that does. John 1:12 says, "Yet to all who did receive him, to those who believed in his name, he gave the right to become children of God." Romans 10:13 says, "Everyone who calls on the name of the Lord will be saved." Both of these verses—and others like them—are ideal for people who don't remember a specific date or time when they surrendered their life to Christ, but they definitely recall an era of life when they knew that they needed to be saved. If you have committed your life to Christ, write the words of one of these verses on your heart so that God's truth will be given a louder voice than any worries about whether or not you're saved.

The Truth about Assurance

Next up is "assurance." Romans 8:1 says, "Therefore, there is now no condemnation for those who are in Christ Jesus."

If you read those words and think, "Okay, so there's no condemnation. Big deal. What does this have to do with me?" then perhaps you've never experienced what it's like to feel terribly, tragically condemned by your own actions and shortcomings.

People who have been closely acquainted with feelings of condemnation understand that "no condemnation" is a *very* big deal. If you've ever felt the looming certainty of oncoming judgment or punishment, or the sting of guilt and shame after having been caught doing something that violated your own standards of morality (or God's), then you grasp how utterly sweet it is to be told that you'll *never* again be condemned.

Recently I spent extended time reflecting on Romans 8:1, just trying to grasp more fully what this "no condemnation" concept truly means. Around that same time, I received a whisper from God that I willfully disobeyed. It wasn't a federal case; it wouldn't have made headlines. But on this particular day, God had clearly asked me to do something—and I had chosen not to do it.

I went for a run later that afternoon. In the solitude of that time, the accuser—the evil one—started in on me: "Bill, after everything that God has done in your life, you couldn't even obey him in this one, small thing? Why?"

I felt a surge of self-reproach.

"Because I'm a terrible Christian," I thought. "*That's* why." I continued further down the path of self-incrimination, wondering why God remains so faithful to me even when I'm deliberately disloyal to him. Example after example of my spiritual shortcomings began to play in my mind's eye like a bad movie.

I rounded a corner and picked up my pace toward home. In the middle of my little shame fest, God interrupted my thoughts. "Therefore there is now no condemnation for those who are in Christ Jesus,"[5] he whispered, straight from that Romans verse. "Enough beating yourself up, Bill. You said you were sorry; now claim my forgiveness. It was purchased for you at the cross. I have no condemnation toward you. Take my hand, and let's move on."

It was a much-needed reminder of truth.

Half an hour later, as I was showering, I sensed God whisper again, "Though your sins are as scarlet, they will be as white as snow; though they are red like crimson, they will be like wool."[6] As the sweat washed off my body, Isaiah 1:18 washed over my soul. *Every sin I've ever committed ... washed perfectly clean by Christ.*

Both verses—Romans 8:1 and Isaiah 1:18—speak to the assurance we can have that we are forever forged into God's family. Let me give you three more truths about assurance.

First John 5:12 says, "Whoever has the Son has life. Whoever does not have the Son of God does not have life." What this verse means is that everyone who has *received* Christ—as defined by those verses on salvation we examined—can be *assured* of eternal life. If you have surrendered your full self to Jesus Christ, then you are promised a vital relationship with God here on earth and even more so in heaven someday.

One verse later, in 1 John 5:13, we read additional words of assurance: "I write these things to you who believe in the name of the Son of God so that *you may know* that you have eternal life."[7] You really *can* live doubt-free, with a rock-solid sense of assurance about your redemption.

Here's another verse on assurance: Romans 5:1 says, "Since we have been justified through faith, we have peace with God through our Lord Jesus Christ." When life feels overwhelming and you need a fresh reminder that your connection with God is unshaken, pull this verse from your memory bank and be assured that with your heavenly Father, all is well.

The Truth about Fear

I don't know anybody who is fearless all the time, but that is precisely how God has called us to live. Second Timothy 1:7 says, "For the Spirit God gave us does not make us timid, but gives us power, love and self-discipline." Romans 8:31 says, "If God is for us, who can be against us?" Isaiah 41:10 says this: "So do not fear, for I am with you; do not be dismayed, for I am your God. I will strengthen you and help you; I will uphold you with my righteous right hand."

You and I will benefit from having one of these verses loaded into our brains and summoning it into service often! If you frequently find yourself operating from a spirit of fear, start claiming these realities: God has given you a spirit of *power*; he is *for* you; and you are *upheld* by your loving Father's right hand.

The Truth about Temptation

I talked to a man at Willow recently who tried to convince me that the reason he sinned so much was that the volume of temptation he received in his life was statistically greater than what the average person received. I kid you not.

Sensing that he could take a little ribbing, I told him that he was off his rocker. Which made his day, I'm sure. "No, I promise!" he protested. "I'm not making this up! I get *far* more temptation coming my way than any normal Christ-follower."

It was time to pull out the big guns. "Biblically, that's just not true," I said.

"Prove it," he challenged.

"No temptation has overtaken you except what is common to us all," I replied, quoting 1 Corinthians 10:13.

He seemed unconvinced.

"The temptations *you* face are common to us *all*, my friend," I reiterated. "You're not getting a disproportionate share. But there's hope. The verse continues, 'God is faithful. He will not let you be tempted beyond what you can bear. But when you are tempted, he will also provide a way out so that you can endure it.'"

This guy wasn't sinning more because he was being tempted more; he was sinning more because when temptations came his way, he was choosing not to take the way of escape that God provides each of us in every tempting situation.

God never will allow us to be tempted beyond what we can

bear. Commit that truth to memory, and you'll save yourself a boatload of grief.

HOW ABOUT TWO MORE, FOR GOOD MEASURE: ROMANS 8:5 says, "Those who live according to the sinful nature have their minds set on what that nature desires; but those who live in accordance with the Spirit have their minds set on what the Spirit desires." And James 4:7 says this: "Resist the devil, and he will flee from you." How much simpler can it get? The next time you feel stymied by Satan's deceitful schemes, refuse to play his game, and he will run.

The Truth about Trials

A couple of years ago I picked up some sort of virus during a trip to Asia. After wrestling with it for more than nine months, I finally went to the Mayo Clinic in hopes of finding some answers. Two days before Christmas, I found myself sitting in a waiting room among a group of very discouraged people, all of whom—like me—were at Mayo looking for medical solutions to difficult ailments. I stared at the festive red and green Christmas decorations, thinking, "Nothing good can come from this situation."

Many of the medical reports I'd received to date were very troubling. Nine months of illness had taken its toll, and that particular December afternoon I began wondering if this was the end of the road for me. But as if on cue, God brought to mind a verse. Romans 8:28 says, "In all things God works for the good of those who love him, who have been called according to his purpose." I wasn't sure what the promised "good" was going to look like (perhaps it was heaven), but I knew that one day it would show up. And many months later it actually did.

By God's grace I was eventually restored to physical health, but perhaps more importantly, I would get stronger on other fronts of my life too. For starters, my illness forged new prayer paths between my family and me. I'd always prayed *for* my kids, but now on a daily basis I received intercession *from* them on my behalf. Todd or Shauna would call and say, "I prayed for you today, Dad," or "Here's a verse that I prayed on your behalf just now...." Lynne would do the same, and the cumulative effect of those well wishes and prayers drew our family even closer together and steadied me even more than I recognized at the time.

I grew stronger in heart, as well. For years I've joked that when God handed out the mercy gift, I must have been sailing that day. Historically, compassion hasn't exactly been my strong suit. And up until now, I'd been blessed with great health. Over the years, when staff members at the church would call to tell me they weren't coming to work because they weren't feeling well, I'd tell them, "Come on. Suck it up and get in here! We're going to have a *ball* today." Then I'd hang up the phone thinking, "That lightweight can't even handle a sore throat!" My compassion level was near-zero.

But during my own illness, I found that it wasn't so easy to just "suck it up." There were days when I literally couldn't get out of bed, let alone charge through my day full bore. As an overachiever, this reality was tough to bear—and humbling.

Several months after my stint at Mayo, a woman at Willow approached me following a weekend service and explained that she had been struggling with chronic fatigue syndrome. There was a day in the not-too-distant past when I would have believed she was faking weariness just to get some time off work—or that her illness was all in her head. But with newfound understanding of what it's like to *really* be sick, I put my hand on her shoulder, looked her straight in the eye and said, "I get it. Really, I do.

And it must be so frustrating for you to want to go places and do things and not to have the energy to do so. I understand how you feel, and I am going to pray for you right now...."

This woman clearly was not a regular attendee at Willow, or she would have lapsed into a state of sheer shock at my unadulterated display of tenderness. (My reputation for being less than sympathetic precedes me.) As she walked away after our prayer, I added a prayer of my own. "Thank you for expanding my heart, God. It's part of the goodness that you have generated from this awful ordeal." On the heels of my own debilitating illness, my empathy factor was definitely heading up and to the right.

THERE ARE THREE CATEGORIES OF PEOPLE IN THE WORLD, AND my bet is that you fall into one of them. Today, you might be what I call a "BP." You're "before pain," which means that up until this point in your life, you've been spared debilitating tragedies and heartaches. For you, God's promise in Romans 8:28 to "work for the good in all things" will be nothing more than theory. I recommend you keep this good theory nearby, nevertheless, because at some point in your life, you just might need it. Which brings me to category two.

You might be an "IP"—someone who is "in pain" right now. In our broken world, pain will eventually find you, and when that day comes—or if you're in the throes of pain as you read these words today—Romans 8:28 is a lifeline, plain and simple. Our God can redeem even the darkest of days for his purposes. Without this promise, your trials and mine could feel overwhelming, and our pain could feel unbearable.

Or, perhaps you're like me, an "AP," which means you've made it over the most recent of life's painful hurdles in one piece. You're recovering and rebuilding as you navigate the waters called "after pain." For you, Romans 8:28 is a treasure. You now can see evidence of how God worked the pain for good, and as you face the prospect of future trials, something in you knows you'll make it through.

Wherever you find yourself on this continuum—BP, IP or AP—I encourage you to commit that Romans verse to memory. God promises goodness for your tomorrows, regardless what realities you're living through today.

The Truth about Pride

If there is one personality trait that is more off-putting than any other, it is pride. Kids hate it in their parents, employees hate it in their bosses, students hate it in their teachers, citizens hate it in their leaders—and the list could go on.

Thankfully, God provides his followers with concrete wisdom on how to navigate our tendencies toward this ugly personality trait. Here are three verses that have served to squelch my own prideful proclivities along the way:

1. God opposes the proud but shows favor to the humble.[8]

Whenever I am out on the water sailing, I am acutely mindful of the tremendous power of an opposing wind. No matter how determined I might be—no matter how many perfectly executed sailing maneuvers I might manifest—I just can't head straight into an opposing wind and overcome it. The angles don't work, and the force of the wind is too strong. This image floods into my mind whenever pride rears its ugly head in my life. God actually *opposes* arrogant people. He resists their forward progress. But, he shows favor to the humble. Ask any boater which he or she would prefer: a stiff breeze on the bow, opposing their forward progress, or that same stiff breeze on the stern, filling their sails and making their journey all the easier. Humility is the easier way, my friend.

> 2. Humble yourselves before the Lord, and he will lift
> you up.[9]

At some point in our lives, both you and I have crossed paths with people who, for whatever reason, feel compelled to point out their own strengths and accomplishments. Sadly, these people often receive the opposite response they seek: they end up repelling people rather than drawing admirers. This verse provides a better recipe for success: Have a right assessment of yourself before God, and trust him to do the uplifting.

> 3. Do not be proud, but be willing to associate with people
> of low position. Do not think you are superior.[10]

If you are looking for something proactive you can do to neutralize your pride, try making it a point to connect with the very people most of society overlooks. I travel with a friend from time to time who makes a special point of having conversations with—and generously tipping—cab drivers, bell hops and room cleaners in hotels. Watching him do this has raised the challenge bar for me, and perhaps you're hearing a whispered challenge yourself. A similar tack can be implemented at home, with grocery baggers, lawn mowing teams or others employed in service-oriented jobs. When you or I are tempted to feel a little superior to those around us, this can be an effective antidote to pride.

The Truth about Anger

Recently I was sitting in my study at the house with my sermon notes spread out on the coffee table next to my laptop, my cell phone and a full glass of water. I heard my two-year-old grandson, Henry, come barreling down the hall toward the room, clearly unaware of his high rate of speed and the coffee table's imminent approach. In a flash I imagined everything going horribly wrong.

Three seconds later, "horribly wrong" came to pass.

Henry crashed, the drink spilled onto the message notes, the computer slid off of the table and the grandfather nearly came undone.

As I scooped up little Henry and salvaged what was left of my notes, I thought, "In your anger, do not sin." It's the first part of a verse I had memorized decades ago, and in that moment it was the exact exhortation I needed in order to remember that two-year-olds can't help but be two. Lynne came to the rescue and after a little cleanup, all was well again.

The second part of that verse, Ephesians 4:26, is perhaps the best marriage verse in all of Scripture: "Do not let the sun go down while you are still angry." If you're frustrated with your spouse and the day is drawing to a close, you don't need some supernatural infusion of insight to know what to do; God already has offered a whisper: Solve whatever problems need to be solved *before* you drift off to sleep.

CAN I GIVE YOU ONE MORE VERSE TO CONSIDER, AS IT RELATES to the topic of anger? James 1:20 says, "Anger will not help you live the right kind of life God wants."[11] In the heat of the moment, it can feel good to yell, say wounding words or slam a door. But lashing out in anger harms those around us and is a barrier to leading the right kind of lives God wants for us.

The Truth about Justice

I met a man last week who is enormously wealthy, and within the first five minutes of our conversation, it was clear to me that he was leveraging his resources for incredible good in this world. I asked what was behind his decision to live such a generous life of compassion, and in response he quoted a verse that is a favorite of mine. Isaiah 1:17 says, "Learn to do right! Seek justice, encourage the oppressed. Defend the cause of the fatherless, plead the case of the widow."

He named this verse as the "most important piece of Scripture" he'd ever read and said that it is his goal to spend however many days he has left on this earth seeking justice, encouraging the oppressed, defending the cause of the fatherless and pleading the case of the widow. When he inhales his last breath, just imagine what a full life he will have led—and how many lives he will have blessed!

God *loves* justice[12] and promises that whoever is "kind to the poor lends to the Lord," who will repay the giver richly.[13] Write these powerful words on your heart, and then be attuned to living them out.

The Truth about Wisdom

At the start of an Elders' meeting recently, one of Willow's Elders began his prayer this way: "God, may we have your mind on the matters we're about to discuss."

God's mind is one of wisdom. He invented wisdom, he loves wisdom and according to James 1:5, he dispenses wisdom freely. The verse says it this way: "If any of you lacks wisdom, you should ask God, who gives generously to all without finding fault, and it will be given to you."

After asking for God's wisdom, heighten your sensitivity to any communication from heaven. God will be true to his promise and will dispense wisdom your way. The challenge isn't whether or not he will send it, but whether or not we will hear and heed it.

Sometimes wisdom from on high shows up fast and clear, and sometimes the path of wisdom is more subtle. But regardless of whether or not you've sensed a clear whisper from God for any given situation you're facing, you can still choose wisdom's course. Jesus counsels his followers in Matthew 10:16: "Therefore be as shrewd as snakes and as innocent as doves." Although God may not be whispering his *specific* wisdom to your particular situation, he has already provided you with *default* wisdom, through the clear, practical principles of wisdom that permeate Scripture. Make the best decisions you can make, based on biblical principles and common sense.

If you find yourself with the opportunity to speak into a situation that demands wisdom, but the wise path is not obvious to you, consider King Solomon's counsel, found in Proverbs 17:28: "Even fools are thought wise if they keep silent, and discerning if they hold their tongues." Perhaps God intends to communicate his wisdom through the lips of another, and your role in this situation is to listen. I've been in more than my share of board meetings when our team was chewing on a complex issue, and although I was straining my ear toward heaven, I was getting nothing. Rather than muddying the issue by adding my "nothing" to the dialogue, I've found my most helpful contribution in those situations is to *not* contribute verbally. (Side benefit of this strategy: Many a time my colleagues have mistaken my silence for my being deep in thought!) Sometimes wisdom's finest advice is simply, "Keep your mouth shut!"

The Truth about Security

Nearly every Christ-follower I know has faced a season or two in life when God seemed distant or uncharacteristically aloof, and I believe that Romans 8:38–39 was written especially for times like those. It says, "For I am convinced that neither death nor life, neither angels nor demons, neither the present nor the future, nor any powers, neither height nor depth, nor anything else in all creation, will be able to separate us from the love of God that is in Christ Jesus our Lord."

For most people, it's an utterly overwhelming idea that a loving and all-powerful God wants to share an intimate bond with the likes of you or me—but this passage assures us that he does. Through one simple verse of Scripture, God seems to remind us, "I know you're going to foul up. I'll forgive you. I know you're going to get scared as well, and I promise to help you with that. You won't always pray as wisely as you hope, but I promise the Holy Spirit will give expression to what you don't even realize you ought to be praying. Just keep your hand in mine, and we'll walk together each step of the way. I'll cover you. I'll love you. I'll never leave you. I'll always be your God."

God wants to be connected to us every hour of every day, for the rest of our lives. What's more, he craves this sort of intimacy not just during our span of life on earth, but for all of eternity—that's your Father's loving heart toward you!

On the darkest of days, you may be tempted to say, "But surely my circumstances (or sin or past—you fill in the blank) must have ripped me out of God's hands." Know that this is a lie, in direct violation of Scripture. In the middle of calamity, disappointment, betrayal—in the midst of the most terrible situation you can conceive—God assures, "*Nothing* can separate us, my child." Hang onto that truth with everything you've got! As we'll discuss further in chapter 6, even on the darkest nights of the soul, our God says, "Rest easy. You're secure."

The Truth about Power

Ready for the truth about power?

The next time you face a weighty challenge and want some whispered empowerment from God, bring to mind Philippians 4:13, which says, "I can do all this through him who gives me strength," or Mark 10:27: "With human beings this is impossible, but not with God; all things are possible with God."

Or, if you're the type who thinks you're powerful enough on your own, you might be better served by the words of Zechariah 4:6: " 'Not by might nor by power, but by my Spirit,' says the Lord!"

The Truth about Contentment

Can you imagine a world in which every single person subscribed to the apostle Paul's worldview as articulated in Philippians 4:11? Paul—who had lived through the most difficult, exhausting, dangerous and painful of circumstances in his journeys as Christ's ambassador—writes, "I have learned to be content *whatever* the circumstances."[14]

Or how about this shot of wisdom from Hebrews 13:5: "Keep your lives free from the love of money and be content with what you have."

And then there is the simple reminder from 1 Timothy 6:6, which says, "Godliness with contentment is great gain."

When you're craving something you presently don't have and wonder about God's take on your craving, wonder no longer! His advice is to *be content*.

I hope you're beginning to catch the idea that God speaks *profoundly* and *powerfully* through his Word. Let's keep going.

The Truth about Peace

As Jesus wrapped up his earthly ministry and prepared to ascend into heaven, he pulled his disciples together and said, "Peace I leave with you; my peace I give you."[15] These words reflect the great value he puts on peace—his peace. Part of what it means to be a Christ-follower is that we now get to implement Christ's peace here on earth. We get to mature from being peace-takers to being peace-makers. When we advocate for the purpose of *peace* throughout the world, Matthew 5:9 declares, we will be called blessed: "*Blessed* are the peacemakers, for they will be called children of God."[16]

Another verse that gives me great comfort in my daily life is Philippians 4:7, "The peace of God, which transcends all understanding, will guard your hearts and your minds in Christ Jesus." When I'm feeling anxious or uneasy, and my inner world feels constricted and tight, I breathe deeply of the spiritual oxygen found in those eighteen words.

The Truth about You

In addition to declaring your go-to verses on subjects like assurance and wisdom, anger and fear, I believe every Christ-follower ought to name a single "life verse"—a verse from which he or she senses God's calling and purpose in their lives. Since I was twenty-two years old, my life verse has been 1 Corinthians 15:58, which says, "Be steadfast, immovable, always abounding in the work of the Lord, knowing that your toil is not in vain in the Lord."[17]

Another translation says, "Always give yourselves fully to the work of the Lord, because you know that your work in the Lord is never wasted."[18] Either way I read it, the verse helps me to remember that each day, I am to approach my ministry role with diligence and passion rather than with a cavalier attitude. Everything around me can be spiraling into chaos, but I am to remain steadfast and immovable, and I am to abound in God's work.

I love the end of that verse as well: "Your work in the Lord is never wasted." Language like that fires me up and helps me stay the course when I'm wondering if my efforts are even making a dent. And the idea that 100 percent of *anything* will count for good is math that adds up, in my book.

When you're choosing a life verse, look for scriptural passages that fine-tune your focus and set your feet more firmly on God's path. For me, it's 1 Corinthians 15:58, but an entirely different theme might resonate with you. My challenge to you is to select a verse that motivates and clarifies God's call on your life—and then memorize it so that you have it close at hand as you walk through each day.

ONE TIME THE APOSTLE PAUL WAS PROBED ABOUT WHY HE was so at ease when he knew he could lose his life for the cause of Christ. In response he said, "To me, to live is Christ and to die is gain."

In essence he was saying, "I'm in a win-win situation here! If God allows me to live, then I will live for him. And if following him costs me my life, then I get to live with him for all eternity."

You might need that kind of resolve in your life today. If so, claim Philippians 1:21 as your life verse, post it where you will see it each morning, memorize it so that you take it with you wherever you go and allow its simple truth to penetrate everything you do.

Another example of a powerful "life verse" is John 15:8, which says, "This is to my Father's glory, that you bear much fruit, showing yourselves to be my disciples." One weekend at Willow, our production team set up a huge fruit stand on stage, which served as a backdrop while I taught from that verse. After one service I met a woman who had adopted that piece of Scripture as her life verse years ago. She had determined in her heart that the most important achievement she could net in life would be to bear much fruit for Christ, and so that is what she spent her time, her energy, her money and her efforts doing. She picked *fruit-bearing* over everything else. Once we dismissed the final service that weekend, hundreds of people took pictures of themselves on stage in front of that fruit stand and then saved the photo as their computer's screensaver. I would be willing to bet that the Holy Spirit has used John's 15:8 and this accompanying visual reminder to prompt those people toward greater "fruit production" for God.

This is the power of stating a life verse: In those critical crossroads moments, when you must choose whether to fully engage in your calling or to simply play passive passenger in the life God created you to live, a few inspired words from your heavenly Father will help you to fight the good fight.

The truth about salvation, the truth about temptation, the truth about contentment and peace—we've covered more than a dozen different categories and barely scratched the surface on the whispers God has provided through his Word.

Colossians 3:16 says, "Let the word of Christ richly dwell within you."[19] To "dwell" is to be at home in, and God desires for his Word to be so at home in us, that his whispers in Scripture are like pieces of conversation with him throughout our day. You and I must be so saturated with the Word of God that when we're caught off-guard by life's circumstances, we reflexively hear his wisdom, his nudges, his whispers through his words that dwell within us. Whether it's in the marketplace, in traffic, in the grocery store or in school, the Holy Spirit actually has a shot of turning every circumstance of our day into his good. He only has to whisper his Word to us!

In John 8:44, Jesus calls Satan the "father of lies." And at every turn the ultimate fraud will try to convince you that peace is not available, that temptation is not escapable and that God's grace is only a temporary gift. God's truth must dwell so deeply in us that we can conquer the evil one's lies.

I mentioned earlier in this chapter that when I was studying Romans 8:1, I had an experience wherein I knowingly disobeyed a prompting from God, and even after I had claimed his forgiveness for my sin, I sensed the suffocating effects of Satan's string of lies. See if any of these lies sound familiar to you.

Lie #1: "A *true* Christ-follower never would have done what you just did, Bill."

Despite my sincerest apologies to God, if I'm not careful I'll revert to believing that based on my careless behavior, I must be a fake and a fraud. "Maybe I just *thought* I was redeemed," I speculate. "Maybe I just *thought* I was a faithful Christ-follower."

Buying lie #1 means playing into Satan's taunt that I'm not really an adopted child of God's. After all, look at the mess I just made! What kind of son would do that?

As lie #1 begins to worm its way into my psyche, *lie #2* starts to kick up some dust: "A holy God never will forgive a sin like that, Bill. I mean, he's the God of the Ten Commandments! He's the God who wiped out entire people groups in the Old Testament for stunts less than what you've just done! He must be spitting angry at you right now, big guy. *Eternally* angry! Good luck garnering forgiveness, pal. In your *dreams*."

It's when I'm already down and feeling defenseless that Satan spews lies three through five.

Lie #3: "Your family and friends will never respect you again when they find out what you've done. They'll see you for who you really are … and bail."

Lie #4: "Your church will never open its arms to you again. The next time you step anywhere *near* that group, you'll swiftly be shown the door!"

Lie #5: "You'll never be eligible to be used by God again. Your sin mocked his holiness, and God will *not* be mocked."

It took me less than five minutes to write down the five-step digression you just read. I've gone down those familiar stairs hundreds of times, refusing to heed the whispers of the Spirit that "there is no condemnation for those who are in Christ Jesus." When I think of all that wasted time and self-reproach, it almost makes me physically ill. Jesus knew a better way! Take a look at his example:

Just before he began his preaching ministry, Matthew 4 says that Jesus was led into the desert, where he was tempted three times by Satan. He had been fasting for more than a month and was tired and hungry when he faced the shrewdest liar the world ever has known. But instead of merely responding to Satan's temptations with a half-hearted, "Nah. Not interested," Jesus answered with hard-core truth. He had the Word of God in his mind and on his heart, so when he was tempted to take a tumble, even in his weakened condition, God's truth steadied his stance.

When the evil one fought dirty, Jesus didn't rely on a community of friends to help him, his amazing prayer life or even his intimate connection with the Father. Rather, in the heat of battle, Jesus relied on the concrete truth of God's Word to counter the temptations leveled his way. Having spent his earthly years saturating himself with Scripture, he was fully equipped with truth to silence Satan's lies.

You and I would do well to follow suit.

***

I don't know if this is true for you, but when it comes to spiritual growth, I tend to follow a predictable trend: I'll grow steadily for a while; and then for reasons even I don't understand, I flatten out. Author Henri Amiel says, "The stationary condition is the beginning of the end,"[20] and based on myriad flat-lined moments I've experienced, I have to agree with those words.

Whenever I find myself in plateau mode, I notice how spiritually restless I become. I feel like my energies bear no fruit, my prayers bounce off of the ceiling and my calling grows cloudy and dim. Inevitably I start playing the blame game with gritted determination, figuring *somebody* must be at fault for my obvious lack of growth. I blame God, I blame my church, I blame my small group, I blame my mentors, I blame my wife and I even blame the planets for obviously not being aligned.

Once I get through those initial indictments, though, I am left facing the truth. "Bill, you're not kidding anybody. You're responsible for your *own* spiritual development. It's no one's job but yours to find your way back."

The last time I felt a sense of spiritual restlessness—when I had reached a plateau and was starting to slide into a serious state of decline—I chose a single chapter of the Bible and decided that instead of continuing to bounce along the surface, I was going to go deep. "I'm going to live in this single chapter of Scripture until the truths in it begin to live in me," I committed to myself. Rather than merely getting through the Bible, I wanted the Bible to get through to me.

I had done this sort of "saturation reflection" before and found that as I immersed myself in God's Word—even in those passages that I had read hundreds of times before—I received fresh insight and fuel for future growth.

Many years ago, I dove into the book of Proverbs and did not come out until I felt its wisdom affecting my thoughts on a daily basis. Years later, I did the same thing with Luke 15, Acts 2 and the entire book of John.

More recently, I spent twelve months parked in the twelfth chapter of the book of Romans, and it proved the most transformational Bible-reading experiment I've done to date. My "plan" wasn't rocket science; I just decided to read one verse at least once each day and then would journal my observations and thoughts. The next day, I'd read through the next verse and pray back various truths to God. On some days I would read the whole chapter. Other days I would see how much of the chapter I could say from memory. If I was traveling and didn't understand a particular concept, I'd Google the verse and spend some time reviewing other people's ideas on what the text might mean. You wouldn't *believe* some of the insights that can be gleaned from believers living in places like Budapest and Kathmandu.

Here's why I bring up the saturation-reflection idea. While it's true that God speaks timely, practical wisdom via various verses of Scripture, it is also true that those pieces only tell part of the story. There is tremendous benefit to be gained from going slowly and systematically through the Word of God, asking him with every turn of events, "What were you up to here, God? Why did you pour favor on that woman or man? What can I learn from this simple verse that I've read a hundred times before?"

God delights when we are quiet and still before him, soaking in the wonders of his magnificent truth, and placing ourselves in a ready state to hear from him. If you need permission to ditch your through-the-entire-Bible-in-thirty-days reading plan, this is it. Slow your pace. Soak it in. And listen for his voice.

GOD, IN HIS KINDNESS, HAS PROVIDED YOU AND ME WITH A lifetime of whispers, found between the covers of the Bible. We may not hear a personal, audible whisper from him for every (or any) situation, but through his Word, every Christ-follower has full access to what he wants us to know—about himself, his character and the life he is calling us to live. And yet we muddle through life's circumstances, forgetting the incredible power available to us through his Word. As we close this chapter, explore with me a story from 2 Kings, which casts a vivid picture of the reality of the power available to us from our Father. In this scene, the prophet Elisha and his servant were walking to town, clueless that upon their arrival they would be ambushed and most certainly killed. There was a war going on, and evidently Elisha was on the wrong side of the opposing king's favor.

Concerning Elijah's traveling companion, 2 Kings 6:15–17 says, "When the servant of the man of God got up and went out early the next morning, an army with horses and chariots had surrounded the city. 'On no, my lord! What shall we do?' the servant asked.

"'Don't be afraid,' the prophet answered. 'Those who are with us are more than those who are with them.'

"And Elisha prayed, 'Open his eyes, LORD, so that he may see.' Then the LORD opened the servant's eyes, and he looked and saw the hills full of horses and chariots of fire all around Elisha." And, as you'd guess, the servant then found nothing to fear.

On more occasions than I care to admit, I find myself thinking, "I know in my head that with the power of Christ living in me, I should be able to face this particular situation, but in my heart, the odds just feel too big." I look at my surrounding circumstances and think, "There is no way this can turn out well."

But then I remember that little story about Elisha and his servant. What might shift in my heart if God were to unveil my eyes and show me that despite my fear or uncertainty, I'm actually surrounded by his powerful protection and presence?

It's time for us to shift our focus. Instead of staring at the obstacles and obstructions that Satan loves for us to see, we must fix our gaze on the path of provision that God already has paved. He has given us full access to his wisdom, full assurance of his faithfulness and full availability of his power through the pages of Scripture. Some scriptural whispers are admonishing, some are correcting, some are filled with delight and some bring challenges our way. But the net effect remains the same: We are steered in a God-ward direction when we act on the truth of his Word.

CHAPTER 6

LIGHT FOR DARK NIGHTS
OF THE SOUL

ALMOST EVERYONE I KNOW IS A SUCKER FOR A RAGS-TO-riches tale, and the Old Testament contains a real page-turner as a simple shepherd boy rises to power and becomes king. While he was still tending a flock of his father's smelly sheep, a young man named David was tapped by God and told that he would one day lead the nation of Israel. It was quite a stretch to imagine this wiry, inexperienced kid assuming such a lofty role.

As David the boy became David the man, his skill and popularity with the people of Israel grew as well. Realizing that the up-and-comer's charisma was overshadowing him, the current king—a man named Saul—resolved to snuff the new guy out. Consequently, David would spend the next ten or so years not as a megastar king of Israel, but rather as a man on the run. With that as context, let's look at what happened next.

In chapter 30 of 1 Samuel, everything is going wrong for David. He had been rushing from town to town, rallying a group of warriors for a big battle against Saul, when he learns that the village he'd been calling home has been raided and burned to the ground. His family has been kidnapped and his possessions are nowhere to be found. To make matters worse, David's men are so bitter over the loss of their own loved ones and belongings that they now are theatening to kill David too. In today's parlance, this is what we call a "dark night of the soul."

Now, here is what I find interesting about this entire saga. In 1 Samuel 30:4, we find David bursting out in loud wails and weeping until he is weak with exhaustion. He misses his family, he misses his bed and he is tired of living on the lam. He knows that God has called him to fulfill a specific purpose in life, but based on recent events, it seems that the divine dream is pretty much dead.

Or maybe not.

Exactly two verses later, the text says this: "But David *strengthened himself* in the LORD his God."[1]

For some time now, I've held to a theory about what took place between David's emotional meltdown and the surge of divine strength that soon would enable him to get his family and property back—and to emerge victorious in the battle against archenemy Saul. I believe that in two brief verses' time, David received a *whisper* from God that spoke light into the darkest of nights.

I HAVE LIVED THROUGH A FEW DARK NIGHTS OF MY OWN, AND perhaps you have too. One of the most vivid memories of my early ministry days includes such a night. A small group of friends and I—all equally inexperienced—had started Willow Creek Community Church four years earlier, and all indications pointed to a mission that was being achieved. We still were meeting in a rented movie theater, but that wasn't hindering God's work in people's lives: men and women were surrendering their lives to Christ and learning to serve others instead of living for themselves. But in 1979, all of that momentum would come crashing to a halt, as a knockout punch caused a ten-count to ring through our team's collective ears.

The near-fatal blow had been caused by an unfortunate collision of bad circumstances, inexperience and sin, a collision that we later would refer to as the "train-wreck era."[2] Various staff members had wandered off of God's path. Some of our best volunteers had gotten sideways with each other. The church's Elders (one of whom was me) were young and inexperienced. As things continued to unravel, people in the congregation withheld their tithes and offerings as a sign of protest. Many quit serving on weekends and stopped supporting almost everything we did.

To complicate matters further, we were in the middle of a building program that Willow could barely afford. The faithful members of our congregation had taken out bank loans to fund our expansion, and yet still we were gasping for air as we sank in a pool of red ink.

Topping it all off was the fact that my leadership was in its infancy, as evidenced by my less-than-stellar response to our church's giant mess. I got wounded by staff members and lost my objectivity along the way. On many occasions my actions were unnecessary and unwise.

In the end, the church was almost destroyed. Those of us who had poured our lives into fulfilling the mission and vision of Willow Creek Community Church came within a hair's breadth of bailing altogether.

On one day in particular, everything came to a head. I remember going home from work, bypassing dinner, telling Lynne good night and finding my way to the family room floor. A knot of thoughts had my mind cinched, and the only thing I could think to do was to lie face down with arms stretched over my head and pour out my heart to God.

I've often heard people say they prayed "all night" when an especially agonizing situation threatened their health or well-being. Those statements are understood to be hyperbole, right? Sort of like the country songs that talk about making love "all night long." I certainly would have assumed so, until my all-night, shag-carpet experience.

As I lay there, my wet eyes shut tight and my cheeks burning from the rough carpet pile, I silently said, "God, I am not getting up from here until there is resolution in my heart. I can't lead this church one more day until you tell me what I'm supposed to do."

I began praying a series of unedited prayers—confessing everything I could think to confess, submitting to every ounce of God's truth I could call to mind, reviewing each excruciating element of the train wreck and asking how I could have averted what had ended in such a mess. I spiraled through round upon round of anxiety: "How am I going to explain to people that we have to shut down the church? How do I tell my friends and family the truth? How do I fire all the staff?"—on and on the desperate conversation went.

As nighttime gave way to morning, something had to give.

AROUND FIVE A.M., I RECEIVED THE LONG-AWAITED PROMPTing from God: "I want you to get up, go to work, put one foot in front of the other and remember that I am with you today. Tomorrow, I want you to do the same thing again. We're going to get through this together, Bill, but it will only happen one day at a time."

"That's it?" I thought, still lying there, face down. "That's what I ate carpet for, all night long?" Tempers had been blazing and people had been resigning, and God's big solution was for me to just "go to work"? Truthfully, I expected more flair. Complex problems require complex solutions, but God's answer was as simple as they come. Still, I didn't have a better idea, so I did precisely as I'd been told.

The previous evening, en route to my prostrate night of prayer, I'd mumbled something to Lynne about the "dream" being "over." But now, here I was, showering and heading off to work like usual—a contrast that wasn't lost on her.

"What are you doing?" she asked her weary husband, who despite being clean still wore carpet creases on his face.

"I'm going to work," I said.

"That's it?" she asked. "In the midst of everything that is happening all around us, your grand plan is just to 'go to work'?"

"Yep," I said with fresh resolve. "That's *exactly* what I'm going to do."

When I got to the office, not one of my circumstances had changed. The congregational letters still were scathing, the financial reports still were miserable and life as I knew it just plain stunk. But in spite of all that, I felt a deep and abiding sense of serenity as God assured, "I will help you stay this course."

With my hand clutching tightly to his, I prepared messages one week at a time, we made construction payments one creditor at a time and I placed one foot in front of the other, step by tiny step. There was no parting of the skies, no blinking neon lights and no immediate resolution to the massive issues that we as a church faced. There was just the constant and comforting accompaniment of God as we somehow muddled our way through. The verse that promises "peace that passes understanding" became a refreshing refrain as I watched Willow slowly get peeled off of the canvas and start standing on its feet once again. God was sustaining—and rebuilding—what remained of our decimated church, one day at a time.

I READ THE BOOK OF JAMES MANY TIMES DURING THAT agonizing season of ministry. Each time, I was struck by the apostle's assertion that people who follow Jesus Christ can actually get to a point of spiritual maturity where they view challenges and hardships as a blessing rather than a curse. We're not asked to smile at the trouble itself—God would never ask his children to be glib about something destructive or sad—but we can grow to smile at the *by-products* of trouble.

"Consider it a sheer gift," we read in James 1:2–4, "when tests and challenges come at you from all sides. You know that under pressure, your faith-life is forced into the open and shows its true colors. So don't try to get out of anything prematurely. Let it do its work so you become mature and well-developed, not deficient in any way."[3]

In February 1981, our congregation relocated from the rented movie theater, where we had held weekend services for six and a half years, to a brand-new lakeside auditorium on property that we could call home. For those of us who had been knitted together since the church's beginning, opening day was nothing short of miraculous. During that inaugural service, scores of us gathered in little friendship clusters, just bawling our eyes out over all that God had done.

Visitors in close proximity to us must have thought, "This place *really* is in trouble if those emotional basket cases are running the show." They couldn't possibly have known that our tears were warranted. We had walked through a terrible valley, but by God's grace we had endured. God had sustained us as he had promised. He had led us, one step at a time.

Since those days, Willow Creek has experienced unbelievable ups and downs. We've seen modern-day miracles and endured unfair media coverage. We've developed leaders and seen difficult staff departures. We've set records and faced unmet goals. We've experienced outpourings of resources and weathered deep financial recessions that required serious belt-tightening. But never again have we returned to that canvas—the ten-count thankfully has been kept at bay by a shag-carpet promise I will never forget.

O n many occasions throughout my adult life I have come to the place where, like David, I needed encouragement straight from the Lord. The situations have varied, but the solution is always the same. When dark nights descend and hope feels long gone, God's voice alone brings light.

Around the same time that the train-wreck era began at Willow, the personal side of my life also suffered a tremendous blow.

On the heels of a heartbreaking miscarriage that Lynne had suffered, I got word that my dad had suddenly died of a massive heart attack. He was only fifty-two years old. He had been on a business trip in Chicago when his heart stopped beating, and now I was supposed to drive downtown to claim his body at the morgue. It was September 28, 1978, and I remember the drive down the JFK Expressway like it happened yesterday.

"What am I going to do without a dad?" I asked God aloud. Harold Hybels had been my strongest supporter, my closest confidant and the biggest personality I had ever known. He was larger than life. He had seen me through the trickiest leadership challenges and had believed in me like no one ever had. "Without my father," I told God, "I don't know that I can handle what you have entrusted to me." I had barely been staying afloat at Willow, and that was *with* my dad's attention and care. Now that he was gone ... I could not bear the thought.

Halfway between Barrington and downtown Chicago I sensed a clear prompting from a loving God. "I will be your Father," he said. "I promise, you're not alone."

As his words sank into my soul, I felt a burden lift from my chest. Immediately, the Spirit brought to mind a phrase from Psalm 68:4–5, which says,

> Sing to God, sing in praise of his name;
>> extol him who rides on the clouds;
>> rejoice before him—his name is the LORD.
> A father to the fatherless, a defender of widows,
>> is God in his holy dwelling.

"A father to the fatherless"—that single truth wedged its way into my mind and offered peace when there was none to be found. *God* would be my father. *God* would be my supporter. *God* would be my confidant. *God* would be my sustenance every day of my life. It would take me some time to learn to lean into him in all of those roles, but eventually I would come to rely on him just as he had invited me to.

I'm pushing sixty years old now and am intrigued by the fact that so many of my contemporaries still have their dads around. From time to time, they'll call to bail on weekend plans with me, explaining that they need to spend some time with their fathers. I still catch myself feeling a surge of shock when I remember that I'm not in that same relational boat. I haven't had a dad since my mid-twenties, but fatherless I am not. It's a distinction I'm sure I'll be drawing until the day I inhale my last breath. And I will never forget the well-timed whisper from God one morning on the JFK.

A FEW YEARS LATER, IN THE EARLY 1980S, THE ELDERS OF Willow and I took a stand in advocating the role of women in church leadership. We had done our due diligence of theological explorations in Scripture for more than two years' time and believed that based on the Bible's teaching, we needed to strongly support the contribution of *both* genders to the God-glorifying mission we were working so hard to achieve.

One Sunday, following a rather contentious meeting in which the Elders explained their position, more than two hundred families decided to leave. They weren't just leaving the meeting; they also were leaving the church. We had just settled into our new auditorium, and their departure stood in stark contrast to the "We made it!" feelings we'd recently shared. Had I led us down a wrong turn?

One day soon thereafter, I was home with my daughter, Shauna, who was just a preschooler at the time. She was chattering away, engrossed in her creative world of imagination, and enjoying being a little girl. As I observed her, God whispered a much-needed message my way. "You might take a hit for what you've advocated, Bill, but every little girl growing up in Willow's family for generations to come will be the beneficiary of your strong stand."

It was precisely the assurance I needed, from the only One whose approval I sought.

AS THE 1980S UNFOLDED, I NOTICED A TREND IN MY WORK LIFE emerge: in three words, *too much teaching*. My entire life somehow had been reduced to the preparation of sermons, the delivery of sermons and the recuperation necessary once those sermons had been delivered. At the time, Willow was holding four weekend services, two midweek services and countless holiday services—in addition to the staff meetings, leadership retreats and church leaders' conferences where I was also expected to speak. The net effect was not pretty. I dreaded my role. I fantasized about going back into the corporate world. And my survival strategy was to economize my relationships, my spiritual disciplines and my emotional health—which thrust me, understandably, into crisis mode.

This dark night of the soul came when I realized that if I didn't make some major adjustments to my life—and fast—I'd flame out of ministry altogether. God had been present on previous hopeless nights; would he prove faithful yet again?

I'll spare you the nuanced details of how it all came down, but the gist of God's just-in-time whisper to me was this: "You're more than a message machine."

My words back to him were simple ones: "Thank you for revealing that to me. Whatever changes must be made or price paid, I'm ready to leave crisis mode for good."

That single prayer ushered in Willow's team-teaching approach, which we (and thousands of other churches these days) have employed ever since. It also paved the way for me to live a healthier life. And it all emanated from a whisper.

⌇

Although the dark nights of the soul I've encountered have been perhaps the most difficult points of my life, they have taught me three truths about God for which I am thankful. Regardless of what dark nights you face, see if these truths resonate with you.

TRUTH #1: God Is Near

In several places in Scripture, God promises he "never will leave" us. This concept is a little difficult to grasp since you and I can only be in one place at a time. But God is not like us. He is spirit, as John 4:24 says. His presence permeates all space; he is fully accessible everywhere at once.

I spend a lot of time in airplanes. Often, as I gaze out my little airplane window at the cornfields of Iowa below, the sprawling metropolis of New York or the vast oceanic expanse between America and far-off lands, it hits me, "The Lord is in this place." He is here on board this plane, 38,000 feet in the air; he is there in the farmhouses below; he is there in every skyscraper office and tenement building; and he is there in the depth of the ocean. He is even in all the places I can't see. Psalm 139:7–10 says, "Where can I go from your Spirit? Where can I flee from your presence? If I go up to the heavens, you are there; if I make my bed in the depths, you are there. If I rise on the wings of the dawn, if I settle on the far side of the sea, even there your hand will guide me, your right hand will hold me fast." No matter where I am, God is near.

WHEN TODD WAS A LITTLE BOY, HE'D SOMETIMES LEAVE HIS blanket or some other nocturnal necessity on the other side of our ranch-style house, a long way from where the bedrooms are located. I would be dozing to sleep in my own bed when he'd awaken, make his way to our bedroom, tap me on the shoulder and whisper, "Dad, I need my blanket. I left it in the living room."

Just for fun, I'd tease, "Well, Todd, if you left your blanket in the living room, then just go to the living room and get it."

Off he'd go. But about halfway down the long, dark hallway, he'd do an about-face.

"Dad?" he'd call.

"What, son? What do you want?"

"How about if you came with me?"

"Go ahead, Todd. You can do it by yourself," I'd assure him. "You'll be perfectly fine."

I'd hear a few more small footsteps, then silence.

"Dad?" a little louder this time.

"Yes, Todd? Are you scared?"

"No, Dad. I just want you to walk with me."

Well, who could say no to that? I'd join Todd right where he had gotten stuck, and together we'd walk the rest of the dark hallway, hand in hand.

You know where I'm going with this. We have a God who loves to make walks down long, dark hallways with us. When we face stiff challenges, wild uncertainties, even violent and raging seas, God says, "I'm going to be near to you so that you don't face the darkness alone."

In the marketplace and in our marriages, in our communities and in our cars, our omnipresent God is with us, offering us courage and giving us peace. His presence is important when things are going well—and it's critical when times get tough.

Psalm 34:18 says, "The LORD is close to the brokenhearted and saves those who are crushed in spirit." Here's what that means to you and me: If you are a believer, then whenever you feel like the ceiling is caving in, you can know that a Comforter walks confidently by your side. The psalmist writes in Psalm 23, "Even though I walk through the darkest valley, I will fear no evil, for you are with me...."[4] Why did he fear no evil? Because he knew that God was *near*.

TRUTH #2: God Seeks

Our God is not only near; he actively *seeks us out*.

Years ago, mid-way through a globe-trotting ministry trip, I contracted a fever that leveled me flat. I'd crossed so many time zones in a handful of days that my wires were starting to cross. I still had twenty-nine days to go before I could sleep in my own bed, and I distinctly remember walking through an airport in

Singapore thinking, "Nobody knows I'm here, and nobody cares. This is what it must feel like to suffer for God."

I'm not wired to be prone to the "poor-me's," but that night I fell headlong into a pit of self-pity.

When I checked in for my flight, I learned that my gate was located near the very end of the terminal, about a third of a mile down a dimly lit, crowded hallway. "Great," I muttered to myself. But as I began to plod my fever-ridden frame through the packed terminal hallway, something unexpected happened. God brought to mind the words from Isaiah 62:12, which say, "They will be called the Holy People, the Redeemed of the LORD; and you will be called Sought After, the City No Longer Deserted."

The verse refers to God as the "sought-after" one, but in a fleeting moment in that crowded hallway, in a busy airport serving nearly five million people, on an island in the middle of Southeast Asia, the King of the universe picked me out of a teeming crush of humanity and whispered, "Tonight, it is *you* who are sought after. I am seeking after you."

God is near. But his presence is not passive. He seeks us out so that he can encourage us to keep going, to move ahead, to *live*. This divine reminder revived my spirit.

As I stood a little taller and left my self-pity behind, I noticed an elderly woman who was struggling to balance her luggage.

"Are you heading to the gate that is a two-zip-codes walk from here?" I asked.

She nodded, eyeing me suspiciously.

"May I carry your bag?"

Reflexively, she pulled her luggage closer to her side.

I grinned. "No, really," I said. "I'm a good guy."

For a few seconds, she hesitated. We stood there, me eyeballing her bag and she eyeballing me.

"Well, all right," she finally conceded. I shouldered her bag and we walked on to our gate.

When it was time to board, I went over to where she sat, picked up her bag again, escorted her onto the plane, stowed her bag for her and then found my seat. It was just a series of small things, but by the time I rested my head against the chair, I felt exponentially better in my spirit.

We both know it was not a world-changing event for this woman that I helped her with her bag. But the small acts of service definitely squared better with my calling to minister in Jesus' name, and they had taken my focus off of myself. The pity party I'd been engaged in ten minutes before had lost its appeal.

God has *good* plans for us to accomplish. And I firmly believe that on our darkest nights of the soul, he unabashedly seeks us out. When life knocks us flat on the mat, we can hop back up, remember that our strength comes from him and get busy doing some kingdom-building good.

TRUTH #3: God Speaks

Given this book's subject matter, the final takeaway I'll highlight won't surprise you in the least. Not only does God draw near to his children and seek them out when they're having a rough go, but also he *speaks words* to them—words of comfort, insight and peace.

Nearly a decade ago, Willow was in the midst of a massive capital campaign that would fund three major initiatives: the building of a new auditorium, the establishment of three regional campuses and the expansion of the Willow Creek Association's international work. Our leadership teams had worked diligently to cast vision toward those efforts, and by the end of our fundraising period we had received pledges for more than 80 million dollars.

But then came 9/11.

As a result of the ensuing tech-market crash and hundreds of people in our congregation losing their jobs, some who had made pledges in good faith no longer could fulfill them. The building construction already was underway and contractors had to be paid. What's more, we had borrowed the maximum amount of capital that we as leaders felt comfortable with, and we certainly didn't want to go any higher than that. Our only option was to re-raise funds to fill the gap.

I was alone on my boat in the middle of Lake Michigan while our chief financial officer crunched the numbers back at Willow. He would email me once he figured out the exact amount of our shortfall, and based on his report, I'd either head back to shore, rally the troops and draw up a plan of attack, or I'd just sail away, all by myself, into the wild blue yonder.

The email finally appeared on my BlackBerry, and holding my breath, I clicked it open. The news wasn't good: we were 18 million dollars behind.

SEVERAL YEARS AGO IN HOPES OF IMPROVING MY OWN LIFE and leadership, I researched the life of Mother Teresa, which is what took me to the book I mentioned earlier, *Come Be My Light*. During that study, I learned that throughout the course of her unparalleled ministry, Mother Teresa suffered spiritual dry spells, times when she didn't detect the love or companionship of God. Despite the fact that she knew God was there, she didn't *feel* him in a visceral sense. Month after month, and in some stretches year after year, Mother Teresa became increasingly despondent because of God's silence; she desperately needed to hear a whisper from him, but she would continue to wait in vain. In spite of his silence, Mother Teresa remained devoted. "Even though I don't feel his presence," she wrote, "I will seek to love him as he has never been loved."[5]

When I came across that quote, it took my breath away. Her sentiment reflected words that are absolutely foreign to my depth of spirituality. I like to think that if I had to endure a long period without communication from God, I'd choose the mature response as well. But would I? Sure, I've had a few dry spells when I wish I "felt" more of God's presence. I've had times when I hoped for a few more warm fuzzies from heaven, a few dramatic "God encounters" to remind me that he is near. But to date, whenever I've been at my lowest, God has faithfully met me with timely words that bring dawn to a very dark night.

The email announcing an 18 million dollar shortfall was definitely one of those "nights." My BlackBerry still in hand, I sat down and said out loud, "God, I can't keep leading until you somehow let me know that you're still with me in all of this."

I wasn't trying to force God's hand or demand some mystical sign; I just knew that I couldn't take one more step without him showing me where it should fall.

Within one hour's time, I received my begged-for direction in ten profound but simple words. Syllable by syllable, here is precisely what the Holy Spirit laid on my heart that day: "You are a treasured child of the most high God."

When I heard this whisper, I was so struck by its beauty and simplicity that I ran down below on the boat, found a pencil and a scrap of paper and captured it in writing, before I could forget one word or lose their exact order. I climbed the steps back into the cockpit area and for the next forty-five minutes picked apart every letter of what God had said. I was struck by the economy of the words he had selected, and as well by the phonetic punch.

"Treasured child"—I'd never heard the two words together, but I knew I would carry them with me the rest of my days. *Each* word, in fact, carried great meaning as I dissected the phrase that day.

"*You* are a treasured child of the most high God"—it was like he was saying, "You, Bill, even with all of your flaws and failings, *you* are a treasured child."

"You *are* a treasured child...." My treasured status is for the here and now. Present tense: I *am* a treasure to God.

"You are a *treasured child*...." I'm not an orphan. I'm not a stepchild. I'm not even merely a mildly appreciated child. I'm a *treasured* child, and of the most high God.

When I got to that last part of the phrase, I reflected back to the day when I had first become a Christian. I was seventeen at the time, and the single most poignant memory I carry from that era is how overwhelmed I felt by the pure, rich love of God. I hadn't known love like that could exist, but upon my conversion I knew it was real. I really was a treasured child, and of the God who is *most high.*

I sat with my scribbled note in hand as streams of tears started to flow. How could I have lost sight of my standing with God? I *wasn't* alone. Far from it! I was accompanied by One who never would leave me, forsake me or abandon me to my fears. In the time it took to convey one straightforward phrase, God revived my commitment for overcoming whatever obstacles stood in my way. He was still with me, and he promised to stay by my side.

When I got back to shore and then made my way to Willow the next morning, not a single aspect of my circumstances had shifted: we were still 18 million in the hole. The only thing that had been altered was my confidence in God's ability to rectify the situations we faced. In Matthew 16:18, Christ says, "I will build my church, and the gates of death will not overcome it."

God's church has survived more than two thousand years of battles, and I was confident that by his grace and empowerment, he'd prove victorious in Willow's battles too.

The end of this story isn't very sexy, but it serves to prove out my point: despite the very real desire I'd had to sail off into the wild blue yonder rather than face our 18 million dollar gap, I approached the situation with renewed hope, called a meeting of our core membership, refreshed them on what it means to steadfastly "listen to God" and then asked them to go home and do just that—listen to whatever God might be asking them to do, in light of our circumstances.

Our building campaign was rescued on the darkest of financial nights, thanks to faithful people who heeded the promptings God gave them as they listened for his whisper.

TWO SUMMERS AGO, I WAS FEELING PRESSED BY ANOTHER SET of circumstances in my life that I was powerless to change. Without going into detail, suffice it to say that I couldn't lead my way through it, power up over it, buy it off or put it in someone else's court. The situation was beyond my control, and the weight of it was wearing me out.

I was in South Haven during my summer study break, and Sunday was coming. For many years now, whenever I'm in South Haven over a weekend, I worship with a small group of African American believers who meet on the poor side of town. They've cycled through four or five pastors in the time that I've been there, and in general the place seems to be in a state of steady decline. Years ago, I made a commitment to stand beside them, and I try to do so through thick and thin.

So, Sunday morning showed up, and out of sheer discipline I decided to head to church. I wasn't expecting God to do anything amazing or the pastor suddenly to deliver a powerful talk. I just went out of obligation and habit: Sundays are for going to church.

Once inside the dilapidated building, I found my usual spot—right-hand side, second pew from the back—and took a seat. A few moments later, an older woman made her way to the front of the room, plopped down on a chair and scooted up to a broken-down organ. As her fingers finally found the right chords, she began to sing, "It's me, it's me, it's me, O Lord, standing in the need of prayer." As she kept singing, I felt the full weight of my crushing circumstance settle in somewhere around my chest.

> *It's me, it's me, it's me, O Lord,*
> *Standin' in the need of prayer.*
> *It's me, it's me, it's me, O Lord,*
> *Standin' in the need of prayer.*
>
> *Not my sister, not my brother, but it's me, O Lord,*
> *Standin' in the need of prayer.*
> *Not my sister, not my brother, but it's me, O Lord,*
> *Standin' in the need of prayer.*[6]

I leaned forward, rested my head on the pew in front of me and I let my request be made known to God: "God, I cannot bear up for much longer under this circumstance. I beg you to change it. Please, change something." The song continued while I pleaded for a word, a whisper, some direction, some insight—*anything.* "Today, it's not my sister, not my brother, but just me, God. I'm sitting here, desperate for your care."

When I opened my eyes and took in the last strains of the song, I felt the unmistakable relief that comes when a burden finally lifts. True, the crushing situation took six more months to be resolved, but in that moment in South Haven, God whispered,

"It's time, Bill. Lay this burden down. I will carry it for the rest of the journey."

Chains of anxiety need not bind us when freedom is ours to claim.

～～～

I have no idea what dark nights of the soul await me in future days, and I don't know which ones you'll be asked to face. They could be medical or relational, financial or emotional, marital or ministerial, brief or painstakingly long. But this much we both can know for sure: when the darkness encroaches, God will be near, he'll seek us out and he'll speak words of insight that cast light onto darkened souls.

Jesus himself faced such a night. After three years of impeccable living, impactful ministry and the forging of a legacy that would inspire believers for thousands of years to come, he found himself sitting in a garden, his soul overwhelmed with sorrow to the point of death.[7]

In just a few hours, he would face torture and crucifixion. The agonizing prospect of this reality caused him to sweat drops of blood. He prayed, "My Father, if it is not possible for this cup to be taken away unless I drink it, may your will be done."[8]

The text tells us he made this request of God not once, not twice, but *three* times in full. And yet *still* Christ had to die.

A seldom-noted moment in this garden scene captures my attention. Between the prayerful sweating of blood and his arrest by a mob of soldiers, Jesus seemed to have experienced a moment when he was emboldened to lay his dark-night burden down and then, simply, to "get up."

"Rise! Let us go!"[9] he told his disciples, who had been snoozing while Jesus fervently prayed. "If ever there has been a dark night, this is it!" I envision him saying. "But trust me when I tell you, *great* light soon will shine again."

That Light can come into your life too. The God who is near to you—the God who actively seeks you out—this God whispers light into your darkest night.

CHAPTER 7

PROMPTINGS
FOR PARENTHOOD

O NE FRIDAY EVENING I HAD SOLE RESPONSIBILITY FOR MY then two-year-old grandson, Henry. Everyone else in the family had made plans to go to a party, so for six hours it was just the kid and me. I dutifully did the diaper drill and the airplane-in-the-hanger trick to get him to eat his dinner, and then I decided I'd take him for a walk. It was eight-thirty or so, which technically meant I should have been putting him to bed. But his parents were nowhere to be found, so I figured we could break some rules.

A few minutes into our stroll, a delivery truck slowly drove by, and on the side of the truck was a picture of a giant ice cream cone. Picking up his stride a little, Henry said, "Ice cream! Ice cream! I *need* ice cream." I figured now was as good a time as any for him to learn the difference between needs and wants, and so bending down to his level I stopped his forward progress.

"Henry," I said, "you don't actually *need* ice cream, because to 'need' something means you have to have it in order to survive, like air. You don't have to have ice cream to survive. You may *want* ice cream, which is okay. But you don't *need* it."

He tilted his face to the side and looked up at me. Two perplexed blue eyes, positioned above his very fat cheeks, seemed to say, "Look, I know you're trying to have a teachable moment here and everything, but I need ice cream. I saw a truck, there was ice cream on the side of that truck and now I *need* to have that ice cream. That's as complicated as I get."

While he and I were engaged in our exchange, the truck eased away from the stop sign and soon was out of sight.

"See?" I said with the certain satisfaction that comes from beating a two-year-old in a debate. "You're not going to get ice cream after all. And for the record, you never needed it to begin with."

We turned back toward the house because it was starting to get cold outside. As we rounded the bend—to Henry's delight—the truck reappeared.

"Ice cream!" Henry cheered. "I need ice cream!"

"You don't *need* ice cream," I said, fully aware that my words were having no effect. As I continued herding him toward home, the truck pulled right up next to us and stopped. Two men hopped out and came over to ask me how to get to a particular address, where they were due to make a frozen-food delivery. After I provided the requested information, one of the guys nodded toward Henry.

"Hey, is that your kid?" he asked.

"Try *grand*kid," I said, "and he's been giving me grief about ice cream ever since he noticed the side of your truck. He keeps telling me he *needs* ice cream, and I keep explaining that while he might *want* ice cream, he does not *need* it."

I don't know why I told the guy all of this. Maybe I was looking for a little validation, but that's not at all what I got.

"Hey!" the guy said, eyes dancing. "I bet I got a spare cone in the back. Hang on." With that, he disappeared into the truck.

Moments later the man reappeared. He gallantly presented an ice cream cone to Henry, who shot me a look that had his clear sentiment written all over it: "I *told* you I needed ice cream."

So much for my big grand-parenting moment—which wasn't so grand in the end.

HOURS LATER, AFTER I'D FINALLY PULLED HENRY DOWN FROM his sugar high, coerced him into pajamas and helped him say his bedtime prayers, I headed toward the living room. I picked up a few scattered toys and lay down on the couch to recuperate for a few minutes. As I lay there, I replayed the night and decided that all in all, I really was a fantastic grandfather. Henry had made it through multiple hours with no adult supervision other than me, and there were no broken bones, bloody noses or major meltdowns to report. In fact, in my honest and objective opinion, I had done a *banner* job of taking care of the little guy.

Partway through my lavish self-praise, I sensed the Holy Spirit saying, "Give it a rest, Bill. You did alright, but you had a pretty good head start, if you'll recall."

As I lay there considering the Holy Spirit's interruption—which although true seemed a bit discourteous to me—a flood of memories came to mind, most of which I know only by way of tattered black-and-white photographs and Hybels' family folklore. God was right: I *had* been given a good head start, courtesy of some Christ-following relatives who had gone before me.

A hundred years ago a man named John Hybels had married a woman named Mary, and together they moved from the Netherlands to Kalamazoo, Michigan. They loved God with all their heart, soul, mind and strength, they were diligent to hear and heed the whispers of God, and they raised a houseful of children, one of whom was Harold Hybels, who would grow up and marry Jerry, my mother. That couple too would live for God and love him with all their heart, soul, mind and strength, and they would wind up having five kids, one of whom is me. I would grow up and marry Lynne, and although we would do an imperfect job of parenting, we would set out with all our heart, soul, mind and strength to hear and heed the input of God and to love our family with every ounce of devotion we possessed.

By God's grace and heaven's humor, our two kids would grow up and choose to love God as well, and our daughter would marry a man who also had been raised by parents who followed Christ with their lives, and who was now choosing to live his life in that same vein. Their union has yielded a little boy, a kid named Henry, who all of us hope will devote his life to God in exactly the same way.

On the couch that evening, in the silence of my living room, I felt an immense wave of gratitude rush over me.

"Thank you, God, for putting me in a family that has generations of faithfulness on its side. Thank you for giving me a spiritual head start, for giving my kids a head start and for giving Henry a head start too." I'll never deserve God's goodness in my life, but I'm grateful for it all the same.

E very serious-minded parent I know wants to pass along good things, not bad things, to their kids. They want to leave a legacy of blessing and wisdom rather than foolishness and pain. They want to be known as ones who followed God's sound instruction rather than going their own way with their lives.

Deuteronomy 6:6–7 says, "Always remember these commands I give you today. Teach them to your children, and talk about them when you sit at home and walk along the road, when you lie down and when you get up" (NCV). Parents who mean business know that spiritual values can't be imparted to kids by words alone. The values lived out through the course of their real-world everyday lives are the ones that will stick. Spiritual dogma doled out in a rigid, militaristic fashion—intended to control, rather than to transform a child's heart—will bear the fruit of some serious resentment and rebellion. Instead, as the verses in Deuteronomy suggest, wise parents adopt the life-lesson approach to helping their kids establish a spiritual foundation upon which to build their lives.

However, it is my contention that even if someone could write the perfect parenting book—and even if every parent on the planet read it and applied its lessons fastidiously—there would still be a few (hundred) times in life when moms and dads would be at a total loss regarding how to coach and counsel their kids.

Even Scripture leaves much to be desired when it comes to turn-by-turn directions for steering our kids toward independence and maturity. God intentionally left out a lot of detail when it comes to solving parenting (and grand-parenting!) dilemmas, which I happen to think is a good thing. When we get in over our heads, when we step beyond our capability, beyond even what Scripture has to say, it brings us to our knees. We get desperate enough to ask God personally to intervene. And then it becomes our job to stay wide open to what he wants to communicate to us. It is whisper time!

One of the earliest, most significant parenting whispers I remember receiving from God pertained to our son, Todd.

It was apparent to me from their earliest ages that our kids, Shauna and Todd, were as different as night and day. Shauna was wired two-twenty from day one. She has always been incredibly verbal, highly extroverted and the life of every party.

At age three, she could carry on adult-level conversations and loved to talk so much that Lynne and I kidded her by saying, "Honey, you've never had a single unexpressed thought, feeling or opinion."

With Shauna, you always knew where she stood. She had a personality type that really resonated with my own. Conversationally, we were like two peas in a pod: I was expressive and candid with her, and she was a verbal light bulb in response.

But Todd was not wired that way.

When he was still quite young, I recognized that I never was going to reach deeply into Todd's soul through the use of words. It was a realization that came to me around our family's dinner table one night. As was typically the case, Lynne, Shauna and I were carrying the conversation, and I noticed that as our banter increased, Todd's involvement decreased. The more we engaged, the more he withdrew, and suddenly the Holy Spirit whispered. "Bill, if you do not adopt a different approach with this little guy, you might just lose him forever."

The prompting was quite upsetting to me. What adjustments could I make as his dad to connect with his personality, so different from my own? During the weeks that followed, I read as many parenting books as I could find, in hopes of discovering the secret to engaging a quieter kid, and thankfully, one author came to my aid.

He suggested that because children are distinct, parents would do well to offer differing parenting styles to each. Now this may sound like Parenting 101 to many, but it was a mind-blower to me. I was raised in a cultural setting where parents employed one parenting style, even though they were raising five or six children with vastly different wiring patterns, preferences and needs. But something rang true in this author's counsel.

With God's whisper still punctuating my thoughts, I thought I would give it a try.

Through another read, I discovered the concept of "love languages,"[1] ways in which people receive love from others. I learned that Todd's "love language" was *quality time.* More than words of affirmation or attempts at deep father/son talks, what Todd needed most from me was unrushed time, and time on *his* terms. So, I decided that if I couldn't reach him through dinnertime conversations—which worked wonderfully with Shauna—I'd offer him my time. This took intentionality, and it looked differently at different ages as Todd grew. During his elementary school years, I would come home after a long day at work and say, "Hey, Todd, what would you like to do for the next couple of hours, just you and me?"

His answer always revolved around one of three things: he wanted to go look at used cars, head to the bicycle shop and look at bike gear, or take a trip to the nearest motorcycle dealership and meander up and down the rows of Harleys, just soaking it all in.

Thankfully, my son and I had some shared interests in each of those areas. But spending multiple hours in these shops two or three times a week—not to *talk*, mind you, but simply to *roam around*—wasn't exactly my definition of "connecting." After making several of these significant investments of time, I thought, "Surely this will open the kid up, and soon he will feel the freedom to talk more."

But no dice. Todd was still quiet. Actually, about every six weeks when we were en route back home from one dealership or another, he would open up a tiny bit and offer something for us to talk about for a few minutes. But I learned that Todd never was going to verbalize his feelings on par with his sister, and the sooner I right-sized my expectations and watched for optimal opportunities that would offer him a chance to talk, the more of his heart he was likely to disclose.

TODD IS IN HIS EARLY THIRTIES NOW, AND HE HAS REMAINED true to his quieter, God-given wiring. As I look back at that first critical whisper from God, it is painfully clear that, had I stayed on the other track—the track of forcing my single-focused parenting style on two very different children—I'd have severely limited my relationship with him.

As it has turned out, we enjoy a wonderfully fulfilling connection these days, mostly because along the way we learned how to use fewer words by using them well. These days, you'd rarely catch us sitting across from each other at a restaurant, engaged in a multi-hour conversation. But you might find us jogging together or boating together or working on one of Todd's jet skis together and, after a substantial amount of quiet, quality time has passed, exchanging a few well-placed, meaningful sentences. I praise God for every single one.

My kids' wiring differences went deeper than just their communication patterns. The entirety of their interpersonal worlds varied as vastly as two people's could.

Shauna has always loved people and parties, and she is not averse to speaking to crowds, large or small. Todd, on the other hand, preferred a behind-the-scenes style of life. This was another area where God by his promptings saved me from a terrible series of parenting mistakes.

Todd played team sports all through grade school—soccer and basketball, mostly. When he was in junior high, he was a starter on his school's basketball team and one of their highest scorers. Once when he was in the throes of try-outs for the eighth-grade team, which he was a shoe-in to make, he caught me totally off-guard. He was just about to head off to bed one night but stopped and said, "Dad, I don't think I want to play basketball anymore."

He knew that I had played basketball most of my life, and that I valued my kids' participation in team sports because of the terrific groundwork I believe it lays for future team-leadership roles. I'm sure he knew his words would hit me hard.

"Why don't you want to play?" I asked, trying to keep my voice neutral and my expression receptive.

"Well, two reasons," he said. "For one, whenever I get fouled during a game, I hate standing on the free-throw line with a whole gymnasium full of people watching me shoot. I don't think I like playing sports in front of big crowds."

"And the second reason?" I asked.

"Dad, none of the other kids are taking the game very seriously. If I'm going to be on a team, I want to practice hard and do my best. It would be fun if everybody felt that way, but they don't. I just don't want to play anymore."

In that moment, I knew that either I could lay down the law and force my son to play basketball, or I could allow for the fact that Todd is different from me, that team sports just might not be his thing.

I asked Todd how much longer try-outs would run—three days, it turned out—and said, "How about you give me three days to pray about this, and you pray about it too, and then on Friday we'll talk again."

Over the course of those seventy-two hours, I felt a strong sense from the Holy Spirit that Todd probably was more wired up to do individual sports as opposed to team sports. He never had been a "public" kid—even when he'd won awards along the way, he had to be pushed to go to the front of the banquet room to receive them. He was a shy boy, plain and simple. What's more, Willow already was quite large by that time, and I wondered if the visibility of Lynne's and my life might also be taking a toll on our son.

By Friday of that week, God was whispering to me, "Let Todd go the way I have created him, Bill. Trust that this new path will lead him in a positive direction." Todd and I talked, and together we agreed that quitting basketball was the right thing for him. The relief on his face was palpable. The following week, Todd and I informed his coach that he would not be playing ball his eighth-grade year, and although the coach was deeply disappointed, my son never once looked back.

Proverbs tells parents to train up their kids in the way they should go. I've heard parents use this verse as a justification for pushing their child into conformity, regardless of his or her God-given temperament. I've since come to understand that there are two layers of wisdom in that verse. Scholars who study this text are convinced that the writer—in addition to encouraging parents to teach a child to surrender to God and practice righteousness—was also challenging parents to discover the natural aptitudes and abilities of their children, and to encourage their children's pursuit of the path that is theirs uniquely to walk. In addition to pouring out massive amounts of love onto your kids and setting appropriate limits along the way, another vital gift you can give your children is a discerning analysis of the special abilities God put into their lives and a gradual drawing-out of those competencies so that a young kid eventually can find his own particular path. It's exactly what I needed to do with Todd.

Incidentally, after Todd quit basketball, he immediately took up snowboarding, snowmobiling, motorcycle racing and surfing

—all individual sports that he became very good at over time. The point is, Todd's life has proven out what I believe God revealed to me in that whisper: my kid's strong need for independence was something he couldn't—and shouldn't—be talked out of. Instead of forcing Todd into *my* predetermined mold, I needed to help pave *God's* path for his life.

~~~~~

Parenting brings varying degrees of difficulty that range from no-brainer stuff, like teaching your kids general civility and basic table manners—things you could teach your dog to do—to mind-bending dilemmas that involve their morals, their character and their future. During those highly intense parenting moments when you're wondering whether to exhibit grace or clamp down, whether to manifest low control or high, whether to forgive them or make them pay, whether to spare them from consequences or let them feel the full brunt, a little divine help is needed. It is then that God whispers, "Stay wide open to my guidance, and I promise to show you the way."

One night when Shauna was sixteen, I was preparing to go to bed when I heard a car pull into the driveway. Thinking it was Shauna arriving home for the night, I remember being glad that I wouldn't have to worry about making sure she met curfew and that for once I could enjoy a sound night's sleep.

That's not exactly how things would go down.

En route to my bedroom, I glanced outside through the front windows and saw Shauna jumping out of a car that was parked in our driveway. The dome light revealed a back seat packed with kids from her school. Seconds later, she burst through the front door and blew past me.

"Hi, honey. You okay?" I asked.

"I can't get into it right now, Dad," she hollered from the

hallway as she dashed toward her room. "My friends are all wait-ing, and I have to get my stuff."

So much for beating curfew.

I suggested to her that right now would actually be a *perfect* time to "get into it," explaining that as her dad, I needed to know where she was going and what she intended to do. "Please slow down and help me understand the plan," I said with as much kindness as I could manage.

In a flurry of sentences she informed me that she was headed to spend the night at a friend-of-a-friend's house, and that she was "pretty sure" it was in Lake Geneva, which is about an hour's drive from our house.

"Dad, I have to go!" she declared. "They're all waiting for me in the car."

"Shauna, I need more information than you're giving me," I said. "Like, who is this friend of a friend, and exactly where in Lake Geneva will you be? And are any parents going to be there?"

I'm not entirely sure what kind of response I expected from Shauna. After all, this was the same kid who at age three fre-quently rode her Big Wheel down the sidewalk, past the fence post that was a declared boundary for her. She knew that riding beyond that certain point on the street was forbidden, but she still would do it. One day, after yet another boundary infraction, Lynne kneeled down, face-to-face with Shauna, put both hands on her little shoulders and said, "Shauna, if you ride past that fence post one more time, I'm going to spank your little rear end. I don't want to, but I will!"

Shauna looked up at her mother, raised her hind side toward the sky and said, "Then spank me now, because I'm going riding!"

But back to our entryway on that Lake Geneva night. In lieu of answering any of my questions, Shauna did something she had never done before. She approached me, looked me straight in the eye and said, "Dad, unless you physically stop me, I am going to go to this party."

My jaw dropped. I was speechless. My little girl! The one whose diapers I had changed! (Well, a couple of times....) The one I had taken to McDonald's every Saturday morning for years, just so we could enjoy dad/daughter time. The one I had dragged with me on speaking trips all over the world, just so she and I could hang out at the hotel after my obligations were fulfilled and have breakfast together the following morning. *Was this the same girl who was now going toe-to-toe with me, defying my authority?*

I stared at her incredulously. Her face bore a defiant look that conveyed, "It's a new day, Dad."

My mind whirred, and my thoughts wrestled to untangle themselves from one another. Clearly, I was out of my league here. What was I supposed to say? Or do?

As I took a deep breath, I sensed a strong prompting from the Holy Spirit: "Don't even *think* about physically restraining this young girl. This thing will go south so fast if you engage in that way. We *are* in new territory now, it *is* a new day, and you're going to have to put her in my hands. There is nothing more that you can do."

I didn't have time to question God on the parenting advice he was giving me. I only had time to obey. I took a step backward, eyed my insubordinate daughter and rattled off the only things I could think to say: "Honey, take my cell phone. You can call me anytime—at any hour of the night—and ask me to come get you. I'll drive to wherever you are and pick you up immediately. *Any* hour. Don't get into a car with anyone who has been drinking. I love you. I'm disappointed in your decision tonight. But I love you. I don't feel good about this at all, but if you're this determined to go, then I will not physically restrain you."

As soon as the last syllable was out of my mouth, Shauna brushed by me.

"Thanks, Dad!"

And she rushed outside to climb into her friend's idling car. The door slammed, and they were gone.

⌇

The Lake Geneva incident would be the first in a series of similarly confounding parenting challenges where Shauna was concerned. One of the more significant occasions happened while she was away at college in California. Through a series of events that are hers to tell,[2] halfway into her undergrad experience she found herself making choices that distanced her from God and compromised the commendable character she'd built. Things eventually escalated to the point that Lynne and I decided I should fly out to California and try to talk some sense into Shauna, face-to-face.

After negotiating a tricky schedule, I designated the day, boarded the jet and later met my daughter at a sidewalk café in Santa Barbara.

After the usual catching-up conversation was behind us, I dove in.

"Shauna, the reason I'm here is that your mom and I are getting increasingly worried about you. We're concerned that you're heading down a dangerous path."

She looked at me intently, seeming almost sympathetic to my concerns.

And so I kept going.

"Honey, we want you to know that we love you, and that it's

never too late to get back on the high road, to choose a God-honoring way of life...."

Still she gazed my way.

"... and so I'm just going to ask you outright: Do you think you might be ready to modify your course a bit?"

The question hung in the air like an invisible matzo ball. She stared at me through her clear, blue eyes. I stared back. The silence lingered.

Then, after the subtlest of lip twitches, she proffered an answer. I felt my eyebrows rise as I anticipated concession on her part.

"Yeah, um, I don't think so," she said. "I've still got a *lot* of life left to live."

Sucker punch. My heart sank. Bewildered and distraught, I headed back to Chicago that night, having no clue what would become of my daughter. But even in the helpless ambiguity, I sensed God saying, "I'm still near."

***

It was around this same season of parenting that Shauna's brother, Todd, was getting his driver's license. His love of cars had been present from an early age. I had taught Todd to drive when he was eight or nine years old, by having him back cars out of the driveway or maneuver boats and equipment whenever opportunities presented themselves. By the time he was sixteen, he was chomping at the bit to get behind the wheel.

When he finally got his license, I noticed that Todd drove a bit too fast. He had been handling cars for years by then, but in my opinion he was simply over-confident. I knew that without some coaching, he could be a threat to himself and to others on the road.

One day I sat down with my son and said, "Todd, you're one

of the best young drivers I know, but you drive too fast. If you don't slow it down, there is going to come a day when you will injure yourself or someone else by your driving. I know how sensitive your heart is, and if you ever caused someone else pain because of your carelessness, I know it would destroy *your* life, let alone the life of the person you harmed."

I thought it was a pretty good spiel—speaking to the sensitive way he was wired—but in response all I got was the teenager's classic yeah-yeah-yeah look. He hadn't been dialed in to one word I had said.

About a week later while enjoying a day off in South Haven with the family, I decided to take a six-mile run. I was about three miles in, when suddenly I heard the screeching of tires behind me. I looked over my shoulder just in time to spot Todd, in his car, doing a power slide as he rounded a busy street corner at forty or fifty miles an hour. It was a perfectly controlled slide and looked like the sort of thing you'd see a professional stunt driver do in a movie. Actually, if it hadn't been so blatantly illegal and dangerous to others, I might have been impressed. In this case, I was not.

Todd hadn't seen me, but I had sure seen him. And I ran home faster than I have ever run before, determined to give him a piece of my fuming mind. I was filled with anger for how he had directly violated my warning of a week prior. I stood outside the cottage thinking, "What are all the possible ways that I can punish this kid so that I can fully get my message of displeasure across?"

But something happened before I entered the cottage; the Holy Spirit intervened. In that instant, the prompting came, "Instead of playing the anger card, let Todd see how much you love him and how brokenhearted you really would be if he got hurt or killed in a car accident. Let him know that you're actually *scared* that you're going to find him in a hospital or in a morgue someday, because of his over-confidence in driving."

The whisper went against my reflexive response. *When children break a rule, they must be forced to pay, right?* That's how I was brought up, and that's how I intended for this situation to go.

I argued with God outside the house: "You want me to show Todd fear instead of anger? He's not going to remember *fear*. What do you want me to do? Bear my soul to this kid, and then let him off scot-free so he can just go out and do the very same thing again?"

The Spirit was unfazed by my cynicism. "Just trust me in this," I sensed him saying. "This time, show Todd your love, not your anger."

I'm not sure if I was more frustrated with Todd or with God as I stormed into the house, but once I found myself seated across from my son, I caved to wisdom from above.

"Todd," I said, "I was jogging right up to the intersection where you did that power slide a few minutes ago. I saw the whole thing, and your actions were in direct violation of what we talked about last week."

I couldn't tell from Todd's expression if he felt any remorse for being caught, but it didn't matter. I knew what I needed to say, even if it would require far more vulnerability than I felt Todd deserved—and certainly more than I preferred giving.

I took a deep breath. "Had you not pulled your car out of that slide just right, you could have hit the curb and rolled the car. And the thought of picking your broken body out of that vehicle and you losing an arm or a leg unnecessarily ... the thought of having to come ID you at the morgue like I had to do with my dad ... it's actually terrifying to me, Todd."

Tears flowed down my cheeks, and when I finished my comments, Todd's eyes too were red and swollen. I wrapped my arms around my son and said, "Please, Todd. Please be careful in your car."

To my knowledge, his driving patterns changed that day. I never had to have another conversation with him on the subject, and based on how I observed him driving from that point forward, I think my plea somehow hit home. Who knows what the anger approach would have done? Can you see why I love whispers so much?

Over the years, there were plenty of trivial parenting conundrums—messy rooms and nose piercings, ill-advised hairstyles and tattoos—that Lynne and I felt it wise to let slide. But when it came to matters of morals or character, or things of safety or legal consequence, we needed infusions of wisdom that could only come from above. And now that my kids are grown adults, I see the benefit of having paid strict attention to every syllable of divine direction received.

Within a six-month period some years ago, I received cards on my desk at work from my kids, both of which proved out the power of letting God guide each of our steps.

The card from Todd read, "Dear Dad, I wanted to tell you how proud I am of you. The older I get, the more I realize why you raised me the way you did. You always challenged me, which made me more confident in myself and in Christ. This past week, I was thinking about all of the experiences I've had that few other kids my age have had, because they didn't have parents who would challenge them. So, thanks for the challenges. And for all of the love and encouragement you've poured into my life along the way. I love you."

I just about lost it as I sat in my desk chair and read that card.

For a timid, non-verbal son to express himself with words like that—it went deep into this father's heart.

Around Father's Day that same year I received a card from Shauna. "Dad, I was just thinking about you," it began. "What a great friend and father you've been to me. You're a person I love to be around and love to share life with. Thanks for all the things you've done along the way, and for the flowers and Diet Cokes and long walks … and for forgiving me."

The sentiment went on, but I don't type well through tears, so I'll let it close there. The point is, there is a payoff that comes when we stay wide open to God. Follow his promptings at key junctures, and you'll benefit from it too.

~~~~~

One of the greatest rewards of living by the well-timed whispers of God regarding raising your family is that one day things might just come full circle.

For many years I craved God's input so that I could steer my kids in the right direction. But last year, during a vacation in one of my family's favorite places in the world, it was my kids who would hear from God—and do some steering of their own.

Eighteen months before that vacation, Todd had embarked on his around-the-world sailing trip. He was midstream on the second half of his voyage, and he took a hiatus from his travels to join us for a family connection. On our first day together—as is our habit when we are together—Todd and I took off for a mid-morning run. Now, typically I would be the one to set the pace, but that day I was sucking air. He glanced over at me mid-stride and said, "Dad, you're in terrible shape! What has happened to you?"

My mind scrolled through everything that had occurred since I had last seen him: staff reductions and reorganizations, budget overhauls, too many back-to-back hundred-hour work weeks and an exhaustingly long international trip. It had been a tough spring. "Just give me a few days," I offered. "I'll bounce back soon enough."

I meant the words, but something deep inside told me I was being overly optimistic at best.

Late that night, after Lynne had gone to bed, Shauna, Todd and I decided to stay up and talk. We were sitting on teak chairs on a terrace that overlooks the harbor, just savoring each other's company, when suddenly I heard myself say, "You know, I'm not sure that my old work patterns are going to serve me well in the new reality I'm leading in...."

The last thing on my mind that night was trolling for free therapy from my kids. But I think my run with Todd had surfaced some stuffed-down feelings about how distracted and disjointed my life had become of late. And for whatever reason, in the safety of that moment, it all came spilling out. Both of my kids engaged immediately, asking questions and scouring my answers for the truth of how I *really* was doing. The attention made me feel quite self-conscious, but I must admit, their concern touched me deeply.

After twenty minutes or so of conversation, and following what I now know was a prompting from God, my wise-beyond-her-years daughter said, "Dad, what are some recent examples of times when you were relaxed and you felt like you were able to connect deeply with God?"

I thought about her question and answered as honestly as I could. "The South American trip I took last month. That single trip yielded the most consecutive days of deep connection with God that I've known in a long, long time."

She probed a little more, until it came out that the reason I had felt such intimacy with God on that trip was because I had fallen into my "trip pattern." I travel more than a hundred days a year, and I find that when I'm on the road, my early mornings in hotel rooms afford me the perfect opportunity to invest extended time studying the Bible, praying and journaling about my inner world. Typically my morning speaking engagements don't start before nine o'clock, so from five-thirty or six a.m. until my ride phones me from the hotel lobby, I can pour a cup of hot coffee, prop up my pillows on the hotel bed, spread out my Bible and study aids, and get centered spiritually. Without people knocking on the door or staff members coming in and out of my office like they do back at Willow, I can perch perfectly justified, uninterrupted in that position until I feel refreshed for my day and reminded of God's presence and power in my life. The added blessing is that none of my leadership-oriented "stacks" are staring at me from various corners of my desk while I do so. Being on the road definitely has its perks!

My kids took in all of this detail before Shauna continued. "So, why don't you take your hotel strategy and turn it into an approach for your life at home?"

I knew my daughter was on to something. Todd nodded in agreement, and although it was nearing the bleary-eyed hour of two a.m., the three of us began talking about what my hotel strategy might look like at home, and how the proper execution of such a plan could potentially restore a sense of sanity and spiritual connectedness to my life.

At this writing, it's eight months into my experiment of instituting my hotel strategy at home, and so far, so good. I awaken early, but instead of hurrying through a shower and rushing off to work, I step into a room that overlooks our back deck and spend the first critical hours of my day with God. The difference it has made in my life could be a whole separate chapter in this book; suffice it to say, this change in my routine has been a much-needed source of sanity for me. And it all started with a two-a.m. whisper from God through my daughter and son.

A dmittedly, there is no perfect parent, there is no perfect child and, consequently, there is no perfect family. I can't conclude this chapter on parenting without relaying an extreme example of this reality: While in a grocery store some time ago, I witnessed a family meltdown I never will forget. The father and the mother started arguing with each other in plain view of everyone else around. Their crudeness and rage kept escalating until one of their three young children got scared and started to cry. Not knowing what else to do to find comfort, the little girl raced up to her father and tried to wrap her arms around his leg. But the father, now completely out of control, was in no mood for affection. He backhanded that child with such force that she tumbled onto the ground and fell on top of her smaller sibling, who then fell against a shelf full of canned beans. Before I or other onlookers could step in, store management and security personnel came to break up the fight.

Talk about a devastating thing to witness! I left the store physically shaken and thinking, "There is nothing uglier than a family that is out of step with God."

When a family is not functioning well, its members often feel diminished and confused and frustrated and alone. And you don't need a Ph.D. in sociology to realize that an alarming number of families are struggling these days, not just with the mundane questions of who gets to handle the remote control or whose turn it is to clean up after the dog, but with significant issues like, *Do we really love each other? Are we going to make it as a family? Will our kids turn out okay?*

But when imperfect people make a point of receiving input

from the One who *is* without fault, it's a game-changer for all involved.

When a wife obeys God's whisper to approach her husband with a tender, carefree spirit once the kids have been tucked into bed for the night; when a father follows a prompting to leave the office a few hours early and surprise his daughter by showing up across town at her volleyball tournament; when a set of parents listen for God's input on how to nurture and mentor their son as he steps into adolescence; when dads invite divine direction regarding drawing out the unique wiring patterns of their kids; when moms pay attention to the supernatural nudges that help them fulfill God's desired roll in the family for them—when these and a thousand other manifestations of being attuned to God's whispers unfold in the life of a family, a legacy of *blessings*, not curses, lives on.

You and I have got one shot at this thing called our heritage, my friend. We will pass on either goodness to generations that come behind us, or we'll pass on something less. My vote is for the good stuff, for the whisper-led way of life.

Parenting has proven to be one of the toughest challenges of my life, but knowing that to the best of my human ability I've invited God in at every turn rather than keeping him at arm's length, I rest in the blessed assurance of knowing that I have done the best job I could do. My kids love God and give him free rein to guide their lives. It doesn't get any better than that!

CHAPTER 8

WHEN GOD SPEAKS
THROUGH OTHERS

During my early days of ministry, I had the misfortune of watching a friend of mine who was an integral part of our church self-destruct. For many months, I had noticed that he was spending quite a bit of time with a woman who was not his wife. I wasn't intentionally doing detective's work; I just kept spotting the two of them riding in cars together or enjoying dinner by candlelight at nearby restaurants.

What's more, I began to notice that periodically when this friend agreed to a lunch appointment with me, he'd fail to show up. I would wait for an hour or more at a table for two and finally bail, figuring he'd been held up in traffic or had to tend to an emergency at work.

The next time I would see him, I'd say, "Hey, I waited for you for an hour on Thursday. What happened?"

"Oh! I got assigned to a two-day trip to New York City and forgot to call you," he'd explain, after scrambling to think up an excuse.

But several days later, when I'd ask about his time in the Big

Apple, he would forget that he had gone. "New York?" he'd ask. "Oh! Yeah, yeah. Uh, it was great! It just seems like so long ago!"

"Hmmm ... I bet it does," I thought. Something just wasn't adding up.

Around the same time that my discernment meter was beginning to register on "high alert," I was teaching a series at Willow based on the life of King David. The title of my final talk in the series was, "Everybody Needs a Nathan." It addressed the idea that, in addition to providing encouragement to fellow members of the body of Christ, being someone's spiritual brother or sister also means warning them of potential pitfalls in their lives—sometimes even before they themselves see trouble on the horizon.

You probably remember the story of David and Bathsheba. In short, from his palace rooftop David eyes a beautiful (although married) woman bathing; he sends his servants to fetch her; he engages in a sexual affair with her; and after later learning that she has become pregnant, he immediately arranges for the murder of her husband so that he can take Bathsheba to be his wife and the mother of their child. It's a pretty bad scene. If David had been asked to keep an annual tally of his sins, this was what you'd call a Very Bad Year.

Interestingly, although everyone around the palace undoubtedly knew what David had done—and that what he had done was terribly wrong—apparently nobody said a word to him. Nobody told him the truth. Nobody, that is, except Nathan—an old friend of David's, now a prophet sent to him by God.

One day, Nathan approached his former-shepherd friend and told him a story strategically targeted both to David's past and present. It was a story about some sheep.

"There were two men in a city," Nathan said. "One was rich, but the other was poor. The rich man had many sheep and cattle.

But the poor man had nothing except one recently purchased little female lamb. It shared his food and drank from his cup and slept in his arms. The lamb was like a daughter to him."[1]

Nathan continued the tale: A traveler stopped to visit the rich man. A meal was in order to feed the traveler, but because the rich man didn't want to use up one of his own sheep or cows to feed the stranger, he stole the precious lamb from the poor man, killed it and then cooked it for his visitor.

David was appalled. The very thought of such a selfish, evil deed enraged him. "As surely as the LORD lives," he bellowed, "the man who did this should die!"[2]

Nathan's tale had struck home.

"You are the man!"[3] Nathan said.

David never saw it coming.

Nathan's wise and bold confrontation ultimately led to David's wholehearted repentance before God.

After teaching this whole story to our congregation, I exhorted them not to shrink back from making high-risk, high-stakes plays like Nathan's in their relational worlds. "Nathan was the only one who would tell his friend the truth," I explained. "We *all* need a little of Nathan's spirit in us."

My own words were still fresh on my mind when I received a prompting from God regarding my friend who was "not" having the affair.

"If you want to be a good brother to this guy," the Holy Spirit seemed to say, "then go ahead and broach the difficult subject, but do it in a non-accusing way. The goal is not to prejudge him; the goal is to find out the truth and remind him of his marriage vows."

The following week, I corralled my courage and approached my friend.

"Listen," I said, "you know how much I care about you, and

you know how committed we're trying to be as a church to shooting straight with each other, to telling the truth at every turn. I need to raise a little concern with you, just to be sure that things are okay...."

My friend nodded and told me to go on.

"Well," I said, "it just seems like you're spending an awful lot of time with another guy's wife...."

As the words rolled off my tongue, he looked at me with a piercing gaze and physically took a step backward. For a split second, I thought he might thank me for raising the issue, since of course he wouldn't want to behave in a way that would cause misperceptions. But his eyes showed a different response.

"Oh, I see how it is," he slowly seethed. "Now that you're a senior pastor of a church—albeit a *tiny* church that meets in a rented *movie* theater—you're going to start playing God and telling people who they can and can't be friends with! You're going to be Mr. Relationship Cop, the guy who snoops into everyone's business and polices their dinner companions! Is *that* how it's going to go, Bill? Is *that* who you've become?"

I wanted to say, "Wait, wait, wait. Don't you remember how the Nathan/David deal wound up? We talked about it in church just last week! After Nathan courageously said his piece, David said, 'I have sinned against the LORD,'[4] he gave Nathan a friendly man-hug, he went and wrote a bunch of great worship music and everyone lived happily ever after! Remember?"

But it was no use. My friend had already stormed off.

Several months after that excruciating exchange, I discovered that an affair had in fact been going on. My friend had missed our lunch appointments and faked those trips back East because he was entangled in a series of secret meetings that involved the "other" woman in his life.

In the end, the guy's marriage and innocent family would get blown apart. Untold amounts of pain and suffering would result from his mistakes, in part because he refused to let a friend shine light into a dark part of his life.

~~~

What I taught in that series back in the early days of Willow is true today: everybody needs a Nathan, and lovers of God all would do well to cultivate a "David" state of mind. Sometimes God routes pain-sparing whispers to us through the ears and lips of another person. And periodically, he chooses us to deliver a message to someone else—regardless of whether or not it will be well-received.

Having a "David" state of mind can mean the difference between continuing down a path destined for self-destruction or turning from that path toward life and restoration. A recent example of this truth played itself out some months ago, when I gave a thirty-five-minute talk at a weekend service on the subject of reconciliation.

I spent the first third of the talk carefully explaining that when you are involved in a relationship that has fractured because of a disagreement, the Bible says that first and foremost, we must clean up our own side of the street before we cross the street and point the blame at the other person. We need to begin by owning our part of the relational breakdown—our attitudes, words or actions—so that when we sense that it is time to build a bridge of reconciliation with the other person, we come to the table with clean hands and a pure heart.

Again, I spent *thirty-five* minutes on this topic, working out for the congregation how to move through the reconciliation process gently, humbly, earnestly and with a deep spirit of grace. Get the picture?

Immediately after the service, one of the first people to greet me down front was a man who introduced himself as a visitor from Ohio. He was a big guy, a linebacker-type whose physique seemed about to burst out of his seams. What's more, he was a close-talker—a space invader. The guy was in my face. And the more he talked, the more uncomfortable I felt.

"My wife is *way* out of line," he said. "She isn't talking to me these days, and based on what I've just heard in your sermon, *she's* the one being unbiblical. *She's* the one at fault!"

With each proclamation, spit from his words sprayed my glasses. I took a small step backward. No use. As I moved back, he moved forward. We were doing something resembling a miserable dance. And anyone who knows me knows I hate to dance, so I stood my ground.

"Tell me those Bible verses you mentioned again," he demanded, "because I'm gonna go home and quote them to her, and straighten her out once and for all!"

This was going nowhere fast. The more the guy talked, the more amped up he became. Something had to give.

Reaching for his elbows, I nudged him back a step. "Let's back up this whole thing a little bit," I said. "And while we're at it, how about you lower your decibel level by about 50 percent?"

He laughed a nervous laugh. "I guess I can get kind of riled up!" he said.

"Your physical presence and proximity are beginning to intimidate me," I said. "Which is a bigger achievement than you likely realize. I can only imagine how your wife must feel, unless she's six-five and pushing three-fifty."

I reminded the man that I had spent the first twelve minutes of my sermon on the topic of handling your *own* business before charging ahead with an accusing spirit toward someone else. I had talked about *humility*; I had talked about *gentleness*; I had talked about *grace*—all things that clearly had not registered with this guy.

"I'm going to shoot straight with you," I said, bracing myself for impact. "You seem like an angry, out-of-control guy." (We have plainclothes security people around Willow, which gives me the confidence to talk big in these kinds of settings.) To his credit, the man shifted his demeanor.

"I've struggled with anger all of my life," he said.

"Now we're getting somewhere," I responded. "You've just given a classic 'David' response, if ever I heard one. Way to go!"

Because this man had graciously received my observations, we were then able to engage in fifteen minutes of productive dialogue. He just needed a Nathan to come alongside him, hold up a mirror and say, "This is who you *really* are." I don't know how this man's story played out back in Ohio, but I admired his willingness to take a look in the mirror during our talk.

If you and I claim to believe God's Word, inevitably the time will come when we will need some help applying it to our lives. God didn't create us to live in a vacuum. We need others. We need someone with skin on to help us achieve the righteousness we crave. Again I point you to Proverbs 11:14, which says, "Without good direction, people lose their way; the more wise counsel you follow, the better your chances" (MSG). As I reflect on the good direction God has whispered in my life, I realize a major portion has come from the lips of trusted friends. I wasn't always mature enough to be thankful for that "wisdom" at the time, but usually (though not always), I'd try to heed the direction I received.

W hen I think about the divine whispers that have been delivered to me by real live people along the way, my mind traces all the way back to my teenage years, when after the burger dinner with a mentor from our church that I described in chapter 1, I lay in my bed, staring at the ceiling with that man's words banging around in my brain. "What are you going to do with your life that will last forever?" he had asked me at the restaurant that night.

It was a radical thought, the idea of turning everything over to a Being I could not see. But forty years later I realize that the trajectory of my spiritual journey was actually set on that single night. The man had told me that to accept his challenge I only had to put my life in God's hands for *as long as* God proved himself trustworthy. The moment God made a mistake, I could bail on the deal then and there.

I've long since given up on the notion that God ever will fumble the ball in my life. Heeding the wise prompting from that man would go down as the most sensible step I've ever taken. One simple whisper. One tentative but receptive spirit. One life *forever* changed.

ANOTHER BIT OF COUNSEL THAT CAME BY WAY OF A FRIEND showed up during the early years of Willow. Lynne and I had become close friends with a family that was part of the church. We were consistently struck by how deeply this family loved each other. We wanted our family to be like that, but we weren't entirely sure where we should begin.

One weekend after the worship service, the father of that family approached me.

"Bill," he said, "I think you're doing a good job of leading our church, but I'm curious if you're open to a piece of advice on the family front."

"Absolutely," I said, and I meant it.

"You might think about using your vacation time more wisely," he said. "Instead of just staying away from church stuff and calling that your time off, consider using vacations as opportunities to make an investment in your family ... to infuse your family with adventure and joy."

What he said gripped me. During my early years of ministry, my tendency whenever I took days off work was either to continue working (from home), or to hang out with a few guy friends. But I wasn't fooling anybody. And my family certainly wasn't benefiting from this trend.

I asked a few questions for clarification and learned that the man and his wife made it a priority to take two family vacations each year. Well in advance of the trips, they would involve their kids in the planning process and build a strong sense of anticipation for what would soon unfold. While they were gone they would squeeze every ounce of family time out of the experience, and once they returned they'd tell stories, share memories and look at photo-album snapshots as they relived the great time they'd had.

For the past twenty-five years, that single prompting from God through that dad has had more of an effect on the Hybels family than any other counsel we've received. We too have prioritized taking a family vacation or two each year—sometimes to exciting places and sometimes to a tiny town in Michigan, where we can just rest and boat and swim. And like the family that modeled this behavior for us, we too watched our family learn to love each other far better as a result.

Several years ago, the kids and Lynne and I were enjoying our final dinner together on one of those vacations, and I asked them to share two or three family memories that were most important to them. Without exception, those memories were made while on vacation together somewhere. As Shauna and

Todd began recounting each trip, Lynne and I were stunned by how vivid their recollections were. They remembered every city, every hotel and nearly every restaurant where we ate. Todd recalled every rental car, truck or boat; Shauna recalled every social activity we engaged in; and *all* of us recalled the years when our vacations were dampened by unwelcomed weather or hijacked by the flu.

Still, through good times and bad, sickness and health, those getaways forged in our family bonds that honor each other and God. All because of one well-placed whisper from a friend.

I WISH I COULD SAY THAT EVERY WHISPER I RECEIVED ALONG the way involved smooth-sailing subjects like feel-good vacations and fond family memories, but that's not the case. A couple of whispers, courtesy of one very good friend, caused huge waves in my life.

For years, Lynne and I had been involved in a small group with friends from church. We would get together once a week to talk about what was going on in our lives and then to pray about various struggles and share with each other what the Bible would advise us to do. In terms of format, we typically would conduct our meeting, enjoy a meal together, pray together and then if possible hang out for a few minutes longer, just to shoot the breeze.

After one such meeting—during that "shoot the breeze" time —one of these close friends approached me with a gale-force whisper from God.

"Bill, I'm concerned about your heart," she said.

She went on to explain that in her view, the way I had conducted myself during the meeting that night bore evidence of a certain "layering over," as she called it.

"When your heart gets layered over by protectiveness because of the tough ministry hits you've taken through the years," she said, "you become less sensitive to the hearts of others. I think this dynamic deserves your honest reflection."

As she spoke these words of truth, her eyes stayed trained on mine. She said her piece slowly, tenderly and with compassion, which didn't surprise me, given how undeniably supportive she and her husband had been of my family, my ministry and me as an individual. I knew she had my best interest at heart, but I wasn't sure how to change this "layering over" that she observed in me.

Several weeks later—again following a small-group meeting—this same friend approached me and asked if we could talk. She had been observing the pace of my life and how it was causing me gradually to pull away from close friendships. Willow had just moved from two services a week to five because the church was growing so fast, ministry to the international church was just firing up, the Willow Creek Association was getting underway and we had just launched a massive building program. I barely could keep my professional plates spinning, let alone carve out time on the personal front. Even worse, I was neglecting the care of my own soul and now was dangerously close to a crash.

"I'm sensing that my words a few weeks ago didn't help, and your ongoing behavior is causing even greater concern," she said. "Bill, I've prayed about this, and I think it's time for you to go see a Christian counselor."

The instant that she conveyed her thoughts, I knew that she was right. God was offering me a lifeline in the form of this friend's advice, and the most foolish thing I could do was to neglect to act upon the input I'd just received.

Her single-sentence whisper from God wound up costing

me hundreds of hours—and thousands of dollars in counseling fees. But in the long run, it saved me far more than it cost. The much-needed investment I made in healing and growing my inner world during that season led to greater relational, emotional and even professional health. Two months ago, when I stood on the platform in our church's main auditorium and said, "Happy thirty-fourth anniversary, Willow!" I thought to myself, *I wouldn't still be here had that friend not taken whispers seriously.*

ONE OF THE MOST PROFOUND WHISPERS I EVER RECEIVED WAS delivered to me around that same season of life. After worship services one weekend, a friend walked me to my car.

The message I'd delivered that weekend, by God's grace, had felt anointed. The congregation's response was overwhelmingly positive. It was one of those experiences that pastors wish they could frame and hang on the wall, just so on tougher weekends they could remember a fonder time.

On the way to my car, my friend said, "God really used you today, Bill. What a tremendous service, and what a powerful message...." When we finally reached my car, he turned toward me and said, "Hey, just one small thing. And don't make too much of it—please—but when you mentioned in one of your sermon illustrations a 'seven-car pileup,' were you referencing the accident that our small group saw last week, when we were on our way back from lunch?"

"Yes," I replied.

"Well, I'm not trying to be a stickler here, but it was a *three*-car wreck at most." He paused for a moment before continuing, while I absorbed his words.

"Bill, God consistently speaks through you in an extremely powerful way," he said. "You don't need to try to spike your impact by another 10 or 15 percent through exaggeration— or any other means. There's plenty of power already coming through. To those of us who know you well, the exaggeration doesn't increase the sense of anointing; it actually *reduces* your credibility some."

I cringed. What he said rang true.

"Listen," he continued, placing a hand on my shoulder. "When you speak, God uses you in amazing ways. My plea is that you'd rest in *his* strength, instead of adding cars to the pileup when you're on stage."

I remember that prompting like it was delivered to me this morning. And still today, whenever I am tempted to add a little pizzazz to my talks, I think about his exhortation: "Don't add cars to the pileup."

"Trust in the LORD with all your heart," Proverbs 3:5–6 advises, "and lean not on your own understanding; in all your ways submit to him, and he will make your paths straight." God straightens our paths by supplying generalized guidance via large-group opportunities, such as weekend worship services or conference sessions where the Bible is taught; he provides insights during the practice of private, spiritual disciplines; and he offers "assistance with skin on it" by whispering to us through caring exchanges like that one in the parking lot that day.

I think back on some of the persistent whispers I've been blessed enough to receive and know that I'd be half the man and leader I am today had I not heeded those powerful words.

Sue Miller was one such conduit of whispers. Sue and I have known each other since we were high-school kids, and our friendship would carry us through serving in a youth group, starting a church and migrating into adulthood. She was in Lynne's and my wedding, and we would later stand by her side when she was the one saying vows. We'd vacation together as families and celebrate the fact that ministry partners could actually be friends.

Sue always has had a passion for seeing children educated in the things of God in inventive and engaging ways. From the get-go, she would tell me, "Bill, kids matter! Children's ministry matters! This vital part of God's church should receive more staff and funding and support from senior leaders." It would take me some time to incorporate that truth, but eventually I did get her point. Her consistent whisper eventually led to children's ministry at Willow getting the staff and funding and support she requested. And today, when I walk through Willow's Promiseland ministry and see the legacy that one woman has left, I think of the countless children who have chosen Jesus as their Leader and Savior because of Sue's vision. I thank God for using her persistent whispers to enlighten me about investing in future generations.

God has sent other whisperers, beating various drums that would serve as instruments of change in my life. From my mentor and college professor Dr. Gilbert Bilezikian, the drumbeat was, "Servanthood matters!" From Nancy Beach, who was a part of the original youth group that eventually gave birth to the church, it was, "Bill, the arts matter! Artists *matter*!" From my wife, Lynne, it was, "People stricken with AIDS matter. People suffering through extreme poverty matter!" From my psychologist friend Henry Cloud, it was, "Your inner world matters, Bill. You can't solve everything with your head." From John Maxwell, the drumbeat was, "Leadership matters—especially leadership in the local church." The list of drumbeats could go on.

In *The Message* transliteration of the Bible, Proverbs 2:1–5 reads like this: "Good friend, take to heart what I'm telling you; collect my counsels and guard them with your life. Tune your

ears to the world of Wisdom; set your heart on a life of Understanding. That's right—if you make Insight your priority, and
won't take no for an answer, searching for it like a prospector
panning for gold, like an adventurer on a treasure hunt, believe
me, before you know it Fear-of-God will be yours; you'll have
come upon the Knowledge of God." What a powerful image, that
of a prospector panning for gold. Just imagine if everyone you
knew searched for insight like that. Imagine if you consistently
did so yourself.

When you and I live wide open to divine direction courtesy
of someone who loves God and loves us—and when we receive
those whispers with humility and grace to spare—those whispers become like beautifully wrapped presents that we can enjoy
throughout the rest of our lives.

Several weeks ago while at a gathering, I engaged in what I
thought was friendly banter with another person in the room. I
think I was giving the guy grief about his golf game, but whatever it was, I thought it was all in good fun.

An Elder of our church was at the same get-together and
happened to overhear the exchange. As the man I was teasing
stepped away to get something to eat, the Elder approached.

"You know I love you, Bill," he said, "but some people are
more comfortable with your bantering than others. Please be
discerning with your teasing."

Though I appreciated the Elder's intent, and the gentle way
he had conveyed this message, I felt a twinge of defensiveness.
"C'mon," I thought, "lighten up. I was only joking."

But then I sensed God saying, "That was a gift, Bill. Reflect
on what he is saying, because he's right. Don't neglect the counsel you are being given."

As the Holy Spirit confirmed what the Elder had conveyed, I
felt my defenses drop. God was letting me know, "No real damage

was done here tonight, but if you don't take heed, you could harm someone in future days." Through the one-two punch of the Elder's words and the Spirit's follow-through, I sensed I had dodged a future bullet, and I was grateful.

Fast forward to a few nights ago, when our Elder board convened for our monthly meeting. Most of us have sat around that Elder table for many years—decades, even—but for one new member, a godly man with long-tenured participation in our church, this was only his second meeting.

The group was involved in a lively discussion about a well-known passage of Scripture when this newest member piped up. "Oh, right. That's found in chapter 14 of the gospel of Luke, verses 14 through 24."

Everyone else knew that he had cited the wrong address, but I kidded him by saying, "You ought to spend a little less time in the Koran and pick up your *Bible* every once in a while!"

There were chuckles all around the table—including from the target of my taunt—as we moved to the next item on the agenda and continued our meeting as planned. But I began to hear a faint whisper.

At the end of the meeting, in typical fashion the chairman of our board led us in a quick assessment of our demeanor and participation that evening. He asked, "Does anybody need to make amends for anything, clarify a point or apologize for a wrongdoing of any kind?"

I eased my hand into the air. "I need to apologize," I said, as I looked at the new member of our team. "You've only been here for two months, and what I said earlier reflected an inappropriate level of playfulness, given your short time with us."

"Oh, come on, Bill!" the guy jumped in. "I listen to you teach every single weekend, and I know you well enough to know that you were just joking...."

"I got a subtle flag in my spirit after I made that wisecrack," I said, "so I want to stick with the apology and ask your forgiveness here tonight."

He graciously granted it, despite believing it was thoroughly unnecessary.

What he didn't know was that God had been taking me on a journey that had started several weeks ago, at a party where I was given some counsel by a trusted, loving friend who truly had my best interest at heart. That journey is one of cleaning up my communication style and using words to build up and not to tear down. Sure, the whisper stung a little that night and took some of the shine off of a great meeting. But I'm learning that if I'll pay attention when the sting is small, I'll be spared greater pain later on.

In John 8:36, Jesus says, "If the Son sets you free, you will be free indeed." And if there is one beneficial by-product to listening to God's whispers as delivered through the people in your life, it is this: the well-timed, well-placed counsel of friends can put you on the fast track to freedom in this life—freedom from the troubling forces people face every day.

For some, the "force" is a self-defeating belief—that they're worthless, incompetent or repulsive to those they love. For some, the "force" is a self-defeating behavior—overspending, overeating, overdrinking, overachieving, over-pleasing or over-worrying.

For others the obstacle deals with relational dynamics: "If I could just control my temper!" the twice-divorced man laments. "If I could just stop manipulating people," says the domineering woman. "If only I could fix the pain inside me that causes me to wound everyone else," says the victim of abuse who many years later still has not found relief.

The list goes on, as controllers and leaners and clingers and stuffers and liars make no progress in the relational wasteland of their lives. Perhaps you silently join their chorus, knowing all too well how they feel. Maybe it's you who have pushed a spouse away, pushed your kids away, pushed your colleagues away or destroyed every decent friendship you've ever known. But your life doesn't have to be this way. By God's grace, you can shift gears, starting today.

The genuine liberation you seek can be found only in Jesus Christ. And part of his strategy for helping you is to provide truthful input through other people in your life. You're not worthless, incompetent or repulsive, but you might need to make a few shifts. And being open to the input of those who will shoot straight with you could be the greatest blessing you'll know.

The next time a trusted friend calls up and asks, "Hey, do you think we could talk about something I'm seeing in your life?" I challenge you to lay down your defenses and to pick up humility instead. Tell your friend you'd love to talk—and mean it—trusting that God might have better days in store for you through the wisdom found in their words. One of the ways both you and I will experience a better, more righteous life is to heed those whispers. Open your ears to the in-the-flesh counsel your Father wants to communicate to you today. You'll never regret the surges of wisdom those interactions may bring.

CHAPTER 9

WHISPERS THAT CHANGE THE WORLD

THINK FOR A MOMENT ABOUT THE CLASSIEST, MOST sophisticated restaurant you've ever visited. Imagine the gourmet chef, working tirelessly in the kitchen, designing each meal as though it were an individualized work of art. Tonight he is preparing *your* dinner: Beef Wellington—a succulent cut of tenderloin, seared just right and topped with marinated mushrooms.

Got the image in your mind?

Now, if I were to ask you, "What is one thing you could do to *really* annoy that chef?", what would your answer be?

I've had more time to think about this question than you have, so I'll give you my answer first. If I wanted to maximally annoy and offend that chef, I would wait until the gourmet meal was placed in front of me, then I'd look up and say, "Thanks! Got any ketchup?"

I dare you to try this sometime. (And, for the record, asking for A1 Steak Sauce will yield the same effect.)

Or imagine a Kennedy Center recital by a world-renowned vocalist, whose perfect pitch and "high C" voice could shatter a crystal glass. In the middle of her beautiful Italian aria, you jump up on stage and join in, singing along at full voice—and at about a half pitch off-key. Your "performance" could maim that musician for life—and she might just return the favor. Don't try it—even musicians can throw a left hook.

If you want to instigate a lively response from a musician or a chef, then try causing harm to the objects of their creativity. On a larger scale, if you or I want to instigate ire in a holy God, then try bringing harm to one of his creations, by playing loose with issues of justice in our world. You can *bank* on a dynamic response.

A quick scan of Scripture makes God's perspective on justice abundantly clear. "Do not pervert justice," Leviticus 19:15 says. "Do not show partiality to the poor or favoritism to the great, but judge your neighbor fairly." "Follow justice and justice alone," says Deuteronomy 16:20, "so that you may live and possess the land the LORD your God is giving you." Or how about Deuteronomy 27:19? "Cursed is anyone who withholds justice from the foreigner, the fatherless or the widow."

"The LORD loves righteousness and justice," Psalm 33:5 declares. "The earth is full of his unfailing love." Check out this litany of justice-loving pronouncements, straight from the heart of a justice-loving God:

> Blessed are those who act justly, who always do what is right.[1]

> I know that the LORD secures justice for the poor and upholds the cause of the needy.[2]

> Learn to do right! Seek justice, encourage the oppressed. Defend the cause of the fatherless, plead the case of the widow.[3]

> For I, the LORD, love justice; I hate robbery and wrong-doing. In my faithfulness I will reward my people and make an everlasting covenant with them.[4]

> He has shown all you people what is good. And what does the LORD require of you? To act justly and to love mercy and to walk humbly with your God.[5]

> Woe to you Pharisees, because you give God a tenth of your mint, rue and all other kinds of garden herbs, but you neglect justice and the love of God. You should have practiced the latter without leaving the former undone.[6]

Clearly, our God fires up pretty quickly when he sees injustice at work in his world. Like a skilled musician who can't help but be traumatized by a series of flat notes, or a chef who reflexively cringes at the thought of ketchup on a tenderloin, injustice rubs God the wrong way. Understandably, it inspires his wrath. God's flawless character can settle for nothing less than justice on behalf of his people.

Now, to be clear, you and I don't respond to injustice quite so strongly. We may read verses like these and think, "Yeah! Preach it, God. I'm right behind you!" But left to our own devices, we sometimes fail to act on that promise. A little oppression here, a little bigotry there—as long as *we're* not the ones being harmed, we can easily look the other way. It's not that we *like* injustice; it's simply that injustice doesn't cut to the quick of who we are. That is, unless God's soul-piercing whispers have their way.

≈≈≈

I 've been in awe of God's character ever since I was adopted into his family. I've noticed that when God finds somebody who is living tuned in to his input—a woman or a man with a serious mind, available hands and an unquenchable thirst for righteousness—he tends to tap that person for help in solving a societal ill. Like the eerie calm just before a storm, God places a quiet whisper of insight into a willing pair of ears—and then sits back to watch as a storm of justice begins to build.

Based on conversations I've had with scores of people who have received these types of whispers, the initial instructions from God often are simple:

> "Read the book."
>
> "Ask the question."
>
> "Watch the documentary."
>
> "Go to the learning group."
>
> "Risk engaging in that relationship."
>
> "Find the funding to take the trip."

But not surprisingly, once the person follows that initial divine direction, all bets are off. More times than not, that person's world gets irreversibly rocked as their role in *this* world takes a radical, justice-focused shift.

If you're a couple of decades on either side of me, you likely remember a woman by the name of Candy Lightner. One day in May of 1980, Candy's thirteen-year-old daughter, Cari, was walking from her house to her school carnival, when she was struck and killed by a hit-and-run drunk driver. The guy behind the wheel had three prior arrests for drunk driving and had been on a three-day drinking binge. Two days before killing Cari, he had been arrested and released for—you guessed it—a drunk-driving hit-and-run. In an instant, Candy's precious daughter had been robbed of life. The injustice of a child dying at the hands of a drunk driver stirred unbelievable passion in this grieving mom. God rocked her world, and Candy Lightner would go on to found

MADD—Mothers Against Drunk Driving—which over the past thirty years has influenced countless local, state and federal jurisdictions to strengthen laws and stiffen penalties for those who choose to drink and drive.

God has moved similarly in scores of other lives. I think of a woman at Willow—a suburbanite, young-but-devoted Christ-follower enjoying a comfortable, upper-middle-class existence until God decided to rock her world. Seeing her able mind, her open hands and her obedient spirit, he said, "I have a special assignment for you."

For the past six years, this woman has resided in Cape Town, South Africa, where she seeks to show God's love to fourteen-year-old prostitutes. Every night she hits the streets, armed with food, wholesome employment opportunities and an invitation to start a new life. One young girl at a time, this woman is right-sizing the injustice of a broken world that uses these girls as disposable objects. And every ounce of progress she has witnessed can be traced back to a single whisper from God—a whisper she could not deny.

Then there is Gary Haugen, the founder and president of International Justice Mission (IJM). In the late 1990s, life was going just fine for Gary, a Harvard-trained lawyer—until one day when God whispered a plea into his ear. "Gary," the Holy Spirit said, "it's time you use your legal background to fight for those who can't fight for themselves." Today, IJM has field offices in fourteen countries and a staff of hundreds, all of whom are laying down their lives to secure justice for victims of slavery, sexual exploitation and the violent oppression that wreaks havoc in our world. Willow is grateful to be one of IJM's many partners.

When God is given the invitation to rock someone's world, *great* kingdom gains get made. The one being rocked joins God on an adventure he or she never could have imagined, and the people he or she serves discover hope and peace and freedom they had never known.

~~~

The first world-rocking whisper I received from God dealt with helping to alleviate extreme poverty. Admittedly, logic would say that I'd be the last person to care about social-action issues such as this. I'm a white Dutch guy of reasonable means who spends his downtime racing sailboats. What do I know of poverty and suffering, of oppression and strife? And yet God would have certain plans for my life that traced their roots all the way back to that Nairobi hotel room I described in chapter 1, when I was a teenager visiting one of Kenya's worst slums.

That particular evening God had whispered, "Bill, if you'll dedicate your life to me, I'll use it to help solve some of the problems you are witnessing." Those "problems" involved bloated bellies, rotting limbs and flies crawling all over the faces of people living and dying in the streets. I was watching the crown of God's creation being forced to subsist on too little money, too little food and *far* too little hope.

I wasn't sure exactly what God meant by this whisper, but I took the deal nonetheless, and over time he has filled in some of the blanks.

WHEN I WAS STILL A STUDENT IN COLLEGE, I BEGAN TO NOTICE and study Scripture that expressed God's strict instructions that the wealthy members of society care for those who were poor. For example, in Leviticus 19:9–10, God says, "When you harvest your land, don't harvest right up to the edges of your field or gather the gleanings from the harvest. Don't strip your vineyard bare or go back and pick up the fallen grapes. Leave them for the poor and the foreigner" (MSG). Later, in Deuteronomy 15, God instructs landowners to carve out a tiny piece from their expansive property and give it to someone who was poor. Landowners were to provide starter seed as well, so that an impoverished family could harvest a crop and feed themselves with a sense of dignity.

To the wealthy, God also says, "Whenever you make a loan to someone who is poor, do not ever charge them interest."[7] They already were poor; why on earth would a rich person want to profit off of their misfortune? Similarly, he tells well-resourced people to cancel the debts of the poor whenever possible—that they would be further blessed by writing off the loans they had made.[8]

Although God is clear in his instructions that his followers help lift the poor out of poverty, sometimes God's people failed to pay attention to what he says. Instead, according to Zechariah 7, they "stubbornly turned their backs and covered their ears. They made their hearts as hard as flint and would not listen to the law or to the words that the LORD Almighty had sent."[9]

God's people actually stopped up their ears so they couldn't hear the cry of the poor! And understandably, God was enraged. I can't help but reflect on times when my own hesitant response to the cry of the poor has equated to "stopping up my ears." During those same young-adult days, I came across a passage of Scripture describing another way to live. Isaiah 58:10–11 says, "If you spend yourselves in behalf of the hungry and satisfy the needs of the oppressed, then your light will rise in the darkness, and your night will become like the noonday. The LORD will guide you always; he will satisfy your needs in a sun-scorched land and will strengthen your frame. You will be like a well-watered garden, like a spring whose waters never fail."

As I pondered up those promised blessings—blessings of

God's constant guidance, of satisfaction and strength—I sensed God handing me a dose of hope: "Bill, you can opt to live this way. The choice is yours."

EVERY HONEST PERSON OF MEANS I KNOW CAN POINT TO A half-dozen moments along life's journey when God opened up a door or brought along the right person, the right creative idea or the right opportunity, and it saved their financial hide. It was certainly true for those of us who started Willow. From 1975 until 1980, both personally and corporately we lived within one week of financial extinction. You don't forget an experience like that. You don't forget the feelings of constant shortage, the worry over lack of provision, the stress of payments you can't make, the embarrassment every time the church phone rings and another angry creditor waits for you on the line.

We didn't get through those days on our own power. God whispered to some adults in our congregation—people who actually wore suits that fit and had "real" jobs and homes that they owned—and moved them to pitch in and help us keep Willow financially viable.

During those years of being under-resourced, I experienced time and again how it felt to be on the receiving end of help. I developed a deep level of gratitude—a humble realization that my life would not be the same, were it not for the doors God has opened for me and the people who responded to his whispers on my behalf.

Nobody reaches well-resourced status alone. It *always* takes the help of another.

I n the Gospel of Matthew, Jesus announced that a distinguishing mark of his followers would be their concern for those who were hungry and naked, shelterless and impoverished.[10] As a young pastor, I wanted to bear this distinguishing mark of Jesus. But what was "concern" supposed to look like? What was *my* role supposed to be?

As opportunities presented themselves, I began traveling to parts of the world where life seemed unbearably broken. I had witnessed poverty in American cities, but this level of societal decimation cast the term "poor" in a whole new light. God began to reveal to me the difference between poverty and *extreme* poverty, and that the latter was something I could actually help fix.[11]

Let me explain what I mean.

Of the more than six billion people alive today, three billion —approximately one half of humanity—live on less than two dollars a day. What's more, these people have virtually no access to capital that would allow them to start a business or buy an acre of farmland that would dramatically change the trajectory of their lives.

That is what is called *extreme poverty*, something most Americans know nothing about.

I watched a short documentary recently about a reporter from CNN who was studying the effects of hunger on the poor. During the creation of the film, the reporter interviewed a man who had lived with pervasive hunger his entire life, a reality that inspired the reporter to boldly state, "Well, I'm going to live your life with you for thirty full days."

The reporter planned to eat exactly what the impoverished man ate—and no more—for one month straight. By day twenty-one he had to bail. The CNN reporter was so dizzy that he nearly fainted and so lethargic that his mind all but shut down. His body began wasting away until finally, he said, "I'm done."

Imagine living your entire life in that kind of poverty.

Once a year at Willow, during the Celebration of Hope experience I mentioned to you earlier, our entire congregation is invited to eat nothing but rice and beans for five days—a full work week—and to drink nothing but water from the tap. It gives you a whole new respect for poverty's devastating effects when you start to cave on the morning of day three.

People in extreme poverty experience a *constant* state of hunger, but their plight certainly doesn't end there. Another tough reality they juggle is not having a place to call home.

I was in Cairo, Egypt, some time ago, and as I walked down the street, I took in the atrocious living conditions all around me. I saw a burned-out automobile lying upside-down on the sidewalk and fleetingly wondered why city workers hadn't come by to drag the eyesore away—until I saw the answer, plain as day: an entire family was living inside. I shook my head and fought off tears that were determined to flow.

While in India a short time after that, I noticed that a construction crew was putting in a new sewage system in one area of Mumbai. Giant pipes, probably eight feet in diameter, lined the road, waiting to be installed. And until those pipes were laid in the ground, they served as home to hundreds of families in need. When a temporary sewer pipe serves as the best shelter around, we can be sure God's ire is stirred.

One night recently I was watching another documentary, this one on worldwide homelessness. In addition to detailing troubling statistics, the film explored what happens in people's psyches and souls when, for whatever reason, they are forced to exist in a tragic, shelterless state. It was a difficult ninety minutes to take in.

Images of gaunt, desperate people enduring cold, windy rainstorms that washed right through their stick huts—and of children who didn't know what it meant to *not* be muddy and wet—flashed across the screen. And then there was a commercial break.

During that four-minute interlude, I channel-surfed through a few stations and stopped when I saw the camera panning a multi-million-dollar mansion. The host introduced the show—*Cribs*, it was called—and then began enumerating the overkill features of the fifteen-bedroom, twelve-bath celebrity home being featured on this week's episode.

The juxtaposition of those two images nearly did me in. More than one hundred million people will sleep huddled on the earth's dirt floor tonight while others rattle around in their nearly empty but luxurious "cribs."

The next day, when I pulled into my own driveway, I stopped and considered my place on the privilege pyramid. "God, I don't understand all of the reasons why blessing has come my way like it has," I prayed, "but by your grace I'm among the most privileged people in the world, especially as it pertains to having food and shelter. Thank you for blessing me this way."

I opened my eyes after praying and caught sight of a torn window screen that had been nagging at me for some time to be fixed. Somehow in the light of that moment, a little tear in a window screen didn't seem like a very big deal.

EXTREME POVERTY INVOLVES OTHER ISSUES AS WELL. SANITAtion is a vital concern—how would you like to wear the same dirty, threadbare clothes each day and never take a warm shower again in your life? The need for clean water is among the top issues on the extreme poverty list. A child dies every fifteen seconds from water-related diseases,[12] some of the easiest maladies to prevent and cure.

Limited access to medical treatment and education top the injustice chart in many parts of the world. With governmental corruption at the highest levels, and violence, abuse and dissension at every turn, I often feel overwhelmed by the level of need. It can be tempting to become numb to these problems because the need for change is staggering. How can *I* make a difference when the challenges are this complex?

"Spend yourself on behalf of the hungry," that verse in Isaiah had said. "Spend yourself ..." I decided to start here.

I began to ask God to show me ways that I could spend my *talents* differently by leveraging relational networks on behalf of the poor. He brought to my attention people who could net big kingdom gains in the battle against poverty. I began challenging construction guys who could build affordable housing, medical people who could staff free clinics a few times a month and computer wizards who could head to Africa and teach entire villages how to navigate online tasks.

I asked him to show me how I might spend my *time* differently. What prayers did I need to pray on behalf of the poor—both in the United States and in far-off lands? What books did I need to read? What service opportunities did I need to invest myself in, so that my eyes and my heart would be further opened to the plight facing so many people around the globe?

I also wanted to know how to spend my *money* differently. Even little expenditures could make a difference. If I'm going to drink coffee every day, for example, it might as well be coffee of the fair-trade variety.

As God provided definite promptings for large and small ways I could effect change, I began sharing those insights with the broader Willow family, who quickly caught God's vision for justice among the poor. And with each stride made—orphans rescued from loneliness in Africa, ministry partnerships forged in Latin America, food banks stocked to the ceiling in the Chicago area, earnest prayers uttered, offerings collected, heartfelt songs sung in thanksgiving to God—I marveled a little more at the incredible people and means and circumstances God has used to make good on a whispered promise to a Dutch teen in a Nairobi slum, forty-something years ago.

James 1:9–10 says, "Believers who are poor should take pride that God has made them spiritually rich. Those who are rich should take pride that God has shown them that they are spiritually poor" (NCV). As I look back on the first fifty-eight years of my life, one of the things I'm most thankful for is that God has revealed the power of this truth. I may be well-resourced compared to the vast majority of the world, but am I ever spiritually poor! But for the grace of God, I'd be a sinner left to fend for myself.

The next verse in that passage says this: "The rich will die like a wild flower in the grass. The sun rises with burning heat and dries up the plants. The flower falls off, and its beauty is gone. In the same way the rich will die while they are still taking care of business" (NCV). Even as I read those words now, I am refreshed in my belief that given the brevity of life, there is no better way to spend my days than on behalf of under-resourced people who desperately need care.

I t was in the midst of my doing a deep dive into the subject of extreme poverty that God began to rock my world on another front as well. I began to sense his whisper on the topic of racial injustice.

It was April of 1999, and I was ready to head out on what was sure to be a picture-perfect vacation—just Lynne, the kids and me; ideal sailing conditions; and the prospect of countless hours of uninterrupted snorkeling and windsurfing. Even as I reflect on it now, the words *sheer bliss* come to mind.

I was more than ready to unwind from what had been a taxing season of ministry. I expected a relaxed pace, agenda-less days and hours of great conversation as I caught up on what was new in my kids' lives. What I didn't see coming was that I was about to be the direct-hit target of a massive spiritual tsunami, courtesy of God himself. What you read in the coming pages may be a spiritual tsunami for you, as well, as I invite you to walk alongside me on an eye-opening journey that still leaves me shaking my head.

The day before I was to leave for my vacation, one of Willow's leaders handed me a book and mentioned that if a rainy day snuck into the scheme of things—perish the thought—at least now I'd have something to read. Thankfully, it didn't rain. But there was a night when everyone else went to bed early. I wasn't sleepy, and having no one to talk to and nothing else to do, I reached into my briefcase, found the recommended book, leaned back in the cockpit of the small boat we were borrowing for the week and turned to page 1 of *Divided by Faith*[13]—a book written by a couple of sociology professors.

Fifteen pages into the book I realized this would be no light read. I had done research on racism before. I had been to seminars and even had given a talk on the subject once. But for some reason the content of this book sneaked into crevices of my consciousness in new ways. I flipped page after sobering page and, for the first time in my life, saw my country's history for what it really was. Now, I absolutely love my country—there is nowhere on the planet I'd rather live than in the United States. But as the authors exposed the historical truths of the early days of America, I couldn't help but feel embarrassed and saddened by the ugliness of it all.

FOR MANY DECADES, MOST WHITE GRADE-SCHOOL KIDS HAVE been fed a glorified notion that when the British came over to occupy American territory, they befriended all of the Indians and then bellied up to a giant Thanksgiving table to enjoy a feast. But the truth, according to historical documents from this era of U.S. history, is a far cry from that.

When British citizens first settled onto American soil, they did so by annihilating the hundreds of thousands of Native Americans who rightfully owned all of this land. The overtakers intentionally introduced smallpox and other deadly viruses into certain Indian villages with intent to kill, even resorting to distributing blankets from virus-infected people to Indian children and then essentially telling them to go home and enjoy a good night's rest.

Once the genocide was successful enough to free up sufficient land on which to establish this country, our ancestors went in search of strong backs. They built ships and sailed them to the Ivory Coast of Africa, where entire clans of families—men, women, grandparents, even children, in total numbering more than ten million people—were kidnapped, chained, dragged to shore, packed like sardines onto boats and shipped off from their homeland to the colonies of America, today proudly referred to as the "land of the free and home of the brave."

About one-third of these first "African Americans" died en route in the holds of those ships. Their inhumane treatment even in death was an indication of what was to come. Rather than being given a proper burial, they were tossed overboard in full view of their spouses and families, left as shark bait in the dark seas below. The two-thirds of that original population who made it to the other side didn't fare much better. Upon arrival, they were cleaned up, sprayed off, stood on auction blocks and sold to the highest bidder. I cringe even as I type this. Who would allow injustice like that?

I found myself thinking that if this abhorrent scheme had lasted a few months, a few years or even a few decades before being righted, then perhaps I would feel less shame than I did. But in reality, the slave-trading practice, which was started elsewhere but was really "perfected" on American soil, lasted more than 350 years. With God's eyes watching the entire time.

God saw white men working black men into a state of exhaustion on their farms, beating, maiming or even killing them if they slacked off. As night fell, God saw white men rape the wives and daughters of the slaves they had abused all day long. God saw slave owners—our early forefathers as well as many pastors of local churches—salve their consciousnesses with lies: African Americans were "less than fully human, did not possess souls, and were incapable of learning."[14] In short, God saw as abhorrent injustice pervaded his beautiful earth—and his Bride, the church.

The raging injustice before his eyes kindled his passion. And the more I read, the more it kindled mine.

IN THE COCKPIT OF THAT SAILBOAT, I WAS REMINDED OF A portion of Scripture in Mark 11 that I'd read dozens of times before. As the story goes, one day Jesus decides to travel all the way to Jerusalem to worship God in the temple. He enters the temple area, expecting to find people worshiping the living God. Instead, he sees slick salesmen who have turned the holy place into a shopping mall. Understandably, Jesus is incensed. He overturns the tables of the moneychangers and the benches of those selling trinkets and doves, and then he forbids anyone from carrying merchandise through the temple courts.

According to the text, he wrapped up the events of the day with these well-known words, "Is it not written: 'My house will be called a house of prayer for all nations'? But you have made it 'a den of robbers.'"

When I was young, I was told in Sunday school that Jesus cleansed the temple because he didn't think greedy people's practices had any place in a church setting. But with an increased awareness of racism floating around in my mind on the boat that April night, I began to reflect on the passage with new eyes. It became obvious to me that there was another form of injustice that needed to be resolved in the temple that day. In addition to the economic corruption unfolding before Jesus' eyes, biblical scholars describe a subplot to the story that involved the Jews squeezing out people of other races—people from "other" nations. Their arrogance and superiority complex didn't sit too well with Jesus, who said in response, "My house will be called a house of prayer for all nations."

For *all* nations.

The One who wore justice like skin essentially said to the Church, "Mono-cultural, mono-ethnic and mono-racial do not fit the dream my Father and I have for you. I want my house to be a house of prayer for all races. For all cultures. For all ethnicities. For *all* nations!"

On that night of my "picture-perfect" vacation, more than enjoying the gentle rocking motion of a boat anchored in a moonlit bay, I experienced a powerful, divinely appointed world-rocking experience I won't soon forget. In a flash of insight God brought to mind everything I had learned throughout my life on the topic of injustice—and of racial injustice in particular—and said, in effect, "Bill, it's time to up the ante on your involvement in this regard."

People matter to God. *All* people matter to God. And there are structural injustices in our generation that need to be torn down in order for God's love for his people to flow through those of us who claim the name of Christ. In not-so-subtle terms God was whispering to me a challenge: "I want you to step up, Bill. And preferably, to do so *now*."

⌇

The reason God's whisper was so jolting to me is that I've never before considered myself racist. For as long as I can remember I have had friends of all ethnicities and backgrounds and have made a point of embracing people for who they are, regardless of the color of their skin.

My mentor since my college days, Dr. Gilbert Bilezikian, had spent part of his life as a refugee in World War II and had seen his beloved grandparents wiped out by racism's evil ways. Because of his experience, he made it a point to drill into his students' minds Scriptures like Galatians 3:28. "There is neither Jew nor Gentile, neither slave nor free, neither male nor female, for you are all one in Christ Jesus," it says.

"The church is the one place in the world where all of these superficial delineations are left at the door!" Dr. B's heavily accented voice would declare. "It does not matter if you are rich or poor, if you are educated or uneducated, if you are successful or unsuccessful, if you are athletic or clumsy. Whether you are black or white, man or woman, young or old, you are welcomed in the church. In this place, all are *family*!"

Since Willow's founding, we have tried to preserve that type of radical acceptance as a core value—not out of obligation, but because it reflects the heart of God.

My respect for people of all races and backgrounds also stemmed from the beliefs of my father. When I was growing up, my dad was determined that his wife and kids would defy the stereotype of our rather homogenous community and instead have open arms to welcome every person from every stripe.

When I was just a little guy—four or five years old, maybe—I used to go to work with my dad. His firm shipped fresh fruits and vegetables from all over the United States into a central warehouse and then distributed them to various places within our community. Truck drivers would load their trucks and then go to the stores, the restaurants, the hotels—and often times, they'd do all this with me in tow. During their deliveries, I was their helper—well, as much of a helper as a preschool kid can be.

One morning, my dad proudly introduced me to a staff member named L.V., one of the firm's African American drivers. He said, "Billy, this is L. V. Perry, one of the finest drivers in the entire company. I want you to spend the next two or three days making deliveries with him. You are in good hands with L.V., Billy. *Very* good hands."

L.V. was the most honorable man you could ever hope to know. He was a friend of our family's for the better part of thirty years—actually, he was a member of our family ... or at least that's how Dad treated him.

Later on, during my high school days, I would hear people refer to African Americans using the n-word or other shameful, derogatory names, and it all sounded so foreign to me. "Obviously, they've never met L. V. Perry," I'd think—or any of the other black people I knew, for that matter. How could they make those blanket statements about an entire group of people? I couldn't get my brain around the insanity of the comments I'd hear. I could dispute every single slur, based solely on the black people I knew and loved.

During those days, it was as if God said to me, "Bill, don't you dare lose your memories of L.V. He—as well as every other person on this planet, whether black, white, red, yellow or any combination thereof—is my kid. I want them treated equitably, with exactly the same tender care as you yourself would want."

So, while I figured I'd enjoyed a decent track record regarding treating all people with respect, I knew upon reading *Divided by Faith* that God was asking for something more. Although my attitudes and actions had not *added* to racial tensions that seemed to abound, it was equally true that I was doing nothing to tear down the systemic inequalities that kept the scales tilted to the white man's side. I happened upon a quote that week that said that most of us weigh a hundred-and-some or two-hundred-and-some pounds, but it's the six pounds of skin on each of us that makes all the difference in the world. What a heartbreaking reality.

The superficial six pounds of skin: that's the part God was asking me to help others learn to look past.

~~~

I returned from that nonrelaxing (but spiritually rich) vacation and couldn't shake the whispers I'd received. I reread Emerson and Smith's contribution two times through, and I picked up everything I could find on the subject of racial reconciliation, opening my eyes to a side of reality of which I had not been fully aware, and immersing myself in the truth. Additionally, I began involving myself in more and more relationships that crossed racial lines, and my wife and I started a small business with a family of a different race, in order to get some graduate-school-level training on the challenges involved in being people of color in a world that favors white. But despite how worthwhile all those efforts seemed, God wanted to further refine my approach.

A BROAD DEFINITION OF BIGOTRY IS A NEGATIVE PASSION toward an entire group of people. It is the tendency to impute to the collective the negative characteristics of the few, and it is something that, sadly, both you and I do. Here's a little proof: bigotry is flying to Charles de Gaulle Airport in Paris, being transported from the airport to the hotel by a cab driver who has a case of the "nasties" that day, then coming back to the States and saying, "French people are jerks!"

There is something evil in us that wants to feel superior and that wants above all else to be big. We want to be seen as smart and strong, as "in" and "with it" and cool. And the cheapest way to accomplish these things is to make others feel "less than" and inferior.

The late British author C. S. Lewis referred to this dynamic as the phenomenon of the "inner ring," and describes its power this way: "I believe that in all men's lives at certain periods, and in many men's lives at all periods between infancy and extreme old age, one of the most dominant elements is the desire to be inside the local Ring and the terror of being left outside."[15]

In picking apart the phenomenon, Lewis exposes human-kind's depraved desire to form themselves and their approved list of friends into an exclusive club that derives a sick and sinful pleasure from keeping other people out. In the final analysis, it is what the Bible calls a pure manifestation of sin.

Let me show you how it works.

I was traveling in Europe many years ago and, after having missed a couple of flight connections, wound up in Heathrow Airport in London. A group had flown me to Europe to do some teaching there, and because they were trying to cut costs, I had a bargain ticket in hand—one that is utterly worthless once you've accidentally missed the flight. Trouble was, I was due to preach at Willow that weekend and sort of needed to get home.

I remember explaining all of this to the disinterested ticket-ing agent, who stared back at me with a look that said, "Where'd you pick up *that* ticket? At a garage sale?" He told me that I didn't have a prayer for resolving my situation, since there was only one flight back to Chicago that would get me there in time to teach, and that the flight in question had been completely booked for well over a month.

He asked me to take a seat in the gate area and offered a non-committal, "We'll have to wait and see."

A few minutes later he began boarding the flight. After everybody else was loaded in, he turned and walked my way, boarding pass in hand. "There is one seat left. If you want it, it's yours," he said.

I thanked him and rushed down the jetway, stepped into the plane and looked for the seat number on my boarding pass. Any guesses as to where my designated seat was located? *First class!* Who says there is no God?

Now, on some domestic flights first class seats are identical to every other seat except for the curtain that says you're big cheese. But international first class is a whole 'nother deal. The seats are more like sofas, and from the moment you reach cruising altitude, it's champagne and caviar for you—until the serious food is served.

Halfway through the flight, while I was enjoying my five-course dinner and stimulating conversation with all the affluent people up front, I noticed a couple of economy-seat people from the rear of the plane infringing on our space. Evidently their assigned lavatories were full, and they thought they'd just borrow ours. As I saw them walk past, I felt a strange urge to summon the first-class flight attendant and say, "You'll want to get that riffraff out of here."

How's that for mature Christ-follower behavior?

But this is the stuff of the inner ring. Something evil lurks in us that wants to hold a privileged place in the world—and we'll push other people down to obtain it.

I'm all for civil rights legislation and for increased education on subjects that really count, but neither of those solutions can cure bigotry's root cause. What keeps racism alive and well is the old-fashioned sin in you and me. First John 4:20 says, "If we say we love God yet hate a brother or sister, we are liars. For if we do not love a fellow believer, whom we have seen, we cannot love God." Translation: You won't see past the six pounds of skin until *love* overwhelms your heart.

I had been taking some worthwhile actions toward racial reconciliation, but my motivations were still a little skewed. And by giving me fresh awareness through his Word, God in essence said, "I don't want the changes that come courtesy of your hands to outpace what's going on in your heart."

～

Every author I read on the subject of ending racial strife agrees that ethnic walls will most quickly crumble as cross-racial friendships are formed. When I first started speaking on this subject nearly a decade ago, many people in our mostly white congregation cast a suspicious glance. They wondered about my agenda and wanted to know where all of this "race talk" was headed. But throughout those years I have noticed a major shift in perspective. Not only has Willow embraced the importance of espousing these ideas, but they also have begun forging relationships across racial lines. Today, when I look out into our auditorium on any given weekend, I smile at the diversity I see. Red and yellow, black and white, they *all* are precious in his sight. And I'm determined they must be precious in our sight too.

Admittedly, there is still a long way to go before the playing field is level for people of color. For example, if a black child and a white child are born in America on the same day, the black child is more than two times more likely to die by his or her first birthday than the white child, mostly due to the lack of prenatal care and the lack of adequate medical facilities in the parts of town where black babies are born.[16] It's the exact opposite of "just."

Here's another reality: African Americans fall below the poverty line more than three times as frequently as non-Hispanic whites.[17]

And one more: while the median net assets for college-educated whites are nearly 20,000 dollars, for college-educated blacks, median net assets are a miniscule 175 dollars.[18]

So, yes, we have a long way to go. But based on how fervently many Christ-followers are praying—and how devotedly they're taking action these days, I believe we'll see the day dawn—and soon—when *all* nations are welcomed home.

～

I've heard God trumpet this all-life-is-valuable idea through other firsthand whispers as well.

When I was a kid, my hunter-type brother talked me into taking down a bird with my BB gun. It was the middle of the afternoon, and the bird was minding his own business, causing no one any harm. Because of my shortsighted willingness to follow my brother's advice, within a few brief seconds a bird that had been happily flitting through the air had unexpectedly nosedived to my feet.

Whatever thoughts I'd had about death to that point were theoretical at best. But now, this helpless creature I'd shot with my gun was bleeding badly, gasping for air and gyrating in unnatural ways. Then all movement stopped, and it was dead. As I stood there looking at the bird's small body, a feeling of deep regret swept over me. I thought, "I never want to cause death again." And in that moment of childhood recognition, I determined that my role was to help protect life.

Because of that experience, the Bible verses dealing with the value of human life stuck to my soul like Velcro strips. I memorized Genesis 9:6, which says, "Whoever sheds human blood, by humans let his blood be shed" (MSG), and wrote 1 Peter 3:9 on my heart. "Do not repay evil with evil or insult with insult, but with blessing," that verse advised, "because to this you were called so that you may inherit a blessing" (NIV).

Do not repay evil with evil—I must have replayed those words in my mind ten thousand times as I grew from boyhood to manhood. Although implementing them in my life was slow progress, eventually I got to the point where I could be cut off in traffic and still maintain my cool. "Wave at the guy and say a prayer," God would whisper. "Then go on about your day."

I delighted in the fact that the values of preserving life and promoting peace were being forged in my spirit. I was unaware that they were about to be challenged one day—big time.

On a particular Friday, I found myself in a concourse at Logan Airport in Boston, waiting for my flight to board. I was standing at one of those countertop coffee bars, drinking a cup of coffee and reading a sailing magazine, when I heard the roar of laughter from a restaurant thirty feet away. The culprits were four twenty-somethings who were clearly liquored up, despite it being barely noon.

I kept a watchful eye on the foursome and looked up when one of the men bolted from his table, walked into the coffee bar and shouted with a slur, "Who stole my sandwich? I want my sandwich!"

He stormed from table to table. "I left a sandwich over here, man. Now tell me who stole my sandwich!"

Instinctively I decided that now would be a very good time to focus on the fine print of my magazine. "The last thing I need to do is get involved with this guy," I figured. And so I squinted my eyes in deep concentration, praying silently that his sandwich miraculously showed up.

Moments later, while the inebriated guy was still terrorizing the café clientele, a busboy appeared from the back room and began clearing garbage from vacated tables. I glanced up and noticed that he suffered from some sort of emotional or mental impairment. No sooner had I made the observation than the twenty-something punk approached him and aggressively grabbed him by the arm.

"Listen, idiot," he shouted into the young man's face, "I know you took my sandwich, and I want it back. Do you hear me? I want my sandwich back. Now!"

"I didn't take a sandwich. I promise, I didn't take it ...," the bewildered busboy sputtered. As this scene unfolded, my heart grew increasingly sick. "I should *do* something," I told myself.

Unrelenting, the aggressor reached down, picked up the boy's full garbage bag and spilled its contents all over the floor. "You get on your knees and find my sandwich now!" he bellowed.

I knew I had to act. With the Bible's clear instructions about defending the defenseless and considering others' welfare as more important than your own in mind, I put down my cup of coffee and walked toward the busboy, who was now on his knees picking through the garbage, the bully towering overhead.

"Hey, Joe!" I heard the bully's three friends yell from the bar. "We've got your sandwich, you moron! It's been over here the entire time!"

They erupted in another round of laughter as the bully made his way back to his friends, shouting expletives at the busboy all the way.

I bent down and began helping the young man pick up sticky cinnamon-roll wrappers and half-eaten turkey wraps. "You know, I'm really sorry for what just happened here," I said. "You didn't deserve this—I saw the whole thing, and I feel terrible about what you've just endured."

He offered a half-smile. "We get all kinds in here," he said.

"Yeah," I said, "but that just was not cool at all."

We finished cleaning up, and I headed to my gate to catch my flight.

ABOUT TWENTY MINUTES AFTER DEPARTING BOSTON, I PUT down my magazine and shut my eyes in hopes of taking a short nap. God had other plans in mind.

"Think this one over, Bill," he said. "Any idea why you didn't defend the busboy right away, instead of waiting for so long to step in and help?"

My reflexive response was that I was exercising sober judgment. I mean, if I had rushed onto the scene too quickly, perhaps the other three drunks would have jumped the busboy and me.

I explained all of this to the Holy Spirit, who was unimpressed. "How about the truth this time?" I sensed him whisper.

In that window-seat at thirty thousand feet, I came face-to-face with the fact that I'd been more concerned about getting punched in the nose than about relieving the plight of someone in need. I can be bold in certain settings, but the strain of cowardice that still lurks within me was tough to deny that day.

~

Over the coming months and years, God would continue to whisper encouragement for me to take that airport lesson to heart. "Prize life," he seemed to say. "Defend life, fight for life and help others to live life in all its abundance until you face your dying day."

I'd be driving down the freeway and would see a car with a bumper sticker that read, "Abortion stops a beating heart," and think, "That makes perfect sense to me. Abortion kills the most innocent of lives, and babies' lives matter to God. This must stop."

Similarly, I'd flip to a channel where pundits were embroiled in a debate about capital punishment and think, "The same life God treasures in the womb matters all the way to the end."

I'd visit someone who was incarcerated and drive away thinking, "He screwed up and now he is serving his time, but I'm someone who has screwed up as well. I'm thankful we both matter to God."

I'd flip through the news channels on TV and watch yet another war break out somewhere on our planet. I'd sit back and sigh and think, "It all starts with the devaluing of life." Someone said or did something that set someone else off, and then they retaliated, and now look at our sorry state of affairs.

"Love your enemies," Jesus said on the Sermon on the Mount, "and pray for those who persecute you."[19] In that same set of instructions, he suggested an even more radical idea: In Matthew 5:21–22, Jesus told his followers to avoid using coarse language when speaking to one other, because such words could incite animosity. "I'm telling you that anyone who is so much as angry with a brother or sister is guilty of murder. Carelessly call a brother 'idiot!' and you just might find yourself hauled into court. Thoughtlessly yell 'stupid!' at a sister and you are on the brink of hellfire. The simple moral fact is that words kill" (MSG).

"Sticks and stones may break my bones," the childhood rhyme says, "but names will never hurt me." You and I both know those words couldn't be more untrue. Jesus recognized that when people call each other names, someone is going to get hurt. He might lash back with a few choice words of his own, and then the escalation begins: the war of words can become the war of fists, which can become the war of knives, which can become the war of bombs that divides one nation against another. And violence and bloodshed were never God's dream for how life on planet Earth would go. His "plan A" for us was that we would partner with him in valuing life—*all* life in all its varied and beautiful forms.

God cares deeply about a litany of things, but in Scripture, certain passions rise to the top. In many places in his Word, God specifically advocates for the poor, the orphaned, the alien, the widow and more. God defends the underdog and asks us to do the same. "If you want to align yourself with your Father's heart," he seems to say, "then pay close attention to these things I care most about."

None of the things that matter to God can be ignored by those who love him, but it has been my observation that sometimes God will assign a few of his issues to particular followers in an accentuated way. He'll hand out specific assignments by saying, "On all of these fronts keep a watchful eye, but in *this* area I want *you* to step up!"

I don't know what that specific area might be for you, but I know the One who does. Persist in asking him what assignment he has in mind for you, and then stay wide open to what he says in reply. Granted, it takes a certain level of spiritual maturity to listen for whispers beyond our immediate needs. If our constant plea to God has centered on asking him to attend to our own injustices—"Fix my husband!" or "Fix my teenager!" or, "Please, God, fix my job!"—it can feel more than a little awkward to suddenly ask, "What justice issue is unfolding in this world that I might be able to help solve?"

But based on feedback from numerous people I know who have risked praying that exact bold prayer, I assure you that maintaining a broader vision for the world—taking up a cause for justice that is dear to God's heart—will yield blessing in your life. I'm taking my own medicine in this regard, as evidenced by the final story I'll share.

FOR YEARS I HAVE BEEN ASKED BY CHURCH LEADERS AND government leaders alike to get involved in reforming this country's immigration policies, but I had not felt God's nudge in that direction—until recently. Through a series of events, I now sense that God is once again rocking my world.

Since 2004, Willow has hosted a Spanish-speaking ministry called Casa de Luz ("House of Light") that meets each weekend on our campus. Their teaching pastor is one of a handful of leaders who convene in my office each week, where together we craft new and inventive ways for continuing to support and strengthen various ministries within the church. For some time now, he has been lifting up the need to come alongside members of Casa's congregation who face deportation and the certain tearing apart of family units—families that are every bit as much a part of Willow as my family is. God started stirring my soul through the simple stories this pastor would tell.

Now, throughout my adult life—and increasingly in recent years as the immigration debate has heated up in our country—I'd certainly been aware of the complexity of this issue. I'd even bought into some assumptions I had never really taken the time to explore: "Illegal immigrants should follow the rules, stand in line and enter the country legally." "Illegal immigrants don't pay taxes." "Illegal immigrants take jobs away from *legal* Americans."

I had figured my assumptions were correct, end of story.

Then, about three months ago, I was given a book titled *Welcoming the Stranger: Justice, Compassion and Truth in the Immigration Debate*,[20] and when I got to the chapter called "Thinking Biblically about Immigration," something in my conscience snapped. I read verse after verse about how God desired his followers to treat foreigners in their midst. How had I not noticed all these passages before? The single thought that kept swirling in my mind was, "Immigrants matter to God."

For the last three Elder meetings, we invited immigration experts to come educate us on the size and complexity of the problem, as well as the role that the local church could be filling to help solve it. Those meetings have proven invaluable as I seek to come up to speed on a situation that is imperiling the lives of so many within Willow's flock—and around our country. Last week, I met with seven pastors from the Chicago area who are serious about seeing our city changed by God's grace. The issue of immigration reform happened to come up, and one of the pastors informed us that he and his wife had just taken in two young girls whose parents were deported that week. "They didn't have anywhere to go," he explained, "so until further notice, they're as much a part of our family as my biological children are."

I stared at him from across the table and thought, "This pastor is describing one of the most Christlike actions I have heard about in recent days." I drove away from that meeting asking myself if I'd be willing to disrupt my life like that. This guy has already raised a family of his own and is nearing the empty-nest years with his wife. Yeah, I know immigrants matter to God and everything—but starting over with two new kids? That's a world-rocker to beat them all!

But isn't this how God often works? He knows that if he can radically rock enough *individual* worlds, the *whole* world one day will change. And I can't help but picture him smiling broadly at the magnificent prospect of a day such as that.

From what I've observed of God's ways thus far, he has no plans for changing his world-rocking approach anytime soon. What's more, my bet is that he has a world-rocking whisper that bears *your* name. Is there a book he has been prompting you to read? A question he has been prompting you to ask? A documentary you need to watch or a trip you need to take? Maybe it is a prompting simply to "linger"—over a verse in the Bible, on a given website, with a particular person, in a specific moment. Whatever his whisper sounds like, I hope you'll heed the instruction it brings. To care deeply about the crown of God's creation—humanity in all its colors, shapes and sizes—and to make sacrifices on its behalf ... there is no greater satisfaction in all the earth.

CHAPTER 10

JUST SAY THE WORD

I MET A MAN MANY YEARS AGO WHO REDEFINED MY UNDER-standing of what it means to say yes to the whispered words of God. Gerry Couchman's path and mine crossed shortly before he surrendered his life to Christ. Although he was a business-man working in Cape Town, South Africa, he happened to be in Chicago, exploring a joint venture with a local company. The CEO of that firm, a man who has long been part of our church, invited Gerry to attend a Saturday night service at Willow.

Gerry had grown up in a mainline denomination and had attended church from ages four to twenty-one. But at no time during that entire tenure had anyone challenged him with the possibility of a personal relationship with Jesus Christ. With-out that necessary anchor in place, he didn't see much use in being part of a church. He married and moved on with life. As you'd imagine, he was less than thrilled when the CEO of that company asked him to go to church. Gerry later told me that in his country, only "strange sects" do church on Saturday nights, but because his host had promised the service would be short, *and* he would foot the bill for pizza and beer afterward, Gerry decided to go.

What he didn't know was that while he was begrudgingly making his way to Willow, his wife, Janine, and the church she belonged to back in South Africa were praying for Gerry to make some kind of spiritual progress while on his trip. They had been praying for Gerry for two straight years, and just before his trek to the States, they had gathered covertly to pray that someone whom Gerry would meet might serve as the catalyst for him to surrender his life to Christ.

As Gerry tells it, if the church of his youth had been anything like what he experienced that Saturday night at Willow, he never would have left. He watched excited kids rushing to get to their children's ministry classes and contrasted that to how his mom had needed to yank him out of the car and drag him to Sunday school. He watched teens from student ministry cleaning various parts of the church (and seemingly enjoying it!). In his own teenage years, hanging out at church was considered anything but fun. As he sat in the service and the offering plates were passed, Gerry was blown away by being asked, as a guest, *not* to give—but rather to just let the service be God's gift to him. On the heels of these and other observations, he received what he now knows to be his very first whisper from God: "The church can be like this in South Africa, Gerry, and I think that you can help."

Everything would change from there.

Two months after that Saturday night service, Gerry was on a business trip in Saudi Arabia. Late one night in the quiet of his hotel room, he surrendered his life to Christ. A year following that major decision, he nearly drained his pension fund so that he and Janine could attend a conference Willow was hosting, a conference on building prevailing churches. Partway through the third session on day two, God whispered again. "Be my hands and feet to the local church," Gerry sensed him saying.

Gerry eyed his wife, who was eyeing him right back. She had received the same whisper and at the very same moment. They were intrigued, but clueless. What did it look like to be the "hands and feet" of Christ? They flew back to Cape Town restless and unsure, but with a sense of anticipation.

GERRY AND HIS WIFE CONTINUED TO FOLLOW THE FIRST whisper he had received—to help their church in Cape Town prevail as it never had before. But all the while, they continued to wonder about the "hands and feet" request.

Months after they received that enigmatic whisper, Gerry's wife felt led to contact the Willow Creek Association in South Africa, to see how she and Gerry might assist other local churches looking for new levels of effectiveness. After a string of phone calls, in-person interviews and heartfelt prayers, the Couchmans packed up their belongings, left their beloved home in Cape Town and moved eight hundred miles away to the city of Pretoria, where they joined the WCA full-time. They have served there in stellar fashion for the past seven years. And it all traces back to a whisper—one that Gerry was still trying to decode.

What does it look like for me to be the hands and feet of Christ? he wondered. The very fact that Gerry was investing so much time and energy answering that question would have amused anyone who knew Gerry well. He came from a no-nonsense family, and his parents, despite encouraging their children to faithfully participate in church activities, had themselves not surrendered their lives to Christ. His dad ran a construction company, and his mom was a hard-nosed accountant. Gerry himself had devoted much of his early life to studying chemistry, so for him, anything that couldn't be proven by scientific facts and figures was hardly worth a second look. Yet here he was, redirecting his entire life based solely on a cryptic prompting from God. It must have pegged his loved ones' weird-meters big time.

It would take nearly four years for Gerry to gain insight into the hand-and-feet whisper that had been mystifying him for so long.

In his role in Pretoria, Gerry served local church pastors as they worked to improve in their ministry leadership. One of those pastors was Tim Hawkridge, minister of Somerset West United Church. The more Gerry got to know Tim, the more impressed he was by the man's strong faith.

As a young man of twenty-six, Tim had been diagnosed with polycystic kidney disease, but because the disease can be slow-progressing in nature, his health wasn't adversely affected until nearly twenty years had passed. At age forty-five, Tim's renal function began to deteriorate, and a month after he turned forty-six, he was diagnosed with end-stage renal failure. The only solution was a kidney transplant, and if a kidney wasn't immediately available, he would need to start dialysis treatments right away.

Tim had known for many years that his condition would someday lead to renal failure unless God chose to intervene. But the reality that "someday" was here still hit him like a ton of bricks. It wasn't death that concerned him; he had committed his life to Christ and knew he would spend eternity with God. It was the potential loss of his quality of life and ministry to others that upset him, the thought of hanging on by a thread in a hospital bed for the balance of his years on earth.

Over the course of several months, many people offered to

donate a kidney to Tim. But well-intentioned members of his family and congregation, one by one, were ruled out. Some had health issues, some had blood issues, and for some the medical risk was too high.

Tim began receiving dialysis a few times a week. During this grueling, three-hour procedure, Tim sat hooked up to a machine that filtered and cleaned his blood, removing impurities and toxins that had built up—a job usually performed by healthy, functioning kidneys. During those agonizing treatments, Tim had plenty of time to hear God's whispers. One particular day, he recalls consciously resolving to trust God with his situation and to quit stewing about what "might be." A verse he had memorized years earlier came to mind: "If we live, we live to the Lord," Romans 14:8 says. "And if we die, we die to the Lord. So, whether we live or die, we belong to the Lord."

Resigned to a rhythm of dialysis as a part of his life, Tim engaged the medical staff wholeheartedly and even led several of them to faith in Christ. He focused on his ever-expanding gift of compassion for those who suffer long-term illness, a compassion fueled by his own painful, physical plight.

Despite his sense of resignation about ever finding a kidney donor, Tim still believed God had something important for him to do. "Dying from the lack of a kidney transplant," he sensed, "just isn't my fate in life." God whispered words from Isaiah 43:2, saying, "When you pass through the waters, I will be with you; and when you pass through the rivers, they will not sweep over you. When you walk through the fire, you will not be burned; the flames will not set you ablaze."

The physical firestorm he was enduring would not burn him up.

About the same time that Tim's hope was being bolstered by God, Gerry Couchman had a spiritual experience of his own. The two acquaintances met for breakfast one morning, and during the meal Tim mentioned his medical situation. In passing he added that for various reasons, neither his sister nor his brother was a viable kidney donor. It was a passing comment, not a plea for help. But something about the situation resonated with Gerry at a deep level. He thought about how much he had enjoyed playing with his kids when they were young and wondered how Tim's two young sons were being impacted by their dad's failing health. He thought of Tim's role as pastor—of the lives God was touching through this faithful man—and pondered how his disease must be adversely impacting his energy and effectiveness in this role.

After the men finished their breakfast, Gerry climbed into his car and drove away. Half a mile from the restaurant, the Holy Spirit brought a verse of Scripture to mind: "Very rarely will anyone die for a righteous person," Romans 5:7 says, "though for a good person someone might possibly dare to die."

"Tim is a good man, Gerry," he sensed God saying. "I am not asking for you to die for him, but I *am* asking for you to help him live."

Gerry arrived home, discussed the matter with Janine and then picked up the phone and called Tim. "God wants me to donate one of my kidneys to you," he explained. "And I have complete peace that this is what I need to do."

Tim was speechless. Was his recently bolstered hope pointing to this wildly unexpected turn of events? While Gerry's seemingly impulsive desire to help Tim was touching, what were the odds that the blood of this man he barely knew would be a match?

Gerry indeed followed through. He went to the medical

center for blood testing, and he and Tim awaited the results. With a mixture of awe and disbelief, they learned that Gerry's blood-type compatibility was a perfect match. Still, Tim found it incredibly difficult to believe that a near-stranger would take such a bold move on his behalf. "How do you thank someone for offering up part of his own body for the simple goal of saving yours?" he asked himself. He believed Gerry had received a prompting from God, but was Gerry *sure* he wanted to obey?

As soon as both men got over the shock that a transplant operation really could await them, Gerry was subjected to a battery of blood tests, kidney-function tests, cholesterol tests and blood-pressure assessments. Everything was a match.

Later, I would ask Gerry what it was like to go through each step of the process, knowing that with every gate cleared, he was one step closer to giving an organ to a guy he barely knew.

"What's the point of taking your organs with you as you're laid in the box," he replied, "when they could save someone's life today?"

He had a point.

During Gerry's hospital stay, each time a technician entered his room to draw blood or conduct further analysis, the soon-to-be donor saw an opportunity to share the message of Christ.

"Is the recipient a family member of yours?" various hospital staff would ask.

"No," Gerry would reply.

"A close friend, then?"

"Not really."

"Then why on earth are you doing this?" they would ask, with looks of incredulity on their faces.

"Because I was prompted by God," came Gerry's straightforward answer.

I can only imagine the conversations that followed.

On December 11, 2007—almost eight months to the day, after that restaurant breakfast—Gerry Couchman found himself lying on a gurney in a South African hospital, being prepped for kidney-transplant surgery. Four hours later, Pastor Tim Hawkridge underwent the same routine—and four hours after that, both men were lying in a recovery room, each with one healthy kidney.

Tim's new organ began functioning right away, cleansing the impurities from his blood, and making his days of dialysis a distant but unforgettable memory. Three months later, Tim was strong enough to teach at his church once more. He had always loved his role as pastor, but after his long-awaited return to the platform, he found new resonance in his work, and that resonance continues today. He attributes this newfound mental and spiritual clarity to the fact that this entire series of miraculous steps was divinely orchestrated by God. "God blesses us to be a blessing," he says. "This story isn't about two men as much as it's about our wonder-working God."

<hr />

I don't know what an account like this does to you, but when I think about Gerry's decision to risk his life and health to obey a whisper from God, something in me can't help but cheer. I wish every Christ-follower in the world could know the same gut-level satisfaction that only shows up when you release your grip on comfortable living and submit to a dangerous prompting from God like Gerry did.

Gerry's sacrificial obedience to God's whisper flies in the face of human nature. You and I (and every other member of the human race) are what I call "clutchers." Left to our own devices, we scrape and claw and fret our way up the ladder, and once our efforts net even a modest amount of status, power or comfort, we hold on to it like pit bulls seizing raw meat.

In the face of this potent, pervasive human instinct, God tells his followers, "Don't be clutchers. Instead, become relinquishers." That's how I read Philippians 2. In the opening verses of that chapter, the apostle Paul says this: "Do nothing out of selfish ambition or vain conceit. Rather, in humility value others above yourselves, not looking to your own interests but each of you to the interests of others." In case we don't fully comprehend what the exhortation means, Paul then offers an illustration by way of the life and legacy of Jesus Christ.

"Have the same attitude of mind that Christ Jesus had," Paul says, and then he unloads a litany of seven voluntarily relinquishments that Jesus himself made.

Seventeen years ago, while soaking in the book of Philippians, this list of Jesus' relinquishments—or demotions—hit me like a Mack truck. So powerful was the section in chapter two of that great epistle that a friend and I eventually wrote a book about it.[1]

I will never forget how verses six through eight speak about Jesus:

> Who, being in very nature God,
> Did not consider equality with God something
>   to be grasped,
> but made himself nothing,
> taking the very nature of a servant,
> being made in human likeness.
> And being found in appearance as a man,
> he humbled himself
> and became obedient to death—
> even death on a cross!

According to this passage, Jesus Christ starts out at the very top. He was "in very nature God," which means that he was not merely vice president of the Trinity Corporation or God's junior partner; he was (and is) a full-fledged member of the Godhead, equal with the Almighty Father in every way, shape, and form. He was just as present and participatory in the creation of the universe as God, and all of the divine prerogatives were not only God's, but Jesus' as well.

Jesus' point of origin is significant, in light of the first demotion I'll cite. Although he started at the top and enjoyed perfect equality with God, Christ did not regard that position as "something to be grasped."[2] Jesus was not a "clutcher."

I don't know about you, but if I ever found myself in a position of equality with God, I'd be hanging on for dear life. Even the most mature believers among us wrestle with letting go of adoration and fame. Not so with Jesus. He as much as says, "I will take a demotion here. I will let go. I will surrender whatever is necessary in order to cooperate with God's mission for me."

And down the ladder he stepped.

Demotion number two is described this way: "He made himself nothing."[3]

Demotion number one dealt with loosening the grip; the next demotion deals with the *consequences* of loosening that grip. In another translation, this verse says he "emptied himself." This doesn't mean Jesus divested himself of his deity; rather, he laid aside those divine characteristics that would hinder him from becoming a man. Nobody stripped Christ of his power; he voluntarily let it go. It was the second in a string of relinquishments. And down the ladder he stepped.

Demotions three, four and five happen in rapid succession. The text says that Jesus agreed to take on the *appearance* of a man, he then was made in the *likeness* of a man, and finally he became a *bondservant* to man. It's a sequence I find utterly breathtaking. The transcendent Creator of the universe came down to the world he had created—not as an emperor requiring subjects to bow before him—but, instead, as an ordinary guy, looking for those he humbly might serve.

When I try to imagine the omniscient, omnipotent, omnipresent God submitting himself to the confines of human flesh, my brain short-circuits. Just imagine what it must have been like for the God of the universe to acquiesce to the limitations of infancy, adolescence and young adulthood. Try to picture a seven-year-old Jesus saying, "Okay, Mom. Okay, Dad. Whatever you say." Creator submitting to creation—it's an astounding thing to take in.

I picture Jesus Christ walking the busy dirt roads of a city in Palestine. "Move it or lose it, Jew-boy!" passers-by might have said, oblivious to who it was they were elbowing out of their way.

THE FIRST TIME I VISITED A POVERTY-STRICKEN COUNTRY AND saw starving kids standing in a food line, an image caught my eye that has stayed with me ever since. One of the smaller kids in line kept inching his way toward the front, but each time he would make it near the food, the bigger kids would shove him out of the way. He would obediently toddle to the back of the line and begin inching his way forward again. I'll never forget him: he wore a tattered blue shirt that stretched tightly over his bloated belly, and below the waist he was stark naked. His dark hair was turning orange, a sure sign of malnutrition, and his skin was chalky white from the caked-on dirt he bore.

On that particular trip, I was staying at a comfortable hotel less than twenty miles away. The following day I would board a jet airplane and fly home to Barrington, Illinois, where a suburban home, clean clothes and as much food as I could possibly eat awaited me. I remember thinking, "What would it take for *me* to voluntarily live in that kid's skin for a year?"

My honest answer sobered me. There wasn't enough money in the world to make me do something as self-sacrificing as that. But Jesus Christ willingly and willfully wrapped himself in human skin and walked this planet—not for one year, but for thirty-three years. He was scorned, misunderstood, rebuked and routinely wronged. And yet he chose to do it anyway. He relinquished the adoration of the angels in order to accomplish his Father's purpose in his life.

And further down the ladder he stepped.

Demotion number six comes to us in Philippians 2:8, which says, "He humbled himself by becoming obedient to death. . . ."

Jesus Christ—the One who initiated all of life and sustains it to this day—stood toe-to-toe with death. "Okay, you win," he conceded on our behalf. He voluntarily laid down his life so that his mission could be fulfilled. The fact that he laid down his life is striking enough—but *how* he laid it down is incomprehensible to me. Did he simply chug some hemlock or chew cyanide? Did he arrange for himself a painless slumber that would lead gently to the blackness of death? Far from it. Which brings us to Jesus' seventh and final demotion.

Whenever I read the last phrase of Philippians 2:8, I do so with awe-filled reverence: Jesus submitted himself to the point of death—*"even death on a cross."*[4]

Crucifixion—death on a cross—was a mode of execution that didn't just kill people; it tortured them to death, allowing every macabre sensation of dying to be experienced in fullest measure. Crucifixion was an excruciating, humiliating way to die.

While Jesus hung on the cross, men and women passed by, spitting and throwing stones, hurling profane accusations his way. Just a week earlier, many of these same people had carpeted his path with cloaks and palm branches, their lips shouting praises, not profanities. This juxtaposition must have made the agony of those hours on the cross all the more complete. When I read these accounts of Jesus' death, something in me wants to cry out, "Is there no depth that Jesus will not go—is there no level to which he will not descend—in order to be faithful to his mission on my behalf?"

The answer is no, there *isn't* a depth to which Jesus did not stoop. There *isn't* a level of pain Jesus didn't agree to bear. There *isn't* a burden our compassionate Savior refused to carry. There is *no* sacrifice our Savior did not make. This realization challenges me to up the ante on my own obedience in following the relatively simple whispers he asks me to obey. Perhaps it has the same effect on you.

Bestselling books these days often tell rags-to-riches tales, but I contend the greatest story history has ever known reflects the exact opposite chain of events. It's a riches-to-rags story—burial rags, that is. It's a highest-height-to-deepest-depth account of One who voluntarily demoted himself. I wrote years ago, in the book *Descending into Greatness*, "The Highest came to serve the lowest. The Creator and Sustainer of all things came to pour himself out. The One who possessed everything became nothing. From the world's perspective, the cross became the symbol of foolishness. Yet in God's eyes, Christ became the greatest of the great."[5] And he did it, not by clutching, but by relinquishing all he had.

G iven the downsizing and downscaling that would be required, why would you or I—or anyone in a right mind—sign up for a life like that? We are trained from a very young age to seek achievement, upward mobility, that sense of "rising above." We are groomed to *become* someone, not to empty ourselves for others. But in order to follow Jesus Christ with any degree of tenacity, we inevitably will be prompted to take demotions. We will be asked to relinquish what is "rightfully" ours. We will inconvenience ourselves to the point of sacrifice, even when others call us fools. And we will do it all for two simple reasons: first, we understand that the kingdom of God never advances without sacrifice; and second, because every serious-minded Christian I know wants to receive a heartfelt "well done!" in heaven someday.

Let's look at each, in turn.

During a particularly tough era around Willow, I felt prompted to remind our congregation on a weekly basis that the only way God's kingdom moves forward is when a Christ-follower is willing to take a hit. I was taking my personal share of hits during those days, and I would tell those gathered in our auditorium the same thing I told you at the end of chapter 1: I would much rather stand before God someday having done his bidding to the best of my understanding than to face him knowing I ignored his voice and sidestepped the tougher promptings I received. Even when the stakes are high—perhaps *especially* so—I seek to be a relinquisher, not a clutcher.

So, what do these "hits" look like? Surely you have taken a few in your life. If you are a Christ-follower, then by definition your pride took a hit when you admitted that you were a sinner, desperately in need of God's saving grace. Submitting to the Spirit—who was whispering, "Humble yourself. Receive Christ. Enter the family of God"—meant taking a *huge* independence hit. Do you remember that experience? Sure, it was a demotion from an ego standpoint, but great gains occurred on the heels of that daring decision. God's kingdom expanded, and your life forever was changed.

Maybe soon thereafter, your vanity took a hit as you considered the waters of baptism. Nobody likes having a bad hair day and standing sopping wet in front of a crowd, but think of the encouragement and example offered to those watching, because of your willingness to lay that superficial stuff down.

If you have grown to the point where you no longer count your life as your own but have given your remaining days to God, I guarantee you've taken some hits. Your agenda has taken a hit. Your finances have taken a hit. Your priorities have been rearranged. Your entire life has been turned upside down as you put Christ first in all that you do. In fact, almost *every* time you hear a prompting from God, something safe or predictable most likely has to go. But you persevere, knowing that when you take the risks he is asking you to take—as you conform to his mission in yet one more way—the kingdom moves forward.

This is what it looks like to live a life fully surrendered to God. It's rarely a walk in the park. Obeying the Spirit instead of your own self-centered whims will lead you to places you've never been, challenge you in ways you have never been challenged and invite levels of sacrifice you never dreamed you could make. This is the power and the promise of full-throttle faith, of living a life fueled solely by God.

There is a second reason average people like you and me sign up for a demotion-laden life. Based on that passage from Philippians, we voluntarily loosen our grip and find a home in humility's grasp because we know that a *serious* reward awaits our arrival in heaven someday.

Philippians 2:9–11 says that after Jesus took these seven voluntary demotions, "God gave Christ the highest place and honored his name above all others. So at the name of Jesus everyone will bow down, those in heaven, on earth, and under the earth. And to the glory of God the Father everyone will openly agree, 'Jesus Christ is Lord!'"[6] He honored Jesus Christ for completing his assigned mission—and someday he will glorify you and me too.

I CONSULTED A WEBSITE THIS WEEK THAT BOASTS THE infamous "death-clock"—a program that claims to calculate when you will die based on various bodily statistics. Evidently, I'm good until November 9, 2025. I can't speak to the reliability of this *particular* estimate—I checked the site several more times just for fun, and each time, remarkably, my day of death radically changed. But this much you and I can hang our hats on: A death date with our names on it *does* exist, and whenever the day may be that God chooses to take us home, that day will undoubtedly seem too soon. Psalm 39 says: "Show me, Lord, my life's end and the number of my days; let me know how fleeting my life is. You have made my days a mere handbreadth; the span of my years is as nothing before you" (vv. 4–5a).

As we looked at previously, the apostle James refers to humankind as "wildflowers"—brittle blooms that are here today, gone tomorrow—just like that.

For anyone living in the Middle East during the days James penned those words, the metaphor of the wildflower rang true. Spring rains would fall for a time and the rocky hillsides of Palestine would become like an artist's palette of rich, vibrant color. But too soon, a stiff breeze would blow and those dry, scorching winds would shrivel the Monet-like landscape in a matter of hours, leaving behind a tangle of twisted, dry vegetation.

"That's just like you and me," James seems to say. One day we are here, looking altogether alive, and then the next moment we are gone, as quickly as a windswept wildflower on a hill.

This is the brevity of life: one day a person is robustly going about his activities, and the next day people are streaming by his casket, saying, "I can't believe it. I just talked to him yesterday." One day a businesswoman is committing to a ten-year strategic plan at work. The next day her family and friends are putting together a different plan—a plan for her funeral service. Or one day a young person is driving to work; the next day her car is in the wrecking yard and her brain-dead body is awaiting organ-donation surgery. Death comes unannounced.

James makes two observations about death: it is often sudden, and it is universal. Here today. Gone tomorrow. We don't get to choose our death, but what remains ours alone to choose is how we'll spend our life.

MATTHEW 8 TELLS THE STORY OF A ROMAN SOLDIER WHO approached Jesus with a request. The man was a centurion, someone who had rank over many subordinates and who was a respectable leader in life. Here's how verses five through thirteen record the appeal he made that day:

> When Jesus had entered Capernaum, a centurion came to him, asking for help. "Lord," he said, "my servant lies at home paralyzed, suffering terribly."
>
> Jesus said to him, "Shall I come and heal him?"
>
> The centurion replied, "Lord, I do not deserve to have you come under my roof. But just say the word, and my servant will be healed. For I myself am a man under authority, with soldiers under me. I tell this one, *Go*, and he goes; and that one, *Come*, and he comes. I say to my servant, *Do this*, and he does it."

When Jesus heard this, he was amazed and said to those following him, "Truly I tell you, I have not found anyone in Israel with such great faith. I say to you that many will come from the east and the west, and will take their places at the feast with Abraham, Isaac and Jacob in the kingdom of heaven. But the subjects of the kingdom will be thrown outside, into the darkness, where there will be weeping and gnashing of teeth."

Then Jesus said to the centurion, "Go! Let it be done just as you believed it would." And his servant was healed at that very hour.

According to this story, the faithful centurion understood his position, relative to Christ's. He also knew the profound power of a single whisper from God. "You just say the word," he essentially told Jesus Christ that day, "and what is wrong will be made right. You have authority over all people, over all rulers, over all events, over all kingdoms, over all of life. You say the word, and your will today will be done."

The text says that the centurion's faith took Jesus' breath away. In one translation, it says Jesus "marveled"[7] at the centurion's assessment, a reaction I have found nowhere else in Scripture, regarding Jesus' impression of a human being's faith. This man had *massive* faith. Unwavering faith. The sort of just-say-the-word faith I covet for you and me.

Every time I read the account of the centurion's faith, I am nearly physically arrested by the desire to follow Christ like that. I want his influence to affect the entirety of my life—my values, my relationships, my vocabulary, my finances, my agenda, my physical health, my decision making, my political ideology. I want Jesus' ways to permeate who I am across the board. More than any other desire of my heart, I want to be a just-say-the-word type of disciple, from this moment until my dying day.

THROUGHOUT THE COURSE OF MY LIFE, FROM TIME TO TIME I have felt the urge well up inside of me to exhibit that kind of total commitment. Perhaps you can relate. Maybe you've felt that kind of commitment athletically—I talked to a marathon runner recently who completed a marathon and afterward said, "I ran those 26.2 miles as fast as I could humanly run. I collapsed at the finish line, and for three or four days following that experience, I felt the exhilaration of having run the best race of my life."

Maybe you have felt that kind of commitment in an academic sense. You received an assignment somewhere along the way and said, "I'm going to do the best job I can possibly do with this term paper." You researched until your brain turned to mush, and you typed your fingers to the bone, but upon submitting that assignment to your professor, something warm swept through your spirit. You walked out of class that day thinking, "I did the best job I could have done."

Sometimes it happens in the marketplace. You are handed a project at work and say, "This time, I'm gonna hit the ball right out of the park. When I finish this project, it will represent my absolute best efforts."

Have you had an experience like that? Have you known the unparalleled elation that comes from going full-out on a commitment you have made?

Over the past couple of decades, one my favorite hobbies has been sailboat racing, and I remember my first race like it was yesterday. The waves were high, the winds were treacherous and we sailed through these adverse conditions for two-and-a-half hours straight. When we finally crossed the finish line, my entire crew and I were completely spent. And yet we were equally exhilarated by having worked as hard as we possibly could work and staying the course with a diligence we didn't know we possessed. Before the race began, we had made a commitment to each other to finish strong—and we kept that commitment right through to the end.

My point is this: It's one thing to say to God, "I want to obey the input I hear from heaven. I want to follow your whispers every step of the way." But it's quite another thing to actually follow through. I speak from experience. Time and again, I have failed miserably in this regard. At various points along my life's journey, I have made bold declarations to God: "To the best of my ability and with regular help from the Holy Spirit, between now and the grave I want to be a 'just-say-the-word' follower of yours.

"You say it, and I'll do it.

"You say it, and I'll follow it.

"You say it, and I'll obey it.

"You say it, and I'll carry it out.

"Whatever it is you want done in order for your kingdom to advance, God, you whisper the word and consider it done."

Did I mean the words I was praying? Absolutely.

Did I always live up to the commitment I had made? Not so much.

But whenever I find myself having failed, I try to confess that failure and to acknowledge that I veered off-track. I try to get back up, allow Christ to dust me off, and then I underscore my commitment once again. I remember the faith of the centurion, and say, "Today, God, just say the word."

Fully devoted Christ-followers experience this desire rising within our souls to wholeheartedly follow our heavenly Father. We want to be flat-out committed to the One who has committed himself to us. We want to blow him away with our "centurion faith" and impress him with how meticulously we obey. We *desire* that. We really do, not because the emphasis is on our works, but because his great mercy, love, forgiveness and grace draw from the depth of our souls such a response. And part of the reason I have written this book is to encourage you that it's actually *possible* to follow through.

You can *choose* today to be a just-say-the-word kind of follower, someone who jumps at the chance to obey the divine whispers sent straight from heaven to your upturned ear. You can *choose* to live with an increased awareness of those whispers, an expanded heart to follow through and an enhanced eternity because of it. You can *choose* to take God at his word—that he has spiritual goodness and blessing in store for you, when you surrender to *all* of his ways.

If we were to boil down Christianity to its core, we'd be left with simply this: *relationship with God.* The living, loving God of the universe has spoken throughout history, and still speaks today—not just to pastors or priests, but to *anyone* who will listen. God will speak to *you.* No matter what spiritual condition you find yourself in, if you train your ear to be open to heaven, God will speak.

A grand adventure with your name on it is on his lips. Tune your ear toward heaven, and he will direct your steps, accompany your path and celebrate your faithfulness one day, in the "flourishing finish" the apostle Paul describes in Philippians 1:6. "There has never been the slightest doubt in my mind," that verse says, "that the God who started this great work in you would keep at it and bring it to a flourishing finish on the very day Christ Jesus appears" (MSG).

And whether we meet Jesus upon his return to earth someday—or we're transferred to heaven ahead of time—imagine standing before him, saying, "We had a ball doing your program, didn't we, God? Thanks for the awesome ride!"

In that moment, you will look back at every intersection in your life and see that it was *worth* saying yes to God's whispers. You'll remember those relational intersections when you heeded whispers for patience and grace. You'll remember those financial intersections and be glad you handled your money in a God-honoring way. You'll recount the vocational forks in the road when he said, "Trust me just one more time"—and you did. You'll remember the moral crossroads you faced, where he saved you from ditch after ditch. And you'll remember myriad spiritual turning points, where your loving Father provided his clear whispers of guidance.

And until that day comes, you can go to bed every night with one priceless thought in your mind: "Today, I furthered not my own kingdom, but *God's.*" This is the power of the whisper-guided life, my friend—a life that culminates in the closing whisper, "Well done, my good and faithful servant." This is the life awaiting you and me, and it starts with having ears to hear God's voice. Listen up. Follow through. And then join your heavenly Father on a whisper-fueled adventure you'll never regret.

SCRIPTURES TO WRITE
ON YOUR HEART

S INCE MY YOUTH-CAMP DAYS AS A KID, I HAVE EXPERIENCED the great benefit of carrying God's Word around with me throughout my day-to-day life, by way of having committed many verses of Scripture to memory. The time I invested toward that end was well-spent, as those passages of truth have steered me clear of many a ditch in life and have served as God's voice to me through countless challenging situations. I continue making these investments today. The verses take a little longer to stick than they did when I was a kid, but the benefits far outweigh the extra effort.

I invite you to commit as many of the following verses to memory as you can. You'll be amazed at how readily—and frequently—these words from God will come to mind, the next time you need fresh insight from heaven.

Salvation

TITUS 3:5 (NKJV): *Not by works of righteousness which we have done, but according to His mercy He saved us, through the washing of regeneration and renewing of the Holy Spirit.*

JOHN 1:12: *Yet to all who did receive him, to those who believed in his name, he gave the right to become children of God.*

ROMANS 10:13: *Everyone who calls on the name of the Lord will be saved.*

Assurance

ROMANS 8:1: *Therefore, there is now no condemnation for those who are in Christ Jesus.*

ISAIAH 1:18 (NIV): *Though your sins are as scarlet, they will be as white as snow; though they are red like crimson, they will be like wool.*

1 JOHN 5:12: *Whoever has the Son has life; whoever does not have the Son of God does not have life.*

ROMANS 5:1: *Since we have been justified through faith, we have peace with God through our Lord Jesus Christ.*

Fear

2 TIMOTHY 1:7: *For the Spirit God gave us does not make us timid, but gives us power, love and self-discipline.*

ROMANS 8:31: *If God is for us, who can be against us?*

ISAIAH 41:10: *So do not fear, for I am with you; do not be dismayed, for I am your God. I will strengthen you and help you; I will uphold you with my righteous right hand.*

Temptation

1 CORINTHIANS 10:13: *No temptation has overtaken you except what is common to us all. And God is faithful; he will not let you be tempted beyond what you can bear. But when you are tempted, he will also provide a way out so that you can endure it.*

ROMANS 8:5: *Those who live according to the sinful nature have their minds set on what that nature desires; but those who live in accordance with the Spirit have their minds set on what the Spirit desires.*

JAMES 4:7: *Resist the devil, and he will flee from you.*

Trials

ROMANS 8:28: *In all things God works for the good of those who love him, who have been called according to his purpose.*

Pride

JAMES 4:6: *God opposes the proud but shows favor to the humble.*

JAMES 4:10: *Humble yourselves before the Lord, and he will lift you up.*

ROMANS 12:16: *Do not be proud, but be willing to associate with people of low position. Do not think you are superior.*

Anger

EPHESIANS 4:26: *In your anger do not sin. Do not let the sun go down while you are still angry.*

JAMES 1:20 (NCV): *Anger will not help you live the right kind of life God wants.*

Justice

ISAIAH 1:17: *Learn to do right! Seek justice, encourage the oppressed. Defend the cause of the fatherless, plead the case of the widow.*

ISAIAH 61:8: *For I, the LORD, love justice; I hate robbery and wrongdoing. In my faithfulness I will reward my people and make an everlasting covenant with them.*

PROVERBS 19:17: *Those who are kind to the poor lend to the LORD, and he will reward them for what they have done.*

Wisdom

JAMES 1:5: *If any of you lacks wisdom, you should ask God, who gives generously to all without finding fault, and it will be given to you.*

MATTHEW 10:16 (KJV): *Be therefore wise as serpents, and harmless as doves.*

PROVERBS 17:28: *Even fools are thought wise if they keep silent, and discerning if they hold their tongues.*

Security

ROMANS 8:38–39: *For I am convinced that neither death nor life, neither angels nor demons, neither the present nor the future, nor any powers, neither height nor depth, nor anything else in all creation, will be able to separate us from the love of God that is in Christ Jesus our Lord.*

Power

PHILIPPIANS 4:13: *I can do all this through him who gives me strength.*

MARK 10:27: *With human beings this is impossible, but not with God; all things are possible with God.*

ZECHARIAH 4:6: *"Not by might nor by power, but by my Spirit," says the LORD.*

Contentment

PHILIPPIANS 4:11: *I have learned to be content whatever the circumstances.*

HEBREWS 13:5: *Keep your lives free from the love of money and be content with what you have.*

1 TIMOTHY 6:6: *Godliness with contentment is great gain.*

Peace

JOHN 14:27a: *Peace I leave with you; my peace I give you.*

MATTHEW 5:9: *Blessed are the peacemakers, for they will be called children of God.*

PHILIPPIANS 4:7: *The peace of God, which transcends all understanding, will guard your hearts and your minds in Christ Jesus.*

"IS THIS WHISPER REALLY FROM GOD?"

O VER THE YEARS I HAVE COMPILED A SHORT LIST OF filters that help me test every whisper I receive. No matter how confusing, challenging or unsettling a prompting may be, if it passes the following five filters, I attempt to obey it every time. Similarly, if a whisper seems like a no-brainer from a human standpoint, but it doesn't stand up under the scrutiny of these five filters, I am reticent to accept it as being from God without further careful examination.

FILTER #1: Is the Prompting Truly from God?

Whenever you receive a prompting—whether from God directly or through the lips of another—take whatever time is necessary to ask, "God, is this message from you? Does this square with who I know you to be? Is it consistent with your character? Is it aligned with your attributes? Is this *you* trying to convey something to me, or are there other voices getting into my head?" Before taking a single step to obey the whisper you've received, be sure you get the all-clear that the voice you have heard could be from God.

FILTER #2: Is It Scriptural?

Scripture is replete with examples of how God would behave in any given life situation, and the Example's name is Jesus Christ. Whenever I sense a prompting from God, I ask myself if I could imagine Jesus doing whatever action the prompting is suggesting I do. If I can't envision Jesus following suit, I fear my wires somehow must have gotten crossed. Check every prompting you receive against the thematic teachings of Scripture. Messages that contradict Scripture are not from God.

FILTER #3: Is It Wise?

God's whispers rarely go against wisdom and common sense. The entire book of Proverbs is devoted to dissecting wisdom and all her attributes. For example, the wise one loves knowledge, while the fool hates it; the wise one practices gentle speech, while the fool uses harsh, incendiary words; the wise one lives blamelessly, while the fool is utterly corrupt; the wise one follows a straight path, while the fool rejoices in the perverseness of evil; the wise one inherits honor, while the fool is held up to shame. Scripture is relentless in exhorting us to be wise in all our dealings, to be wise in all our ways.

God's direction rarely violates the wisdom test. Be sure you're not sidestepping what is wise in favor of acting quickly on whispers. If God is indeed in the plan, it will likely not involve blatantly unwise action.

FILTER #4: Is It in Tune with Your Own Character?

I caution people against running headlong into a field that is totally foreign to their wiring patterns, their education, their expertise and their experience in life thus far. It's not that God can't endorse a dramatic 180-degree turn. It's just that typically when he does so, it gets affirmed through a series of whispers, from several sources, in a variety of different ways.

FILTER #5: What Do the People You Most Trust Think about It?

Whenever you sense that God is speaking to you, find two or three veteran Christ-followers—preferably people who know you well and who are further down the spiritual path than you are—and take some time to describe the situation to them in detail. Humbly ask them, "Do you think God really did speak to me? Is this the voice of God I'm hearing, or in your estimation did I get my wires crossed?" Then, listen openly and intently to the answers you receive, because they might just save your hide.

Subject every prompting to the godly counsel test. It will save you from boatloads of heartache and just might affirm God's best will for your life.

NOTES

CHAPTER 1: Samuel's Ear

1. 1 Samuel 3:4b, MSG.
2. 1 Samuel 3:5b, MSG.
3. 1 Samuel 3:9a, MSG.
4. 1 Samuel 3:9b, MSG.
5. 1 Samuel 3:10b.
6. James Drummond Burns (1823–64), "Hushed Was the Evening Hymn," also called "Samuel" in some hymnals, from *Church Hymns with Tunes* (London: SPCK, 1874).
7. Titus 3:5, KJV.

CHAPTER 2: Our Communicating God

1. 1 Kings 19:10, MSG.
2. 1 Kings 19:11, MSG.
3. Ibid.
4. 1 Kings 19:12, MSG.
5. I Kings 19:13, MSG.
6. Genesis 3:8.
7. Genesis 8:15.
8. Genesis 12:1–9.
9. See Genesis 46:2.
10. Exodus 3:2.
11. Exodus 20:1.
12. See Exodus 25.
13. Numbers 22:37–38.
14. Deuteronomy 5:23–24.
15. See Judges 6 and 7.
16. Judges 13:6–8.
17. 2 Chronicles 18:13, MSG.
18. Isaiah 30:21.
19. Isaiah 6:8.
20. Isaiah 50:4–5.
21. Jeremiah 1:7.
22. Amos 3:7.
23. See Luke 1.
24. Luke 1:28.
25. Matthew 1:20–21.
26. Luke 2:10–11.
27. See Mark 4.
28. John 11:14–15.
29. Acts 8:26.
30. Acts 10:15.
31. Acts 15:28.
32. Acts 27:23–25.
33. 1 Corinthians 2:7.
34. 2 Corinthians 2:17.
35. 2 Corinthians 12:8–9.
36. Hebrews 1:1–2.
37. See Acts, chapters 11, 13 and 16.
38. See James 1:2–5 and Hebrews 12:5–11.
39. Acts 9:4.
40. Acts 9:5a, author's abridgment.
41. Acts 9:5b, author's abridgment.
42. Dallas Willard, *Hearing God: Developing a Conversational Relationship with God* (Downers Grove, Ill.: InterVarsity, 1984), 18.
43. Hebrews 10:19, 22.

CHAPTER 4: How to Know When You're Hearing from God

1. Psalm 46:10, emphasis added.
2. Matthew 10:16, ASV.
3. Proverbs 11:14, NKJV.

CHAPTER 5: God's Written Whispers

1. Ephesians 4:32, NKJV.
2. Proverbs 3:5–6, NKJV.
3. See Romans 13:1–2.
4. Titus 3:5, NKJV.
5. Romans 8:1, NASB.
6. Isaiah 1:18, NASB.
7. 1 John 5:13, emphasis added.
8. James 4:6.
9. James 4:10.
10. Romans 12:16.
11. James 1:20, NCV.
12. Isaiah 61:8.
13. Proverbs 19:17.
14. Emphasis added.
15. John 14:27a.
16. Emphasis added.
17. 1 Corinthians 15:58, NASB.
18. 1 Corinthians 15:58, NCV.
19. Colossians 3:16, NASB.
20. Henri-Frédéric Amiel, *Amiel's Journal*; *The Journal Intime of Henri-Frédéric Amiel* (New York: A. L. Burt, 1900), 16.

CHAPTER 6: Light for Dark Nights of the Soul

1. 1 Samuel 30:6, NASB. Emphasis added.
2. For more on this era, read Bill Hybels and Lynne Hybels, *Rediscovering Church: The Story and Vision of Willow Creek Community Church* (Grand Rapids: Zondervan, 1995).
3. James 1:2–4, MSG.
4. Psalm 23:4a.
5. Brian Kolodiejchuk, ed., *Mother Teresa—Come Be My Light: The Private Writings of the "Saint of Calcutta"* (New York: Doubleday, 2007), 263.
6. "Standin' in the Need of Prayer," a traditional African American spiritual.
7. See Matthew 26:38.
8. Matthew 26:42.
9. Matthew 26:46a.

CHAPTER 7: Promptings for Parenthood

1. For more information on this concept, see author Gary Chapman's books on the five love languages.
2. Shauna published a book in 2007 titled, *Cold Tangerines: Celebrating the Extraordinary Nature of Everyday Life*, (Zondervan), in which she recounts the details and tough lessons learned during this era of life.

CHAPTER 8: When God Speaks through Others

1. 2 Samuel 12:1–3, NCV.
2. 2 Samuel 12:5, NCV.
3. 2 Samuel 12:7a, NCV.
4. 2 Samuel 12:13, NCV.

CHAPTER 9: Whispers That Change the World

1. Psalm 106:3.
2. Psalm 140:12.
3. Isaiah 1:17.
4. Isaiah 61:8.
5. Micah 6:8.
6. Luke 11:42.

7. See Exodus 22:25.

8. See Deuteronomy 15.

9. Zechariah 7:11b–12a.

10. See 2 Corinthians 8:9; Proverbs 19:17; Matthew 25:31–46.

11. Undoubtedly, the best book I have read on the subject of extreme poverty is Bryant Myers's *Walking with the Poor* (Maryknoll, N.Y.: Orbis, 1999). Your heart never will be the same after you understand the truth about poverty in our world. Read at your own risk!

12. Number estimated from statistics in the 2006 United Nations Human Development Report.

13. Michael Emerson and Christian Smith, *Divided by Faith: Evangelical Religion and the Problem of Race in America* (London and New York: Oxford University Press, 2001).

14. Ibid., 22.

15. C. S. Lewis, "The Inner Ring," *The Weight of Glory* (Grand Rapids: Eerdmans, 1965), 58. The essay was originally a Memorial Lecture at King's College, University of London, delivered in 1944 and was originally published in the collection *Transposition and Other Addresses* in 1949. For a fascinating discussion of this concept of the Inner Ring, go to lewissociety.org/innerring.php.

16. Emerson and Smith, *Divided by Faith*, 14.

17. Ibid, 93.

18. Ibid, 94.

19. Matthew 5:44.

20. Matthew Soerens and Jenny Hwang, *Welcoming the Stranger: Justice, Compassion and Truth in the Immigration Debate* (Downers Grove, Ill.: InterVarsity, 2009).

CHAPTER 10: Just Say the Word

1. Bill Hybels and Rob Wilkins, *(Find True Satisfaction by) Descending into Greatness* (Grand Rapids: Zondervan, 1993).

2. Philippians 2:6, NIV.

3. Philippians 2:7a.

4. Emphasis added.

5. Hybels and Wilkins, *Descending into Greatness*, 19.

6. Philippians 2:9–11, CEV.

7. Matthew 8:10, NASB.

The Power of a Whisper Audio CD

Hearing God.
Having the Guts to Respond.

Bill Hybels

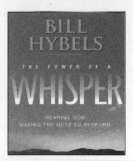

"Without a hint of exaggeration," says pastor and author Bill Hybels in this unabridged audio CD, *The Power of a Whisper: Hearing God, Having the Guts to Respond*, "the ability to discern divine direction has saved me from a life of sure boredom and self-destruction. God's well-timed words have redirected my path, rescued me from temptation and re-energized me during some of my deepest moments of despair."

In *The Power of a Whisper*, vision is cast for what life can look like when God's followers choose to hear from heaven as they navigate life on earth. Whispers that arbitrate key decisions, nudges that rescue from dark nights of the soul, promptings that spur on growth, urgings that come by way of another person, inspiration that opens once-glazed-over eyes to the terrible plight people face in this world.... Through firsthand accounts spanning fifty-seven years of life, more than thirty of which have been spent in the trenches of ministry, Hybels promotes passion in Christ-followers' hearts for being wide open to hearing from God, and for getting gutsier about doing exactly what he says to do.

The Power of a Whisper DVD Curriculum

Hearing God.
Having the Guts to Respond.

Bill Hybels

God still speaks — is anyone listening? Join bestselling author and pastor Bill Hybels in this four-session video-based study where your group will learn to navigate life through whispers from God. Through this dynamic teaching and group study, you will learn to practice hearing from God, surrender to the voice of God, obey his promptings and become a more effective kingdom-builder. Use with the *Power of a Whisper Participant's Guide* to help facilitate group discussion and further study.

Just Walk Across the Room

Simple Steps Pointing People to Faith

Bill Hybels

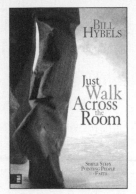

What if you knew that by simply crossing the room and saying hello to someone, you could change that person's forever? Just a few steps to make an eternal difference. It has nothing to do with methods and everything to do with taking a genuine interest in another human being. All you need is a heart that's in tune with the Holy Spirit and a willingness to venture out of your "Circle of Comfort" and into another person's life.

Just Walk Across the Room brings personal evangelism into the twenty-first century. Building on the solid foundation laid in *Becoming a Contagious Christian*, Bill Hybels shows how you can participate in the model first set by Jesus, who stepped down from heaven two thousand years ago to bring hope and redemption to broken people living in a fallen world. Now it's your turn. Your journey may not be as dramatic, but it can have a life-changing impact for someone standing a few steps away from you — and for you as well, as you learn the power of extending care, compassion, and inclusiveness under the guidance of the Holy Spirit.

The stakes are high. The implications are eternal. And you may be only a conversation away from having an eternal impact on someone's life — if you will just walk across the room.

Available in stores and online!

Just Walk Across the Room
DVD Curriculum

Four Sessions on Simple Steps Pointing People to Faith

Bill Hybels with Ashley Wiersma

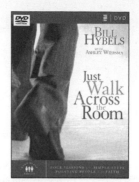

In *Just Walk Across the Room*, Bill Hybels brings personal evangelism into the twenty-first century with a natural and empowering approach modeled after Jesus himself. When Christ "walked" clear across the cosmos more than two thousand years ago, he had no forced formulas and no memorized script; rather, he came armed only with an offer of redemption for people like us, many of whom were neck-deep in pain of their own making.

This dynamic four-week experience is designed to equip and inspire your entire church to participate in that same pattern of grace-giving by taking simple walks across rooms—leaving your circles of comfort and extending hands of care, compassion, and inclusiveness to people who might need a touch of God's love today.

This DVD is designed for use in conjunction with *Just Walk Across the Room: The Four-Week Campaign Experience*, which consists of three integrated components:

- Sermons, an implementation guide, and church promotional materials provided on CD-ROM to address the church as a whole
- Small group DVD and a participant's guide to enable people to work through the material in small, connected circles of community
- The book *Just Walk Across the Room* to allow participants to think through the concepts individually

Available in stores and online!

Courageous Leadership

Bill Hybels

The book you hold resonates with this conviction: that leaders such as you have the potential to be the most influential forces on planet Earth. Yours is the staggering responsibility and the matchless privilege of rallying believers and mobilizing their spiritual gifts in order to help people who are far from God become fully devoted followers of Christ. Life transformation and the eternal destinies of real people depend on the redemptive message entrusted to the local church. Are you willing to do whatever it takes to lead your church effectively so God's message of hope can change the world? Then this book is for you.

Courageous Leadership is Bill Hybels' magnum opus, a book far too important to be written before its time. Only now, after nearly thirty years leading his own church from a handful of people with a burning vision into a globe-spanning kingdom force—only after almost three decades of victories and setbacks, of praying hard and risking big—is Hybels ready at last to share the lessons he has learned, and continues to learn, about Christian leadership.

In this passionate, powerful book, Hybels unpacks the tools, tasks, and challenges of your calling. You'll discover the power of vision and how to turn it into action. You'll gain frontline insights for developing a kingdom dream team, discovering your leadership style, developing other leaders, making decisions, walking with God, embracing change, and much, much more. Drawing on his own richly varied life experiences, Hybels fleshes out vital principles with riveting first-hand stories.

Available in stores and online!

ZONDERVAN®
.com

Becoming
a Contagious Christian

Bill Hybels and Mark Mittelberg

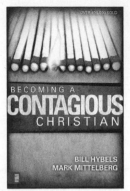

Evangelism doesn't have to be frustrating or intimidating. Bill Hybels and Mark
Mittelberg believe that effectively communicating our faith in Christ should be
the most natural thing in the world. We
just need encouragement and direction. In
Becoming a Contagious Christian, Hybels and Mittelberg articulate
the central principles that have helped the believers at Willow Creek
Community Church become a church known around the world for
its outstanding outreach to unchurched people. Based on the words
of Jesus and flowing from the firsthand experiences of the authors,
Becoming a Contagious Christian is a groundbreaking, personalized
approach to relational evangelism. You will discover your own natural
evangelism style, how to develop a contagious Christian character,
to build spiritually strategic relationships, to direct conversations
toward matters of faith, and to share biblical truths in everyday language. This landmark book presents a blueprint for starting a spiritual epidemic of hope and enthusiasm for spreading the Gospel.

Axiom

Powerful Leadership Proverbs

Bill Hybels

The best leaders not only lead well but also reflect on their leadership long enough and thoughtfully enough to articulate the philosophies that cause them to do so. Whether serving in the marketplace or in ministry, as executives or rank-and-file employees, as salaried staff or volunteer servants, good leaders can pinpoint the rationale for their actions and decisions with the ease of reciting their home address.

In *Axiom*, author Bill Hybels divulges the God-given convictions that have dictated his leadership strategy for more than three decades as senior pastor of Willow Creek Community Church. Oriented toward four key leadership categories ...

1. Vision and strategy ("Promote Shameless Profitability," "Take a Flyer")
2. Teamwork and communication ("Obi-Wan Kenobi Isn't for Hire," "Disagree without Drawing Blood")
3. Activity and assessment ("Develop a Mole System," "Sweat the Small Stuff")
4. Personal integrity ("Admit Mistakes, and Your Stock Goes Up," "Fight for Your Family")

... *Axiom* brokers accessible wisdom from one leader's journey, as well as emboldens you to nail down the reasons why you lead like you lead.

Axiom
Audio CD
Powerful Leadership Proverbs

Bill Hybels

The best leaders not only lead well but also reflect on their leadership long enough and thoughtfully enough to articulate what philosophies cause them to do so. Whether serving in the marketplace or in ministry, as executives or rank-and-file employees, as salaried staff or volunteer servants, they can pinpoint the rationale for their actions and decisions with the ease of reciting their home address.

In *Axiom*, author Bill Hybels divulges the God-given convictions that have dictated his leadership strategy for more than three decades as Senior Pastor of Willow Creek Community Church. Oriented toward four key leadership categories — vision and strategy ("Promote Shameless Profitability," "Take a Flyer"), teamwork and communication ("Obi-Wan Kenobi Isn't for Hire," "Disagree without Drawing Blood"), activity and assessment ("Develop a Mole System," "Sweat the Small Stuff"), and personal integrity ("Admit Mistakes, and Your Stock Goes Up," "Fight for Your Family") — *Axiom* brokers accessible wisdom from one leader's journey, as well as emboldens you to nail down the reasons why you lead like you lead.

Available in stores and online!

Holy Discontent

Fueling the Fire
That Ignites Personal Vision

Bill Hybels

What is the one aspect of this broken world that, when you see it, touch it, get near it, you just can't stand? Very likely, that firestorm of frustration reflects your holy discontent, a reality so troubling that you are thrust off the couch and into the game. It's during these defining times when your eyes open to the needs surrounding you and your heart hungers to respond that you hear God say, "I feel the same way about this problem. Now, let's go solve it together!"

Bill Hybels invites you to consider the dramatic impact your life will have when you allow your holy discontent to fuel instead of frustrate you. Using examples from the Bible, his own life, and the experiences of others, Hybels shows how you can find and feed your personal area of holy discontent, fight for it when things get risky, and follow it when it takes a mid-course turn. As you live from the energy of your holy discontent, you'll fulfill your role in setting what is wrong in this world right!

WILLOW CREEK ASSOCIATION

This resource is just one of many ministry tools published in partnership with the Willow Creek Association. Founded in 1992, WCA was created to serve churches and church leaders striving to create environments where those still outside the family of God are welcomed—and can more easily consider God's loving offer of salvation through faith.

These innovative churches and leaders are connected at the deepest level by their all-out dedication to Christ and His Kingdom. Willing to do whatever it required to build churches that help people move along the path toward Christ-centered devotion; they also share a deep desire to encourage all believers at every step of their faith journey, to continue moving toward a fully transformed, Christ-centered life.

Today, more than 10,000 churches from 80 denominations worldwide are formally connected to WCA and each other through WCA Membership. Many thousands more come to WCA for networking, training, and resources.

For more information about the ministry of the
Willow Creek Association, visit: **willowcreek.com**.

Share Your Thoughts

With the Author: Your comments will be forwarded to the author when you send them to *zauthor@zondervan.com*.

With Zondervan: Submit your review of this book by writing to *zreview@zondervan.com*.

Free Online Resources at

www.zondervan.com

Zondervan AuthorTracker: Be notified whenever your favorite authors publish new books, go on tour, or post an update about what's happening in their lives at www.zondervan.com/authortracker.

Daily Bible Verses and Devotions: Enrich your life with daily Bible verses or devotions that help you start every morning focused on God. Visit www.zondervan.com/newsletters.

Free Email Publications: Sign up for newsletters on Christian living, academic resources, church ministry, fiction, children's resources, and more. Visit www.zondervan.com/newsletters.

Zondervan Bible Search: Find and compare Bible passages in a variety of translations at www.zondervanbiblesearch.com.

Other Benefits: Register yourself to receive online benefits like coupons and special offers, or to participate in research.